Web Host Manager
Administration Guide

Run your web host with the popular Web Host Manager software

Aric Pedersen

BIRMINGHAM - MUMBAI

Web Host Manager
Administration Guide

First published: August 2006

Production Reference: 1110806

Published by Packt Publishing Ltd.
32 Lincoln Road
Olton
Birmingham, B27 6PA, UK.

ISBN 1-904811-50-7

www.packtpub.com

Cover Image by www.visionwt.com

Credits

Author

Aric Pedersen

Reviewers

Tony Butler

Brian Coogan

David Mytton

Development Editor

David Barnes

Technical Editor

Divya Menon

Editorial Manager

Dipali Chittar

Indexer

Mithil Kulkarni

Proofreaders

Martin Brooks

Chris Smith

Production Manager

Patricia Weir

Layouts and Illustrations

Shantanu Zagade

Cover Designer

Shantanu Zagade

About the Author

Aric Pedersen has been using cPanel and WHM on a daily basis for over six years both as an end user for his own websites and as a systems administrator. He currently works as a systems administrator for several hosting companies and also for Netenberg.com, the creators of Fantastico Deluxe (a popular script auto-installer for cPanel). Aric has been providing companies and end users with web hosting and related documentation for several years.

As always, this book could not have been completed without the assistance of numerous people. I'd like to take the time to thank a few more of them:

To my mother and Allen: You're the best.

To my brothers Ken, Big Steve, and Michael: You're the best bunch of brothers a kid ever had. Thanks to all of you for keeping my life interesting.

To Ilias: Not only do you make some great products, you've also been great to work with.

To Tony: For once again stepping up to the plate in a time of need.

To Pete: I hope this helps. ☺

And finally to the readers: I hope you will find my cPanel and WHM books are a valuable resource that you will refer to time and again.

About the Reviewers

Tony Butler has been an IT Consultant and systems architect to some of the largest financial institutions in Europe for the past 10 years. He has also been using cPanel and WHM, both personally and professionally for over five years. He started a web hosting business in 2002 targeting the SME market with a strong focus on customer service, and in 2004 he acquired another successful host with similar customer-centric philosophies. In December 2005, Tony's hosting business was bought out as he shifted his focus more towards his family and personal life.

Although my part in this book was small, it took no small amount of time to acquire the experience which allowed me to act as technical reviewer. As such, I would like to thank:

My wife Yvonne for her love and support over the years, and for being so tolerant when I spent many a long night and weekend supporting my web hosting clients!

My sons, Lucas and Daniel, for providing so much joy in my life.

Aric for his invaluable support, both technical and otherwise over the past five years, and for giving me the tools to help me to help him with this book :-)

My web hosting clients, who were so tolerant and understanding in (rare) times of crisis, and a pleasure to deal with at quieter times.

Brian Coogan is owner and technical director of White Dog Green Frog, a cPanel-based Webhosting company in Melbourne, Australia that has been hosting sites for over 4 years. Brian has had over 20 years of experience with Unix administration, including working for over 10 years as a consultant and trainer in Unix Administration for Fortune 100 companies including Hewlett-Packard and Telstra. Brian has also worked as an IT manager, software developer, youth crisis worker, and high school teacher and has interests in health and longevity. Brian is based in Melbourne, Australia.

David Mytton is a young web developer based in the UK. Although he spends much of his time programming for the Web, he is also a keen writer, having written articles for web development resource SitePoint.com and *International PHP Magazine*, as well as for his own website. These articles have also included interviews of famous personalities such as Andi Gutmans and Zeev Suraski (PHP architects & Zend Founders), Matthew Mecham (Invision Power Services CEO & Lead Developer), and Nick Lindridge (ionCube Founder). In between running his software development company, Olate Ltd. (www.olate.co.uk), he enjoys scuba diving and fencing.

Table of Contents

Preface

You've finally decided to buy a **dedicated server,** or **Virtual Dedicated Server,** or **Virtual Private Server (VDS/VPS)** with **cPanel** and **Web Hosting Manager (WHM)** management software and host your own websites. A dedicated server is a single piece of computing hardware that serves as a web server. A VDS/VPS is a single dedicated server that has been segregated into 2 or more equal parts. Each VDS/VPS acts as if it was a separate physical server, except that memory, CPU, and disk space are divided among each VDS/VPS on the physical server hardware. Since VDS and VPS are two names for the same product, we will refer to it as a VPS from now on.

Perhaps you've chosen to get a server because you have numerous personal sites you need to host and you want complete control over your sites, or perhaps you've chosen to start your own web-hosting company and you want a dedicated server or VPS so that you can maximize profits. Either way, if you've never had a dedicated server or VPS before, the prospect of it can be a bit daunting. What should you look for when you are shopping for hardware? How do you set it up initially? How do you manage accounts? What do you do if you have problems? It's enough to cause many people to give up and keep hosting through someone else.

However, it is possible for almost anyone to successfully manage a dedicated server or VPS with a little preparation and some basic knowledge. The goal of this book is to help you with both the preparation and knowledge you need to successfully manage your new server with WHM, and help you grow your business.

This book assumes that you already are reasonably familiar with cPanel, the end-user companion software to WHM, and web hosting in general. If you aren't, or would like to understand it better, you should consider buying my book on cPanel: *cPanel User Guide and Tutorial* from Packt Publishing (ISBN 1-904811-92-2) or `http://www.packtpub.com/cPanel/book`.

What This Book Covers

Chapter 1: Introduction to WHM and Dedicated Server/VPS Hosting
In this chapter, you will learn what WHM is, how it relates to cPanel, and what sort of things WHM can and cannot do. You'll also learn how to find a good host for your dedicated server or VPS.

Chapter 2: Setting Up Your Server with cPanel and WHM
In this chapter, you will learn how to download and install cPanel on your server and finalize the installation by configuring some settings in WHM.

Chapter 3: Additional Server Configuration
In this chapter, you will learn how to access root WHM and do some basic (but important) server configuration. You will also discover how to update WHM and learn about WHM/cPanel build tracks.

Chapter 4: Apache, PHP, Perl, and Databases
This chapter will teach you about Apache, Perl, PHP, databases, and other important web features. You will learn to configure these items to meet your needs.

Chapter 5: Working with User Accounts
In this chapter we will discuss how to create and manage user accounts on your server.

Chapter 6: Working with Reseller Accounts
In this chapter, you will learn about reseller accounts and what they can do. You will also learn how to manage what those accounts can do.

Chapter 7: IP Address, SSL/TLS, and DNS Management
In this chapter, you'll learn how to manage IP addresses, SSL/TLS certificates, and DNS entries.

Chapter 8: Ongoing Server Management
This chapter will examine the many tools WHM provides to help you keep tabs on your server and will help you take appropriate action if necessary.

Chapter 9: Customizing your Server with Themes and Add-Ons
In this chapter, you will learn how to customize your server using cPanel and WHM themes, how to modify and add themes, and also how to work with add-on modules for WHM and cPanel.

Chapter 10: Where to Go for Help with WHM
In the final chapter we'll look at some other places you can turn to for help with WHM and cPanel.

You can download the appendices of this book from
`http://www.packtpub.com/web_host_manager/book`.

Conventions

In this book, you will find a number of styles of text that distinguish between different kinds of information. Here are some examples of these styles, and an explanation of their meaning.

Code words in text are shown as follows: "We can include other contexts through the use of the `include` directive."

Any command-line input and output is written as follows:

```
ssh -lroot 111.111.111.111 -p6731
```

New terms and **important words** are introduced in a bold-type font. Words that you see on the screen, in menus or dialog boxes for example, appear in our text like this: "clicking the **Next** button moves you to the next screen".

Some data in the screenshots have been obscured to protect privacy. These will be displayed as (██████████████)

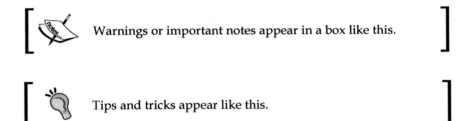

Warnings or important notes appear in a box like this.

Tips and tricks appear like this.

Reader Feedback

Feedback from our readers is always welcome. Let us know what you think about this book, what you liked or may have disliked. Reader feedback is important for us to develop titles that you really get the most out of.

To send us general feedback, simply drop an e-mail to `feedback@packtpub.com`, making sure to mention the book title in the subject of your message.

If there is a book that you need and would like to see us publish, please send us a note in the **SUGGEST A TITLE** form on `www.packtpub.com` or e-mail `suggest@packtpub.com`.

If there is a topic that you have expertise in and you are interested in either writing or contributing to a book, see our author guide on www.packtpub.com/authors.

Customer Support

Now that you are the proud owner of a Packt book, we have a number of things to help you to get the most from your purchase.

Errata

Although we have taken every care to ensure the accuracy of our contents, mistakes do happen. If you find a mistake in one of our books—maybe a mistake in text or code—we would be grateful if you would report this to us. By doing this you can save other readers from frustration, and help to improve subsequent versions of this book. If you find any errata, report them by visiting http://www.packtpub.com/support, selecting your book, clicking on the **Submit Errata** link, and entering the details of your errata. Once your errata have been verified, your submission will be accepted and the errata added to the list of existing errata. The existing errata can be viewed by selecting your title from http://www.packtpub.com/support.

Questions

You can contact us at questions@packtpub.com if you are having a problem with some aspect of the book, and we will do our best to address it.

1

Introduction to WHM and Dedicated Server/VPS Hosting

Thanks again for showing interest in this book. Based on your choice of reading material, it is clear that you are seriously considering buying a server that comes with cPanel and WHM. However, there are several things you'll probably want to take into account before we jump into working with WHM, such as:

- What WHM is and how it relates to cPanel
- What the system requirements for use of WHM and cPanel are
- A few important considerations about what kind of server or VPS you may need for your business
- How to shop for a dedicated server or VPS that includes WHM and cPanel

These are the things this chapter will deal with. If you have already purchased a server and are clear about what WHM is, then you can safely skip this chapter and head to Chapter 2, where you will learn how to set up your server and ensure it has the proper settings before moving paying clients (or yourself) onto it.

What are WHM and cPanel and How Do They Work Together?

cPanel and WHM are two sides of the same coin and are always sold together as a single product. **cPanel Inc.** is the name of the company that makes cPanel and WHM. **cPanel** is the name for the web-based hosting control panel for end users (customers or clients of yourself or your resellers). **WHM** is the web-based control panel for both server administrators (you) and resellers (clients of yours that host other clients' websites).

WHM helps you manage your entire server, install and maintain software, check systems, create accounts, assign features, and view the usage of resources on the server. It also helps your resellers manage their client accounts and features. The feature set of WHM on dedicated servers and VPS servers is very similar, since a VPS acts just like a *mini* dedicated server.

In order to understand just what WHM can do for us, we also need to be clear on what WHM *cannot* do.

What WHM Can Do

As noted above, WHM can do many important things, including:

- WHM can be used to control vital services, and install and manage important software that every web server needs. This includes web server software (**Apache**), databases (**MySQL** or **PostgreSQL**), mail server software (**Exim**), DNS (**Bind**), SSH (**OpenSSH**, which provides secure access to the command line interface for your server), and other important services and software.
- WHM can install, manage, or remove clients from the server for both you and resellers.
- WHM can control which features clients and resellers have available to them.
- WHM can scan and notify you or your clients when certain problems arise (services go down, clients use too many resources, there are some security issues that need to investigated).
- WHM can help you move accounts from one server to another (assuming you have appropriate access to both servers).
- WHM can automatically update itself and automate some tasks (site backups, updating critical system files, process web log files, and more).

What WHM Cannot Do

For all of the wonderful things WHM can accomplish, there are a few tasks that it cannot do. In most cases you will have to go to third-party software if you want to help automate these things (or do them manually).

- WHM cannot handle client billing.
- WHM cannot handle automated setup of new accounts. (It can create the accounts, but you need to provide the information manually or rely on third-party software to automate the process.)
- WHM cannot automatically remove (terminate) old/inactive hosting accounts or backup files. You have to handle these things manually in WHM or through some other software.

- WHM cannot notify you of serious problems if the server is overloaded or offline for some reason (because it won't be able to contact you). WHM may tell you about the problem after the server gets back to normal, but then it's probably too late. You'll need to use third-party services or software to let you know about such serious problems, so you can deal with them quickly. You can learn more about third-party add-ons in Chapter 9.

Understanding what WHM is and isn't capable of will help you make better decisions about how to run your business and what other tools you might need to use.

System Requirements for WHM and cPanel

In order to install cPanel and WHM on a server, it must meet certain basic system requirements. At the time of publication of this book, the requirements are as follows:

- Intel Pentium 2/266 MHz CPU or better (or equivalent CPU)
- 256 MB RAM
- 4 GB of free hard drive space

A clean install of one of the following supported operating systems:

Operating system	32-bit OS versions supported	64-bit OS versions supported
cAos	2	2
CentOS	3.x – 4.x	3.4 – 4.x
Debian	3.0*	Not supported
Fedora Core	1.x – 5.x	3.x – 4.x
FreeBSD	4.2, 4.3, 4.4, 4.5, 4.6, 4.8, 4.10, 5.0, 5.3, 5.4	5.3, 5.4
Mandriva	7.2, 8.0, 8.1, 8.2, 9.0, 9.1, 9.2, 10.0, 2006	2006
Red Hat Enterprise Linux	2.1, 3.x, 4.x	3.x – 4.x
Red Hat Linux (Fedora-Legacy)	7.3, 9	Not supported
SuSE	9.0, 10.0	9.0, 10.0
Trustix ES	2.0, 2.2	Not supported
Whitebox Enterprise	3	Not supported

* Debian support is currently in beta testing.

The latest system requirements and supported OSes can be found at: `http://cpanel.net/`

As with most published minimum system requirements, you could successfully install the product on such a system, but you wouldn't have much room or horsepower left to actually host any customers. A more realistic minimum would be:

- Intel® Celeron® 2.0 GHz CPU or higher (or equivalent CPU)
- 512 MB RAM
- 10-20 GB free hard drive space
- The latest supported version of a supported OS (listed above)

For VPS systems, you should try to at least match the minimum requirements with the resources allocated to your VPS (though it is likely that you won't have a choice of what operating system your VPS uses).

Important Considerations before Shopping for a Server or VPS

Before you fire up your web browser to go shopping for a server or VPS, you should take some time to sit down and flesh out your needs and business plan. Hopefully, you've done this before picking up this book, but if not, now is the time to do it before you waste money or time on something you don't need or that doesn't make good economic sense. Given below are a few things you need to consider.

What Do You Plan to Do with Your Server or VPS?

Are you planning on hosting paying clients' websites, or just host personal friends/family? Friends and family are more likely to be forgiving in case of interruptions in service. If you're hosting paying clients you don't personally know, don't expect them to be so forgiving. Are you going to primarily sell hosting, or do you also want to offer other services like game servers or streaming media services? Generally, it isn't a good idea to offer cPanel hosting and run other CPU-intensive services from the same server, as this will adversely affect server performance and slow down your clients' websites. If you really are serious about offering other services, you might want to consider getting a separate dedicated server just to run these other services on or putting fewer accounts on your existing server.

Do You Currently Have Any Experience of Offering cPanel Hosting to Paying Customers?

If not, you might want to consider cutting down on your up-front costs and looking for a reseller account from a reliable web host first. This will allow you to focus on learning how the business works, without the added stress of learning to manage an entire server or multiple servers; then when you are sure your business can support the costs of a dedicated server or VPS, and you are familiar with running a hosting business, you can trade up.

What Kinds of Hosting Customers are You Going to Focus On?

Generally, you can divide hosting customers into three segments—low-end, mid-range, and high-end.

Low-End Customers: Cheap and (Hopefully) Cheerful

Low-end customers are typically very *price-conscious*. Mostly, you'll find individuals looking for bare-bones hosting and very small "mom and pop" type businesses, who aren't looking to do much (if any) business online but do want people to be able to find their business contact information on the Web. They may be looking to upgrade from a free web hosting service that offers them more flexibility and better support. This group will typically be somewhat more accepting of a certain (limited) amount of downtime or connectivity problems (since they aren't paying much). Also, this group's resource (disk space and bandwidth) usage will be modest. However, you are also much more likely to need to provide very basic support to this group. They may not be familiar with how to create web content or how to get the content they do have onto the web, and they will turn to you for help.

If you host low-end customers, you can often pack several hundred accounts on a single mid-range server, and you'll probably need to, because you're not going to be getting much money per customer. It may also be helpful to offer a site building program of some kind because that will directly fill a need many customers in this category will likely have (see Chapter 10 for more information on some site-building programs that work with cPanel).

Mid-Range Customers: Growing Needs, Growing Profits

Mid-range customers are less price-conscious and typically more concerned with reliable and flexible service. Resource usage is going to be more. This class of customers includes small business owners, and individuals with more popular websites or more complex needs.

Basic support costs are likely to be less, since users in this category typically have some experience already with putting content on the web. However, these customers will probably be looking for more advanced features and assistance. They may request things like remote database access, additional functionality from PHP and Perl, and advanced mail handling. These customers are going to look for a certain amount of uninterrupted service and are going to want to know what you plan to do if service drops below that percentage.

High-End Customers: Welcome to the Big Time!

High-end customers are going to primarily be concerned with reliable service and top-notch 24/7 support, preferably via multiple methods of contact (phone, e-mail, live online chat). Basic support needs will be almost nothing, but they will expect fast and flexible service, and plenty of available resources. Support requests from these customers are likely to be complex when they do come. They'll want access to advanced services like **SSH**, **FXP**, **SFTP**, and **WebDAV**, the latest versions of PHP and Perl, and perhaps even additional languages like **Ruby on Rails** or **ASP**.

High-end customers include small to mid-sized businesses that cannot afford their own server, individuals who have very popular websites, or who are programmers and looking to design or run web services. Price isn't going to be an issue, but you'd better be able to provide the service and resources to back up the higher prices. These customers often outgrow shared web hosting, and may come to you looking for VPS or dedicated servers. It will be harder for a small company to attract these sorts of customers, but if you have the skill and resources to provide properly for these customers, their business can be quite lucrative for you.

 If you are just starting your business, you should probably try focusing on the low-end and mid-range customers until you have the infrastructure to support the high-end customers.

What Kind of Server do you Need?

If you have outgrown reseller hosting, getting a VPS may seem like the next logical step. VPS are cheaper than full dedicated servers and provide much of the same flexibility for your business. A VPS may run at 40 USD to 100 USD per month or more, while a dedicated server rarely starts under 70 USD per month. So if money is a serious concern, a VPS is a good idea. It may also make sense if you're just hosting your own sites and need more flexibility than a reseller account or shared hosting provides, but cannot afford the increased costs of a dedicated server.

However, a VPS does have some limitations. There may be several VPS on a single server, so you share CPU time with other VPS customers on the same server. In addition, there are some limitations to what you can do as an administrator in a VPS environment. In order to protect the division between VPS customers on the same machine there will be certain commands you won't be able to use in the command line, and certain files and directories may be "protected" so that you cannot edit them. The exact limitations will depend on which VPS software your host is using.

Some commercial software may require that you purchase a special version that works with VPS, especially software that typically gets licensed on a "per server" basis. So always be sure to check before you purchase expensive software, whether it will work on a VPS if you plan to use it on one. Later, if you upgrade to a dedicated server, you may need to pay an additional fee to relicense. Contact the software provider to see if this is the case.

Finally, moving paying clients from one server to another can be a tricky business, so it's a good idea to try to keep such moves to a minimum to avoid bothering them too often. If you've outgrown a reseller account and think your hosting business will continue to grow at a steady pace, it might make sense to move directly to a dedicated server. Of course, you'll need to do the math to be sure that it makes best economic sense.

Shopping for a VPS or Dedicated Server

Once you have a clear business model and a vision of where you want your business to go, you are now ready to go shopping for a VPS or dedicated server.

Just as with standard web hosting, there are a bewildering number of companies offering VPS and/or dedicated servers for sale. Some even offer **colocation**. Colocation means that you buy your own server and ship it to the company, and rent space in their facility specially designed to host servers often referred to as a **data center** (DC) or **network operations center** (NOC). They then provide the Internet access and maintain your hardware for you, but it is owned by you. If you don't wish to colocate with the company, they will send your server back (though they will likely charge you a fee).

Finding Deals

It will be very helpful for you to know what sort of product you are looking for (VPS/dedicated server/colocation) and how much you are willing to spend for that service.

Once you know what you want and how much you're willing to spend, it's time to go looking for deals. Dedicated server and VPS offers change even more often than shared hosting offers do with new hardware, features and prices, so it is a good idea to shop around awhile before ordering.

Thankfully, many of the places you'd go to look for opinions and deals on shared hosting are also places that you can go to explore VPS and dedicated servers.

Here are a few good places to start your search:

- `http://webhostingtalk.com/`: *WebHostingTalk* (or WHT as it is often referred to) is a central hub for information and discussion about all things related to hosting. This includes dedicated servers, VPS, and colocation. Lots of companies advertise specials here, so if you are very price sensitive this is a good place to visit regularly.
- `http://www.findmyhost.com/`: *FindMyHost* is a hosting search engine that also includes dedicated server hosting in their database. Customers also come here to rate their hosts.
- `http://forums.cpanel.net/forumdisplay.php?f=22`: In cPanel's own forum, you can find special deals on servers, hosting and services in the Ads and Offers area.

Of course, doing a search for VPS, dedicated server or colocation on a search engine will turn up a number of other options.

Important Things to Consider Before Sealing the Deal

Hopefully, now you've got a sense of what is available out there, and perhaps, you even have your eye on a few deals that seem to be most interesting.

So what should you look for in a company that you are going to buy a VPS, colocation or a dedicated server from? (Other than pricing that meets your needs, of course.)

Support is Critical

The importance of good support cannot be underestimated. Even if you are a seasoned server administrator, you need to make sure the company you work with has support policies that meet your needs. Remember, even if you don't think you'll need much support, it's unlikely that you will have physical access to the hardware, and you'll need to have someone at the data center reboot your hardware or check for hardware problems occasionally. In those instances, you definitely don't want slow or sloppy support.

The problem is that every company promises top-notch support. So how do you figure out which companies are the best at support? One good way is to watch what customers say about the companies you are interested in. You can see this at some of the sites mentioned above. Some companies also have public forums that you can visit. Of course, people are more likely to complain when there is a problem than they are to praise a company when everything is going well, so you'll want to take such reports with a grain of salt. Still, if you see many complaints about a company or if you see clients complaining about negative forum posts being removed, then that isn't a good sign.

In addition to that, it is important to understand what sort of support you can expect, and what it will cost you. Many companies offer some free support, but what that support covers varies. Does the company offer support by phone, e-mail, or live chat? Is the support available all the time or only during business hours?

If a company tells you that a VPS or dedicated server is self-managed, this means you can only expect the most *cursory* support for free. You are expected to handle your own server. If you need assistance of almost any kind, expect to pay (probably lots of money) for it. Self-managed servers tend to be cheaper, but the costs for support if you need it can quickly wipe out any savings.

If a company offers managed servers, this typically means that some amount of support is included for no additional charge. Every company is going to have a different definition of what sort of support is included. Be sure you know what kinds of support are covered for free before signing up, especially if you are new to dedicated server hosting. Managed free support could include server reboots, setup assistance, software installation assistance, general hosting assistance, service monitoring, administrative time (this typically refers to anything that requires an employee of the company to access your server that isn't covered in other categories of service), hosting account transfers, and security scanning and consultation.

Additional Fees, Included Extras, Upgrade Charges

Lots of companies offer cheap deals on VPS and dedicated servers. Be sure you understand the terms of any deal before you give a company your money. Often the cheapest deals don't include important software (like cPanel/WHM) or skimp on the hardware (a slow Celeron processor with 512 MB RAM and a 20 GB hard drive, for example). Some companies will allow you to upgrade your server later, but be sure you know what the options and charges are.

On the other hand, some companies will throw in extra hardware or software to attract more customers. Make sure you know what you are getting and what, if any, limitations there are on these extra products. Don't forget, when comparing deals between companies, to factor in what it would cost you to purchase these extras separately, if you didn't receive them for free.

The Data Center Itself

Look for data centers that have multiple connections to the Internet through various large providers (MCI, Level 3, AT&T, etc.) and lots of well-maintained networking equipment. Sometimes, a single bandwidth provider will have problems, so it is important to host in a data center that has more than one major connection to the Internet, or people won't be able to access your server. Make sure that the data center can survive a major power outage in their area and that the interior of the data center is carefully temperature controlled. Lots of hot servers in close proximity without good temperature control are a recipe for disaster.

Location, Location, Location

While the physical location where your VPS or server will be located isn't as important as the quality of the data center in which it is hosted, it can make a difference. Generally, a server hosted in a data center that is close to the bulk of your customers will perform more quickly than one that is many thousands of miles away. However, a high quality data center thousands of miles away from your customers may still outperform a local data center that doesn't have as many or as good connections to the Internet. Most companies will offer test links if you ask them, so that you can measure the speed of service from their data center to your location.

Billing and Cancellation Policies

Billing costs and times should be clear. Do you get charged for your server on the anniversary of the date that you first paid for the service or does billing always happen at a particular date? What happens if you are late with payments? Do they offer a grace period or do they disconnect your server immediately? Is there a fee to reconnect your server if it is disconnected due to late payment? How much does additional bandwidth cost if you go over your monthly allotment and how and when does it get billed?

Even if you are thrilled with the company you choose, there may come a time when you need to cancel a server. What is the company's policy on cancellations? Is there a money back guarantee if you cancel soon after signing up because you don't like the service? How much notice are you required to give before the next billing cycle so as to avoid further charges? Are there any additional fees for cancelling the service? Are you required to pay for a server for a set period of time (a contract) or can you cancel whenever you like?

The company you choose should have all of these items clearly articulated somewhere, or at least be clear about the policy when you ask. If a company doesn't answer to your satisfaction, you may want to look elsewhere.

General Purchasing Advice

A dedicated server or VPS is not something you want to skimp on. Purchase the fastest hardware with the most resources (disk space and bandwidth) that you can afford based on your planned usage. Low-end hardware may look like quite a bargain, but these servers typically won't be able to handle lots of business. You may find that your old reseller account was faster than your new low-end dedicated server, if your old host used high-end hardware. You also don't want to spend so much on your server or VPS that your business is losing money. Don't forget to factor in the cost of your cPanel/WHM license also if the server or VPS you've purchased doesn't come with it. Most NOCs will provide reduced cost cPanel licenses, so it's generally a good idea to get your license from them. The key is for you to find the best balance possible between performance, reliability, and overall cost.

Summary

In this chapter you've learned what WHM is and how it relates to cPanel, and what sorts of things WHM can and cannot do. We explored the minimum system requirements for a server with cPanel/WHM. We delved into some important things to consider before purchasing a server, including what you plan to use the server for, what types of customers you want to attract, and what those customers are probably going to want from you. Next, we looked at when purchasing a VPS makes best sense, and when purchasing a dedicated server is called for. Finally, we learned where and how to shop for our VPS, dedicated server, and colocation needs.

In the next chapter we will discuss proper initial setup of your new server or VPS with cPanel/WHM. Even if your host has done this setup for you already, you should definitely read the next chapter because there are a lot of settings that most hosts don't bother with during setup that may be important for your business.

2

Setting Up Your Server with cPanel and WHM

You should now have access to your dedicated or VPS server. Depending on the policies of the company you obtain your server from, it may already have cPanel and WHM installed. However, even if that is the case, you should review the items that we will cover in this chapter to make sure nothing was missed. We will discuss how to install cPanel and WHM on your server, and also how to finish initial configuration in WHM.

If you are certain you have this covered already, you can move on to Chapter 3, where we will discuss other settings that you should check before moving on to setting up Apache, PHP, and databases in Chapter 4.

Accessing Your Server for the First Time and Determining if You Need to Install cPanel and WHM

No matter how or where you host your server, the company that hosts it should provide you with basic information about how to connect to your server so that you can begin working with it.

You should have the following information:

- The main IP address of your server
- A list of any additional IP addresses your server has been assigned as well as netmask information, if you are going to be expected to bind these extra IPs to your server yourself

- The root password of the server (or information about where you can find it)
- Confirmation that you do have a cPanel/WHM license, and that it has been activated

If you are missing any of this information, contact your host to obtain it.

Getting the Tools You Need to Access Your Server

Our first order of business is to access the server and figure out what we need to do to get cPanel and WHM working. To do this, you will need two tools: an **SSH** client and a web browser (and Internet access, of course).

If you are running Windows on the computer you will be accessing your server from, then you will need to download and install an SSH client. One good free one is **PuTTY**: `http://www.chiark.greenend.org.uk/~sgtatham/putty/`

On the download page, there are a number of different applications and sub-projects available for download. If you've never used an SSH client before and don't know what you might need, you should probably download the Windows installer version that installs most of the tools available on this site (called `putty-VERSION#-installer.exe`). Just run the installer, and follow the recommendations.

On **Mac OS X** and **Linux**, your operating system most likely includes a full-featured SSH client. Linux/Unix users can also choose to install PuTTY if they prefer. PuTTY is not available natively for Mac OS X, though you might be able to get the Unix source to build.

On Mac OS X, you can use the Terminal to access the command line and use it for SSH. Typically, you will find the Terminal application here:

`/Applications/Utilities/Terminal`

Once you've identified the SSH client you are going to use, you will also need a graphical web browser. Any *modern* web browser should work fine: Firefox, Internet Explorer, Safari, Konqueror, Netscape, Opera, etc. The only thing you should be sure of before beginning is that you are using the latest version of whatever web browser you choose. Old or discontinued web browsers may not work properly with WHM and cPanel.

Log into Your Server

Now that you have the required tools, you can log into your server for the first time. Start up your SSH client or Terminal or whatever method you choose to use.

You will be logging into the server as the user called `root`, which is the master administrator account for machines running Linux/Unix.

 You do need to be careful when logged into your server as `root`, because unless you have a VPS, the root user can do anything on the machine, including removing critical files that the operating system needs to operate thus causing your server to fail, and perhaps even requiring all data to be removed and the operating system to be reinstalled. Think before you act when you are logged in as root!

Log into Your Server Using Windows

Start the PuTTY application, and you will be presented with a session configuration window:

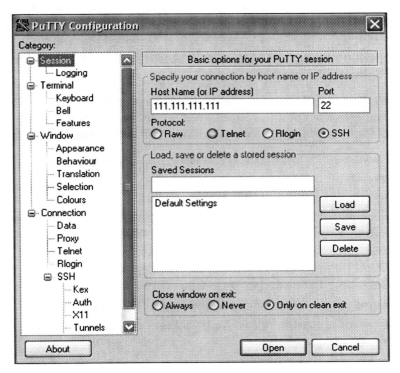

There are a wide variety of settings that you can change, but this book cannot go into great detail about this or any other SSH client. The only critical information you will need to enter is the information on the **Session** screen. Type your server's main IP address (which you'll have from your host NOC's welcome letter). Leave the protocol set to SSH and the port set to 22, and click **Open** at the bottom of the window. You should shortly be prompted for your username which is `root` and the user's password. Enter it, and you will be at the **root shell** (similar to a DOS command line). Now you can skip down to the *Are cPanel* and *WHM Installed Already* section.

Log into Your Server Using Mac OS X or Linux

You should be at a command line at this point (from now on referred to as a shell). Type the following to log into your server:

`ssh -lroot IPADDRESS`

`ssh` is the command itself that tells your computer to try connecting to the specified IP address via SSH. `-lroot` is a combination of the option `-l` which tells SSH what user to try logging into and the actual name of that user (`root` in this case). No space is necessary between the option `-l` and the username. This is followed by a space and the IP address of your server. The SSH command always assumes you want to use the standard SSH port number 22 to connect unless you add `-pPORT#` to the command. Here's an example: `ssh -lroot 111.111.111.111 -p6731`

This example will try to connect to the server at IP-111.111.111.111 as the user `root` using port 6731 (instead of port 22).

Since this is the first time you've connected to this server, you will probably be prompted if you actually want to connect to it, or not before you actually get to the login prompt. Here's an example from my Mac (your own display may differ):

```
Last login: Mon Apr 24 18:49:02 on ttyp2

Welcome to Darwin!

Computer:~ aric$ ssh -lroot 111.111.111.111

reverse mapping checking getaddrinfo for 111.111.111.111.reverse.
layeredtech.com failed - POSSIBLE BREAKIN ATTEMPT!

The authenticity of host '111.111.111.111 (111.111.111.111)'
can't be established.

RSA key fingerprint is d3:9b:46:6e:1d:ba:60:50:2c:85:26:bb:24:c1:81:a4.

Are you sure you want to continue connecting (yes/no)? yes

Warning: Permanently added '111.111.111.111' (RSA) to the list of
known hosts.

root@111.111.111.111's password:

Last login: Mon Apr 24 18:47:04 2006 from support.ltsvnoc.layeredtech.com
[root@82 ~]#
```

After you attempt to log in for the first time, your computer may warn you that reverse mapping checking failed for your new server. If so, ignore it for now, it is something we can get the host to fix later. You may also be prompted if you want to continue connecting to this machine. If so, type *yes*. This is just your computer's way of letting you know that it has never connected to this machine before and so doesn't recognize it.

After the first connection attempt, the RSA key for the server will be saved on your computer. Every time you connect to this machine from now on, the server's key will be compared against the saved local key. If they match, you'll be able to continue connecting. If not, you'll probably get a warning about mismatched keys and may have to delete the local key if you want to continue connecting. However, if you get such a warning, you should make sure that you're connecting to the correct server and not getting redirected to some other server.

You will be prompted to enter the password for the user you specified in the SSH command (root). Type in the root password you were given by your host. Linux does not display what you are typing as a form of security, so just type carefully and press *Enter/Return* when you've finished. If you typed it properly, you should now see a line letting you know what time and date someone last logged into this server. It should also display the IP address (or host name) of the computer that connected to your server (be sure you recognize the login time/location to be sure someone else isn't accessing your server other than your data center or yourself). You will then be at the server's root shell command prompt (which may end with a # or $, or even some other character).

Are cPanel and WHM Installed Already?

To figure out if cPanel and WHM have been installed, you can check this in several different ways (assuming your host hasn't already explicitly told you if it is installed or not). One way is to check and see if cPanel is installed and functioning via the root shell. You can try to determine it by looking for unique files:

```
ls /scripts/upcp
```

If you can see the upcp script in that location, then cPanel and WHM have been installed already. If that script doesn't exist, then you will probably have to install cPanel and WHM yourself.

Alternately, you can try connecting to your main server IP address via your web browser: `http://111.111.111.111/`

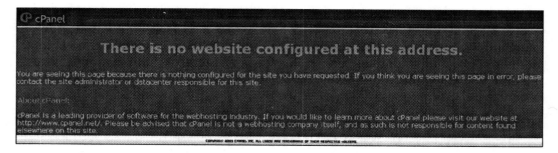

If you see a screen similar to the previous one, cPanel and WHM have already been installed. If not, then you may have more work ahead. Just to be absolutely sure, try also connecting to your server via port 2087 (secure) in your browser: https://111.111.111.111:2087/ or https://111.111.111.111/securewhm

You could also connect via port 2086 (nonsecure) in your browser: http://111.111.111.111:2086/ or http://111.111.111.111/whm

If you get prompted to enter your username and password, then WHM and cPanel are installed. For now though, don't bother logging in even if WHM is active (unless you plan to skip ahead in this book).

How to Install WHM and cPanel

If you are certain WHM and cPanel haven't been installed on your server yet, and that you do have an active license for it, you will need to install it. Thankfully, cPanel Inc. has made the process fairly easy on supported hardware and operating systems (see Chapter 1 for more on supported hardware and OSes).

First, make sure the server itself is as pristine as possible. If you've had another control panel or other similar software installed, you may have problems installing cPanel. If you've just gotten your server details from your host NOC, then it's probably ready for cPanel right now.

To install WHM and cPanel, you will need to log into your server as root first. Once you are at the shell prompt, type the following to begin the installation process:

```
mkdir /home/cpins
cd /home/cpins
wget http://layer1.cpanel.net/latest
sh latest
```

Note that this process is the same for all supported operating systems. The installer will figure out what hardware and software you have and install the appropriate files.

This will create a directory to hold the installation files and then fetch the latest cPanel installer script and run it. The script itself will take care of everything else.

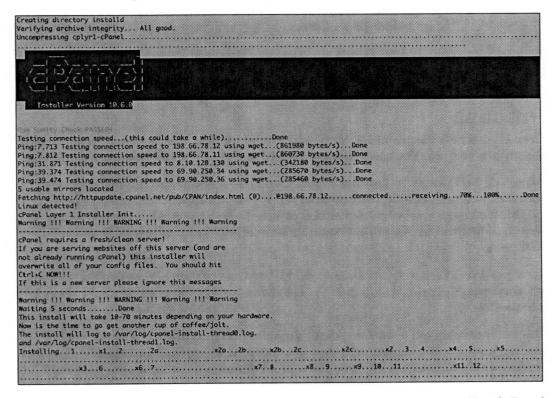

As you can see, the script will warn you about not trying to run this installer if cPanel is already installed, as it will wipe out your existing configuration files. Press *Ctrl+C* if you want to quit the installer before the installation begins. After it starts, you should not interrupt it for any reason or you may end up with an unstable system.

The actual installation process, once begun, can take quite a while, so you may want to go get some coffee or tea while you're waiting. You won't be required to enter any information at all during the installation, so you might as well relax. The time it takes for the installation to complete depends on how fast your server is. Low-end hardware like a Celeron or Sempron will obviously take longer than a dual Xeon or dual Opteron server. The listed time to finish the install (10 to 70 minutes) is fairly reasonable.

During the installation process, the install script downloads and installs critical files and services needed to run both WHM and cPanel. When the process finishes, hopefully without any errors, you will be returned to the root shell prompt.

 If you get any errors during the installation, or if the installation fails, contact your host or cPanel license provider for assistance.

Accessing WHM and Finishing the Installation Process

Even if your host has installed WHM and cPanel for you, they may not have finished the process for you. You need to access WHM and check before doing anything else.

Accessing WHM may be familiar to you if you had a reseller account with another web host before obtaining your own server. If you were a reseller, you accessed WHM to manage your client's cPanel accounts. Even so, you'll be shocked at the wealth of features in WHM that you only have access to when logged in as the user root.

To access WHM securely, access the main IP address of your server like this in your web browser: https://111.111.111.111:2087/ or https://111.111.111.111/securewhm.

You will probably get a warning about the server **SSL certificate**. If so, accept the certificate and continue. You will then be prompted to log in. To access WHM as the server administrator, you log in as the user root and use the same root password you used to access your server via SSH earlier.

If you have problems accessing your server using the secure method above, you can access it without SSL/TLS like this: http://111.111.111.111/whm or http ://111.111.111.111:2086/. This is *not* recommended unless you simply cannot get into WHM securely because it is possible for hackers to intercept insecure communications between your computer and your server. The username and password are for the same as the secure login method: the user is root and the password is your server's root password.

Finishing Installation

Once you log in, you will either be greeted by the main WHM screen with lots of text in the sidebar and icons in the center, or by a screen that is mostly empty, except for some writing in the sidebar on the left:

`Welcome to Web Host Manager®!`

`It appears this is your first time using Web Host Manager®. This wizard will guide you through setting up your server.`

If you see the full WHM screen, then your installation is complete, and you can skip to the next section.

WHM Setup: The License

If you see the Welcome text mentioned earlier, click the **Next** button to be shown the cPanel license agreement. You should read this agreement, and then you must click the **I Agree** button at the bottom of the agreement if you want to continue using WHM and cPanel.

WHM Setup: Basic Information

The screen will change once you accept the license agreement, and you will be asked to fill out some information. Note that you won't need to actually make any changes to this section right now if you don't want to, but you will need to revisit this screen by clicking **Basic cPanel/WHM Setup** at the top of the WHM sidebar once you've finished the installation process.

Basic Information: Contact Details

These details will be used by the server to contact users in case of downtime.

Depending on which version of WHM and cPanel you have installed as well as what operating system/hardware you are using, the options in this basic setup section may be slightly different or rearranged.

Server Contact E-Mail Address

* Enter an email address you can be reached at in case a problem arises with this server.

Examples: john@doe.com, john.q.public@anonymous.com, user@host.com

`admin@domain.com`

Server Contact Pager Address

Enter an cellular phone or pager email address that can be messaged in case a problem arises with this server.

Examples: john@cellphone.com, 8005551212@provider.com, user@host.com

`admincell@vnobl.com`

Server Contact AIM

Enter an AIM name you can be reached at in case a problem arises with this server.

Examples: user54044

`adminaim`

AIM Username

The username that this server should use for login to AIM when sending alerts. You can register a new aim name: here.

`serveraim`

AIM Password

The AIM username password for sending alerts.

`password`

Server Contact ICQ

Enter an ICQ user identification number you can be reached at in case a problem arises with this server.

Examples: 1234567, 11223344, 1020304

`1234567`

ICQ ID

The ICQ ID the the server should use for sending alerts. You can register for a new ICQ number: here.

`1234568`

ICQ Password

The ICQ ID password for sending alerts.

`password`

The **Server Contact E-mail Address** will be the address e-mail is sent to, when there are problems with the server (the server is overloaded, services fail and need to be restarted, etc.). Exactly what kinds of warnings you will get via e-mail depend on what you set in the **Contact Manager** (discussed later in Chapter 3). Keep in mind that this e-mail address will automatically appear in every account's **DNS zone** on this server (see Chapter 7 for information about DNS zones). Therefore, make sure this e-mail address is a real e-mail address that you check regularly, but one that you don't mind the public having.

The **Server Contact Pager Address** is an e-mail address where the server can contact you if there is a problem. Note, the server cannot handle SMS messages, so your provider must provide a standard e-mail gateway for your pager or cell phone. What you are contacted about this way depends on the settings in the **Contact Manager**.

Server Contact AIM Address is the screen name or AOL Instant Messenger (**AIM**) username where you can be contacted if there is a problem with your server. Again, contact is governed by the **Contact Manager** settings.

AIM Username is the AIM username the server itself should log into in order to contact you via that messaging service. You may need to set up a special AIM username for the server. You can do this by clicking the word **here** in the item description.

AIM Password is the password of the AIM account you want the server to log into when there is a problem in order to AIM you. This password is stored in plaintext on this screen, so don't use a password you use for any other service and especially make sure it is not the server root password.

The **Server Contact ICQ** item is the ICQ number (another instant messaging service also owned by AOL) you can be reached at in case of an emergency with the server. What you get contacted about depends on the settings in the **Contact Manager**.

ICQ ID allows you to set the ICQ number the server should log into in order to send you a message via the ICQ instant messaging service.

ICQ Password is the password for the ICQ ID number the server will use to contact you. Again, this password is stored in plaintext on this screen, so be careful with what password you use.

Basic Information: Default Themes and Directories

You can set up a default cPanel theme and a default home directory for all your accounts.

Default cPanel Theme

* Enter the default cPanel theme for newly created accounts whose package does not specify a theme.

Examples: x, monsoon, bluelagoon

`x`

Default Home Directory

* Enter the location where you wish for new users' home directories to be created. By default all directories matching the "Home Directory Prefix" are checked for available disk space and the directory with the most free space will be used.

Example: /home

`/home`

Home Directory Prefix

Additional home directories matching the following value will also be used for new home directory creations. **This option only takes one value.** A blank value disables this feature.

Examples: home matches /home, /home2, /newhome, /usr/home, /anythingwith/homeinit

`home`

The **Default cPanel Theme** setting allows you to specify which theme you want all new accounts to use by default. This setting can be changed at the time of account setup. (See Chapters 5 and 6 for more on working with accounts.) Oddly, this item is not a drop-down box of choices. You need to manually type in the name of the default theme as it appears in the **List Installed cPanel Themes** item in the **Themes** section of WHM (see Chapter 9 in this book, or Chapter 12 in *cPanel: User Guide and Tutorial*, ISBN-1-904811-92-2, Packt Publishing for more about cPanel themes). The default is **x**, which is cPanel Inc.'s own theme, updated automatically with cPanel, so it generally will offer access to new features and content before third-party themes, which may take a while to update. If you don't know what to choose, **x** (**X-Skin**) is a good default choice.

The **Default Home Directory** is the name of the directory where you would like to store cPanel users' accounts including their mail, web, and FTP-related files. Typically, the default entry of /home is fine. If you have more than one hard drive or prefer that users' home directories get stored elsewhere, enter the directory name here prefixed with a forward slash (/). Entering a name here will not create that directory; it will be up to you to do so. /home is automatically created on all cPanel servers. Also, this is just the default directory. If you have more than one home directory, you can switch accounts manually between directories at any time. However, it is generally not a good idea to move an account to a different home directory unless you absolutely have to do so. This is because some web scripts require specifying the absolute path on the server to some content and if you switch the user from /home to /home2, those scripts will break until the user edits them.

The **Home Directory Prefix** lets WHM know what directories are home directories by specifying part of the name that every home directory will contain. This item should not contain a forward slash. The default is **home** and that is fine under most circumstances. Keep in mind that whatever you type here will act as a wildcard selector, matching any directory with those letters in it. For example, if the prefix is home then a directory with the name home2 or homersimpson is considered a possible location for additional user accounts. If you don't put any value in this box, WHM won't look for other home directories. This item cannot be more than a single value.

Basic Setup: User IDs and Networking

These basic settings are related to networking.

```
┌─Minimum UID──────────────────────────────────────────────────────────────────────┐
│        The minimum user ID value used when creating new accounts. Leave blank to use the    │
│        OS defaults.                                                      [                    ]│
│        Values below 500 may result in a very broken system!                        │
└──────────────────────────────────────────────────────────────────────────────────┘

┌─Main Shared Virtual Host IP──────────────────────────────────────────────────────┐
│        * The IP address that will be used for setting up shared IP virtual hosts. This can only │
│        be one address. Do not enter multiple addresses.              [111.111.111.111       ]│
│                                                                                    │
│        Example: 10.11.133.14                                                        │
└──────────────────────────────────────────────────────────────────────────────────┘

┌─Alternate Main Ethernet Device───────────────────────────────────────────────────┐
│        If you are using a device other than the first ethernet device (eth0) as your public │
│        interface, enter it here.                                        [                    ]│
│                                                                                    │
│        Examples: eth0:3, eth1, eth2 venet0:0 (virtuozzo servers)                    │
└──────────────────────────────────────────────────────────────────────────────────┘
```

Minimum UID allows you to set a number under which new Linux users will not create new user accounts. In Linux, every new account and group gets assigned a unique number. Don't type anything into this box unless you know what you are doing because setting this number too *low* will cause very serious problems on your server.

Main Shared Virtual Host IP will be automatically set to the first IP address set up on this server. You can switch it to any other IP address bound to this server if you wish. Don't try to set the IP address to 127.0.0.1 (localhost) or any IP address not publicly bound to this server or no one will be able to access the accounts you set up. The main shared IP address is the one on which all new accounts that do not have a dedicated IP address specified will be bound to. You may not set this to more than one IP address. If you want resellers to use a different IP address for their shared accounts, you can set that up in the **Reseller Center** (see Chapter 6 for more about reseller accounts).

The **Alternate Main Ethernet Device** item allows you to specify which Ethernet controller is the public one (the one connected to the Internet). You can leave this blank if you wish, but if you try to add additional IP addresses to this server and that process fails even though you've entered it correctly, you probably need a different interface listed here. Most common are eth0, eth0:1, and eth1, but you should ask your host NOC what interface you should be using.

Basic Setup: Hostname, Nameservers, and DNS Values

The basic setup of WHM has options to set up the server's current hostname and up to four default nameserver.

Hostname displays your server's **hostname**. People who are new to the world of dedicated servers are often confused about the concept of a hostname. A hostname is a unique name for the server itself. When set up properly, you can access your server via one of its bound IP addresses or the hostname. A hostname always looks like a subdomain or what is more properly called a **Fully Qualified Domain Name (FQDN)**. That is, it has three parts like this: servername.domain.com. It should be a real domain, something that you personally own or have control over. It should also never match the name of an existing subdomain in that domain. You could call your server *powerful.myhostingcompany.com* so long as you own the *myhostingcompany.com* domain name. You won't be able to use "powerful" as a subdomain, though, so choose carefully. (Learn more about DNS management in Chapter 7.)

When the hostname is set up properly, you will be able to access WHM using the server hostname rather than the main IP address if you prefer. You should make sure that the hostname properly resolves to this server. This means that you will have to set up an A record in the DNS zone for the domain name you are using for the server hostname. Note, changing the hostname in this area doesn't actually reset the real server hostname; you will need to do that by using the **Hostname** feature under the **Network Setup** section of WHM once installation is finished.

The **Primary, Secondary, Third,** and **Fourth Nameserver** items all do the same basic thing: Set up the nameservers that this server will use by default. You must define at least two, and you can optionally set up to four. Type the name of the nameservers you want to use in the appropriate boxes (**ns1.domain.com, ns2.domain.com,** etc.) and then click the **Assign IP Address** button next to each entry, one at a time. This should assign the nameserver an IP address from your server (unless it is already set up to point to another IP address). The box that pops up will display the nameserver's assigned IP address. Once it does that, you can close it and click the **Add an A Entry for this Nameserver** button, and WHM will set up a DNS zone if needed for this IP address or add an A record to an existing domain on the server if needed. You will need to log into your registrar for the nameservers you want to use and point these nameserver addresses to the IP addresses that WHM just displayed for each one. How you set this up at your registrar differs, so you should discuss the matter with your domain registrar if you are unclear what to do.

This is followed by DNS related **Time to Live** values.

Domain Time To Live

This value defines the caching time for host name lookups for domains hosted on this server. When a caching nameserver queries the authoritative nameserver for a resource record, this value defines the number of seconds before the record will expire. Shorter TTL values can cause heavier loads on the nameserver, but can be useful for zones that contain frequently changing records. The range of values in seconds as defined by RFC 2181 is 0 to 2147483647.

`14400`

Nameserver Time To Live

This value is similar to the Domain Time To Live setting, but is specifically the value used for newly created zone file's authoritative nameserver entries.

`14400`

Master Nameserver

This setting is deprecated. Please consider using the Cluster configuration instead. Enter the IP address of the primary nameserver that will be sent domain and subdomain updates (if this is not the primary nameserver). **Setting this value will make this server a slave nameserver.** A *trust key relationship* must be established before entering the hostname.

Examples: trusted.server.com, ns1.myhost.com, ns2.anotherhost.com

[Save]

Domain Time to Live (TTL) defines how much time (in seconds) DNS servers will cache the domain host lookup information before checking for changes and re-caching it. The default value is OK, but shorter times will cause the local DNS server to check for changes more often. Shorter values may also increase the load on the local DNS server process, since it must re-cache information more often. If you're not certain what value would be good, leave this set to the default value. All new accounts created will use this domain TTL value when the DNS zone is set up.

Nameserver Time to Live controls the default setting in seconds that nameserver values will be cached.

Master Nameserver is a depreciated setting that will probably be removed altogether at some point. It allows you to set up a master and slave relationship between multiple DNS servers. Don't bother with this feature. If you want to use a separate master nameserver (instead of one DNS server for each server you own), you will want to use the **DNS Clustering** feature in WHM's **Cluster/Remote Access** section. See Chapter 7 for more about DNS clustering.

Basic Setup: CGI and Apache Logging

In WHM you can enable or disable an alias for cgi-bin scripts. You can also change the style in which you receive your Apache logs.

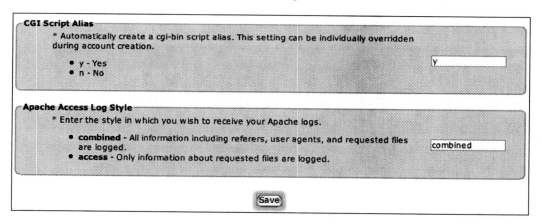

The **CGI Script Alias** setting allows you to set the default for cgi-bin directory creation. If this item is set to **y**, then every new domain and subdomain will have a cgi-bin directory created so the user can use CGI scripts (like Perl scripts). Setting this to **n** will turn off the CGI feature by default for new accounts. You can change this setting for each account you set up.

The **Apache Access Log** setting can be set to **combined** or **access**. This changes what is reported in Apache raw logs. Generally, you'll probably want the added information that **combined** provides.

After making the necessary changes remember to click **Save**.

After you have finished working with the basic cPanel and WHM settings, click the **Next** button in the WHM sidebar to continue to the next installation step. Don't forget to come back to the **Basic cPanel/WHM Setup** later if you've skipped any important settings.

WHM Setup: Disk Quota Setup

This will start a process on the server that will set up disk quotas on the server so that WHM can keep track of how much disk space each user is using. This process may take a while.

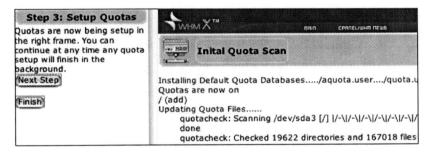

Thankfully, you don't have to watch the display until the process is finished if you don't want to. You can click **Next** in the sidebar at any time, and the quota setup will be completed in the background while you work. Just don't reboot the server in the middle of this process.

WHM Setup: Nameserver Setup

Now you can choose to set up the local DNS server on this server. cPanel uses a program called **Bind** to serve DNS information about the domains on this server. Generally, you will want to set up the nameserver process.

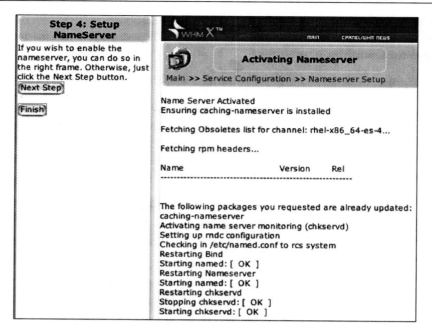

This should not take long. Once finished, click **Next Step** in the WHM sidebar to continue with setup.

WHM Setup: DNS Resolvers

Now you will want to specify at least two off-server, working DNS servers. Typically, your host NOC can provide you with this information. If you don't have anything else, you can set this to two IP addresses from your own server. However, for security reasons (which we will discuss in Chapter 3) this isn't a good idea, and it is thus best if you can avoid it.

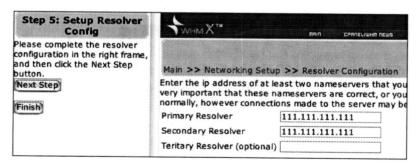

Specify at least two different IPs and then save the changes and click **Next Step** in the sidebar to continue with setup.

WHM Setup: Setting the MySQL Root Password

Since every cPanel server comes with **MySQL** (a database server) set up, you will need to set a root (master) password. Don't confuse the root user password with the MySQL root password. They are, and should always be entirely different. It is unlikely you will ever need to remember this password unless you plan to connect to the MySQL as root. Even if you do decide to do so later, you can change the MySQL root password again at any time. Make it long and random. Include upper and lower case letters and numbers, but do try to stay away from extended characters and symbols, or **phpMyAdmin** may not be able to connect to the MySQL server.

Type the password into the box, save the changes and then click **Finish** in the sidebar to finish the installation process. Congratulations on the successful setup of your server!

Summary

In this chapter, you've learned how to download and install cPanel on your server. You have also learned how to finish the installation by configuring some settings in WHM. In particular, you've configured how your server will contact you in case of problems. You now know how to set up what default themes and directories WHM and cPanel will use, and also know about minimum user IDs and basic networking interfaces.

You have learned about the server hostname, configured nameserver values and basic DNS settings, and also defined how CGI and Apache logging are handled. In addition, we have seen how to set up initial disk space quota tracking on your server, start the nameserver process (Bind), configure the DNS resolvers, and set the root MySQL password for your server

You've finished the basic setup of your server, but there is still more work to be done before you can move paying customers onto your server. Chapter 3 will deal with all of the additional settings you will want to configure, before moving on to Apache, PHP, and database configuration in Chapter 4.

3
Additional Server Configuration

Your server now has cPanel and WHM installed, and is at least minimally configured. In this chapter, we will take the configuration further in our quest for getting our server ready for paying customers (or our own websites). We will explore:

- The root WHM interface and how to navigate it
- How to choose a cPanel/WHM build track
- Setting your server's hostname, time, and date, as well as other important settings
- Setting up additional services and hardware
- How to set up automated backups of data using WHM

Even if you think you're ready for paying customers now, I suggest you read through this chapter before continuing to Chapter 4, where we will discuss Apache, PHP, and databases. There are so many features in WHM, it can be easy to miss at least a few important ones, and reading this chapter will ensure a smoother roll out of your server.

Welcome to Root WHM!

You've finally finished the setup process and now you have your first glimpse of the full root WHM interface:

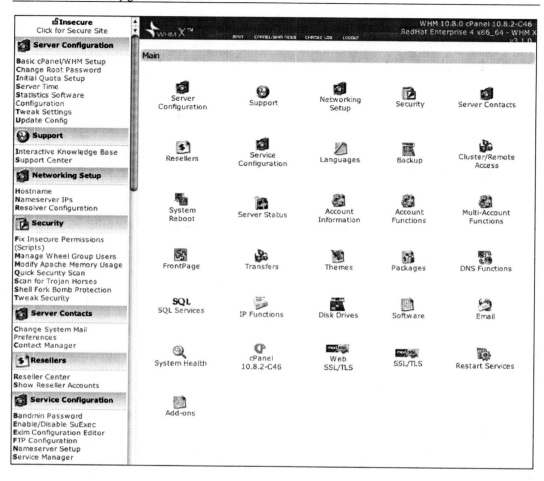

The interface can be a bit overwhelming at first, but the basic setup is fairly simple. On the left side of the screen you have the WHM features sidebar. Every function can be accessed from the sidebar at any time. The top of the interface gives you some basic information about WHM and cPanel as well as a few links to additional information about WHM and cPanel, including the cPanel change log and main interface buttons. Below this area and to the right of the sidebar is the main interface screen. It is here that the various WHM features will appear. Right now you should see a bunch of icons. Clicking the icons allows you to navigate all WHM features that you find in the sidebar.

At the top of the WHM interface are several links and some information about what version of WHM and cPanel you are running.

The first link is **MAIN**. Clicking this will cause the icon interface of WHM to reappear in the center panel, just as it does when you first log into WHM.

CPANEL/WHM NEWS will take you to a page that displays information about Apache, and also some news from cPanel Inc.

---

cPanel Training Seminar

Do you want to advance your knowledge and understanding of cPanel Software and how to troubleshoot various issues? Would you like to receive hands on training directly from cPanel's own Technical Support and Development Staff?

If so, cPanel's first ever Training Seminar is for YOU! From level 1 techs to system administrators, everyone who handles technical support for cPanel software is invited AND encouraged to attend. At only $25 per person, attending this Seminar will prove to be extremely beneficial to you and your staff.

Additional information on the Training Seminar and how to sign up can be found on the cPanel Training Seminar page.

Apache Security/Version Table			
Module	Latest Version	Installed Version	Status
Apache Core	1.3.34	1.3.34	🔒
Gzip Module	1.3.26.1a	1.3.26.1a	🔒
Mono	1.0.1	1.0.1	🔒
Jk (Tomcat) Module	1.2.6	2.0.0	🔒

Unfortunately, cPanel Inc. doesn't update the news or "latest version" information very often, so this screen isn't as useful as it could be. However, it will still provide some important information. In addition to cPanel Inc. news, it displays the version of Apache web server and the various Apache modules you have installed. The Apache modules are all listed in the **Apache Security/Version Table**. The **Latest Version** column is supposed to reflect the most recent version of that module which cPanel supports (it is usually the version that cPanel's **easyapache** script will install—see Chapter 4 for more information about the easyapache script and Apache itself). Next to that is the **Installed Version** column. This reflects the version you currently have installed on this server. The **Status** column will display a closed lock if cPanel Inc. believes that the version you have installed on your server is secure. If the module might be insecure, an open lock icon will appear there.

Just because this table suggests that your module versions may be secure, you shouldn't rely on this information exclusively. Since new issues can be discovered daily, there may be insecurities or new versions of modules not reflected in this table.

The **Change Log** link at the top of the WHM interface will display the latest changes that cPanel has documented for the latest builds of cPanel.

By default, the change log shows all of the latest builds of cPanel for all supported platforms. You can filter the displayed results or view the **change log** in different formats by clicking on the appropriate link at the top of the **change log** list (under the title). You can show all changes, only **Linux x86** (32-bit Intel or AMD CPUs) specific changes, **Linux x86_64** (64-bit Intel or AMD CPUs) specific changes, **FreeBSD**-specific changes, and view the changes in **RDF** (Resource Description Framework) or **WML** (Wireless Markup Language) format.

Every entry in the change log can only be assigned to one type of computer and OS. If there are changes that affect more than one platform, then cPanel Inc. currently assigns that change to the Linux 32-bit x86 platform. If you use some other platform, always watch the Linux x86 **change log** in addition to your platform-specific changes, because some of those changes and bug fixes may affect you as well.

Unfortunately, cPanel Inc. does not note every change made to every build, so it can sometimes be difficult for you to know exactly what is different.

You don't have to be logged into WHM to view the cPanel change log. You can access it from any web browser at: http://changelog.cpanel.net/

The next link at the top of the WHM interface is **LogOut**. If you click on this it will end your session in WHM. After clicking on that link, you will be prompted if you want to access WHM again as another user.

At the far right side of the top of the WHM interface, you will see the currently installed version number of WHM and cPanel, and under that, which platform your server is running. If you click on the WHM and cPanel version information, this will take you to the screen that allows you to manually update cPanel and WHM.

Finally, at the top of the WHM sidebar on the left, you will see a link that will let you switch to a secure SSL connection to WHM if you aren't already in the secure interface, and if you are, the graphic will confirm that.

cPanel Builds: Choosing the Right One for You

cPanel and WHM are updated a bit differently from other types of software you may be familiar with. cPanel Inc. makes updates to WHM and cPanel nearly every day, and you can use a version with the very latest changes and bug fixes updated regularly or rely on one or two build updates each year. (A build is a version of the software code released either internally for testing or exernally to use by consumers.) cPanel Inc. has designed build tracks that allow you to choose how often you'd like WHM and cPanel updated with new features and bug fixes. There are five build tracks to choose from:

- **Stable**: Stable builds typically get released one to two times a year. Since updates come rarely and there is a lot of testing of the code prior to getting a new stable build released, support becomes easier for you, the systems administrator.

- **Release**: Release builds come out more often than stable builds (typically two to five times a year). This is cPanel Inc.'s recommended default build track, and when you first install cPanel, it is this build track that gets installed. The code in release builds typically sees less testing than stable builds, but it should generally perform well while still permitting you to keep up with new features and bug fixes.

 If you don't know what type of build track you want to use, you should remain on release.

- **Current**: The current builds of cPanel have had less code testing than either release or stable builds, and updates can come frequently (up to hundreds of times a year). If you want the latest features and bug fixes, and aren't overly concerned about the new bugs you may experience, then this is the build for you. There is very little testing done on current builds before releasing them to the public, so watch the cPanel **Change Log** and make sure you know what you are getting into if you choose **Use current**.

- **Edge**: You should generally not use edge builds on an in-production server (one with paying clients or where stability is required). Edge builds have almost no testing done on them. If you use edge, you are a guinea pig for cPanel, helping to test the latest bug fixes and features. There are new edge builds almost daily. It is recommended that you only use edge if you are running it on a test server or if you absolutely need some bug fix or feature included in the latest edge build.

- **Beta**: Unlike the other build tracks, if you want to use a beta build you must manually edit the `/etc/cpupdate.conf` file and change CPANEL=*build* (where *build* is whatever build track you are currently using) to CPANEL=beta. Beta builds are designed to allow cPanel to test new features or bug fixes without the worry of affecting in-production servers. If you want to test a special feature, you can manually update to a beta build. Beta builds are not updated regularly. They are only released when new feature testing needs to be done. You should *never* remain on the beta build track permanently. Always update to one of the other tracks as soon as you can.

Generally the version of cPanel and WHM are denoted by a version number, an S, R, C, E or B for stable, release, current, edge or beta build tracks respectively, followed by the build number. For example:

cPanel 10.8.1S114 stands for cPanel version 10.8.1, stable build track, build number 114.

No two build tracks can share the same build number, so if a particular set of features gets released for more than one build track, the build numbers will be incremented by one. So cPanel 10.8.2S65 and 10.8.2R64 may have the same basic feature set and fixes with only minor changes (if any) between the two build tracks.

You may look at the list of build track descriptions and wonder why any company uses anything other than stable builds. After all, stable builds are the ones that receive the most testing before release, and there are fewer updates to worry about. For those reasons, many companies do choose to use stable builds on their servers. However, there are a few drawbacks:

- Security and bug fixes do not get back-ported (released) for any previous builds. If you are running cPanel 10.8.1S114, and a new critical bug fix comes out for cPanel in cPanel 10.8.2E170 or later, then your server will not have the benefit of that fix until the next time the cPanel stable build track is updated, which may be months away.

- Stable builds are not bug-free builds. There may be numerous bugs in the current build in the stable build track. If you stick with stable builds, you may be stuck with the same set of well known bugs for a long time.

- Sometimes you may update certain components on your server (perhaps by updating the operating system), and stable builds may not work well with the new changes. You may be forced to update to another build track if this happens.

For these reasons, the release build track is probably the best choice overall. It gets updated often enough that you're not usually waiting long for security or bug fixes and new features, but not so often that it is going to create a support nightmare for you.

The current and edge build tracks all have their uses. For example, cPanel may fix a critical bug that is affecting your server. You can use those builds if you need that fixed right away and then switch back to the release build track once the changes have made it into release.

The most important thing you can do to make sure you're using the right build track for your needs is to keep track of what's happening with cPanel development. Unfortunately, there's no one particular location where you can get all the information you need. Here are a few of the best places for information about cPanel development (see Chapter 10 for more information about these resources):

- `http://changelog.cpanel.net/`: This is where information about newly released builds can be found. Unfortunately, not every build makes it into the change log, nor does every new feature or bug fix get logged. However, this is still a good place to start.

- `http://forums.cpanel.net/`: The cPanel customer forums aren't the place for official cPanel support from the company. However, a lot of proposed changes, problems, and fixes are discussed there by both customers and staff, so it's an invaluable tool.

- `http://layer1.cpanel.net/`: You can find a list here of the latest build number for every build track for all supported platforms. In addition, this is where you can download a copy of certain critical software for use with cPanel, like the cPanel installer and latest supported version of Perl for cPanel.

- `http://bugzilla.cpanel.net/`: All bugs in cPanel get filed here. You can and should search the bug tracker if you are experiencing a problem and want to see if there is a fix for it. If you think you've found a bug that no one else has reported, you can put in your own ticket so that cPanel Inc. is aware of the issue. If someone has already filed a bug that you are also having problems with, you can vote for that bug so cPanel Inc. understands that there are more people with the same problem. You will also be notified if a bug you file or vote for gets updated. Often the cPanel developers will fix the bug or tell you how to fix it. In some cases they may ask you to try the latest edge build to see if the problem goes away.

Whatever build track of cPanel you decide to use, you should set cPanel to use that particular track now and update cPanel if need be.

Updating cPanel

Once you've decided on what build track you'd like to use, you need to decide if you want to have cPanel automatically update itself or not. If you have lots of servers, having cPanel automatically update itself every night will help keep all servers in sync without your having to take time to update them yourself. However, cPanel Inc. has been known to push updates out (even in the stable build track) that cause serious issues for users. Typically, when this happens, cPanel is quick to issue a fix, but your clients may be stuck with the bugs until that happens. For this reason, many hosts prefer to manually update cPanel themselves once they are sure an update won't cause serious problems. If you have hundreds of servers this can be a bit of a pain. Of course you can choose never to update cPanel at all (but this isn't a good idea unless you need the version of cPanel to remain unchanged because of testing you are doing).

> It is a good idea for you to check http://layer1.
> cpanel.net/ and then check places like the cPanel forums
> http://forums.cpanel.net/ for complaints or issues
> about the new update if you plan on manually updating.
> This way you'll be better prepared if issues arise.

Click **Update Config** under the **Server Configuration** section of WHM. Here, you can choose the type of build track you want to use for cPanel and also control how cPanel updates itself.

```
┌─────────────────────────────────────────────────────────────────────────┐
│                    Cpanel/WHM Update Preferences                          │
│ ┌─cPanel/WHM Updates──────────────────────────────────────────────────┐  │
│ │ ○ Automatic (STABLE tree)                                           │  │
│ │ ◉ Automatic (RELEASE tree)                                          │  │
│ │ ○ Automatic (CURRENT tree)                                          │  │
│ │ ○ Manual Updates Only (STABLE tree)                                 │  │
│ │ ○ Manual Updates Only (RELEASE tree)                                │  │
│ │ ○ Manual Updates Only (CURRENT tree)                                │  │
│ │ ○ Manual Updates Only (bleeding EDGE tree)                          │  │
│ │ ○ Never Update                                                      │  │
│ └─────────────────────────────────────────────────────────────────────┘  │
│ ┌─cPanel Package Updates──────────────────────────────────────────────┐  │
│ │ ◉ Automatic                                                         │  │
│ │ ○ Manual Updates Only                                               │  │
│ │ ○ Never Update                                                      │  │
│ └─────────────────────────────────────────────────────────────────────┘  │
│ ┌─Security Package Updates────────────────────────────────────────────┐  │
│ │ ◉ Automatic                                                         │  │
│ │ ○ Manual Updates Only                                               │  │
│ │ ○ Never Update                                                      │  │
│ └─────────────────────────────────────────────────────────────────────┘  │
│                              [Save]                                        │
└───────────────────────────────────────────────────────────────────────────┘
```

Build Types

EDGE	Edge is the bleeding edge tree. While it has the newest features; It has undergone the least amount of testing (if any). You generally shouldn't run this build unless you need a bug fix or feature in it. Once an equivalent CURRENT or RELEASE build has been released, you should switch away from this.
CURRENT	Current builds are more mature than the EDGE builds since they have been tested in a production environment.
RELEASE	Release builds are the prefered builds to run. They are generally current enough to have the latest bugfixes and new features, but without the worry of new bugs being introduced.
STABLE	Stable builds are for the consverative people who do not wish to run the latest release.

The **cPanel/WHM Updates** section controls whether cPanel/WHM updates itself automatically or not, and what build track it uses when updates are done. Note that you cannot automatically have your server updated to edge builds. If you want to use an edge build, you can only update cPanel and WHM manually. You can also choose to never allow cPanel and WHM to be updated. If you are uncertain what option to choose, set this to **Automatic (RELEASE tree)**.

The **cPanel Package Updates** section allows you to control how critical updates for packages are handled. These packages aren't directly part of WHM or cPanel itself, but are required for proper functionality. You can let cPanel automatically update the packages, or do it only on manual updates or never update the packages. You should permit cPanel to automatically update this unless you have a particular reason not to want this.

The **Security Package Updates** section controls updates to system packages for security purposes. You should allow cPanel to automatically update these as well.

Remember to click **Save** when you've finished making your choices.

There are two ways to initiate a manual update of cPanel and WHM. The first is from within WHM itself. Click the **Upgrade to Latest Version** item in the **cPanel** section of WHM. You will then be informed that if you choose to upgrade now, you will be upgrading to whatever your chosen build track is. If you click the **Update Settings** text here, that will take you directly to the **Update Config** item in WHM. Click **Update** to begin the manual update of cPanel and WHM.

You will see the progress of the update on screen. Watch for errors or other reported problems, as you may need to address them before the update will complete successfully. If you click on another link in your web browser after the update has begun in WHM, it will continue in the background, so don't start a new update process right away. Give the current one 10-15 minutes to finish.

You don't have to update cPanel and WHM from within WHM. You can also log into your server as root via SSH and manually update from the shell. To do so, just type:

`/scripts/upcp`

and the update process will begin. You should allow it to finish naturally as far as possible. If you can't for some reason, pressing *Ctrl+C* will stop the update in most cases. Even if you press *Ctrl+C*, the update process may continue in the background; to make sure it stops, issue the command `killall upcp` after you have returned to the root shell prompt. Note that if the update didn't complete properly, you may have problems with WHM or cPanel until you update again, so I don't recommend doing that unless you have no choice. Of course you can suspend the update temporarily by typing *Ctrl+Z* during the update. You will be returned to the shell. Don't forget to allow the update to finish by typing:

`fg`

as soon as you are ready to do so. Waiting too long may cause problems with the update process, as certain processes may time out or files may have changed since the process began.

Sometimes you may be running the latest version of cPanel and WHM, but you suspect that one or more files may be corrupt. If so, forcing a manual update may help. To do the manual update, type the following into the root shell:

`/scripts/upcp --force`

This will cause the updater to ignore the currently installed version of cPanel and WHM, and download and install all new files for the build track you have chosen.

Note that, if there is some set of commands that you need to have executed after the update process has finished, you can create a `/scripts/postupcp` file (with 0700 permissions — see the following section for more about file and directory permissions). This file should be set up like a shell script that will be run as root. Anything in this file will be executed after the update has completed. Some third-party items may require that you make/restore certain changes to cPanel or WHM after every update and this is the best way to do so (unless you relish doing this manually).

About File and Directory Permissions

If you work with files and directories on a Linux server, it is important to understand a bit about permissions. In order to make sure that only those people who are supposed to have access to a directory or file can actually do so, Linux has a file and directory permission system. Every file and directory has permissions set for three kinds of users:

- **User**: The owner or creator of the file or directory.
- **Group**: A group of users who are permitted to use a directory or file in some way.
- **World**: Everyone else who isn't the owner, or creator, or a member of the correct group. (You can think of "world" as public permissions.)

For each kind of user, there are three basic categories of permissions:

- **Read**: Any type of user who is allowed Read access can do just that, read a file. If a user only has this permission, they can open the file or directory, and see the contents, but they may not make changes.
- **Write**: If the user has Write permission, they can make changes to a file and save those changes or in the case of a directory, they can put files and directories inside that directory. It is possible to have write-only access to a directory or file.
- **Execute**: In the case of binary files (code designed to run on Linux), a user with Execute access can run that file or items in that directory. Think of this permission as the ability to launch an application (though it is a bit more complex than that).

The most common method of referring to permissions is using a three-digit number. If you work with web applications (scripts), you will often be told to set permissions on files or directories to some three-digit number. The way this works is, every type of permission has a certain unique numerical value: Read permission is 4, Write permission is 2 and Execute permission is 1, no permissions at all is 0. These numbers are added together for each kind of user.

For example, a user with Read and Write but not Execute permission is assigned a value of 6. Every type of user has their own numerical value expressed in the order of User, Group, World, like this: 755 (User has Read, Write, and Execute permissions; Group has Read and Execute permissions only and so does World). The maximum number for each kind of user is 7. So 777 is Read, Write, and Execute access for everyone (no restrictions at all). It is much easier to figure out these numerical values by setting up a grid, like cPanel's **File Manager** does:

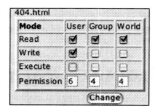

If you want to figure out numerical Linux permissions but don't want to use the cPanel File Manager, you can access an online version of this permissions calculator at http://wsabstract.com/script/script2/chmodcal.shtml. This page also offers the code for this web-based calculator, so you can add it to your own website if you wish.

Setting Up Server Contact Information

It is important for you to properly set up how and what your server contacts you about. You've already set some of this up in the **Basic cPanel/WHM Settings** area, but there is more to do.

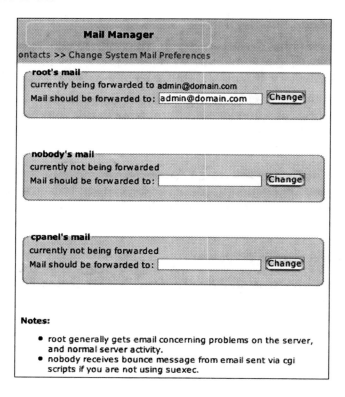

Click on **Change System Mail Preferences** in the **Server Contacts** section of WHM. Here you can choose to forward certain kinds of special system mail to a particular e-mail address.

root's mail is any mail that gets sent to the root (system administrator) user on this server. If you don't specify anything, this e-mail will remain in the root mail account. If you forward no other kind of mail, you should definitely forward root mail to a valid e-mail address that you will check regularly. Some examples of important mail that typically comes in for the root user (unless you configure it otherwise) are **logwatch** (a program that examines your server's logs every day and e-mails you a synopsis of important data), notification of server problems, and output from some system cron tasks and other programs you may have set up on your server. If you prefer not to receive mail, you can set this item to nothing (blank) or **:fail:** (reject mail sent to root@yourserver.com and send a bounce message to the sender) or **:blackhole:** (delete the mail without sending a bounce message to the sender).

Mail addressed to nobody@yourserver.com is typically output or responses from scripts that send e-mail on your server (if you don't use **phpsuexec** or **suexec** on your server). This can potentially mean that you could get a lot of mail (bounces, people responding to improperly set up mailing lists, and other similar types of communication). However, forwarding this sort of mail can also help you track down spammers, scammers, or improperly set up mail scripts. As with root mail, you can also set this item to nothing (mail goes nowhere), **:fail:**, or **:blackhole:** if you prefer.

cPanel's mail is mail sent by cPanel itself. As with the others, you can set this to a valid e-mail address, nothing, **:fail:**, or **:blackhole:**.

Don't forget to click the **Change** button if you make changes to these settings.

The Contact Manager

There are many events on your server that WHM can inform you of when they happen. To make sure you get the right types of information to the correct people or locations, you can set up what WHM does when a particular event happens. To do this, click the **Contact Manager** in the **Server Contacts** section of WHM.

In the first area of the contact manager, you should assign a rank from 1 to 4 for each contact method (all of which are set in **Basic cPanel/WHM Settings**, discussed in Chapter 2). You will see the e-mail and pager address listed next to those two items, so you know where messages sent to those contact methods will go. The lower the number you set, the more likely that contact method will be used if the server needs to contact you.

In the next section, you actually set what contact methods you want to be used if a particular event happens. You enter a number next to each event you want to be contacted about. It is important to note that alert types are cumulative. If you set an event to 3 and the event happens, any contact methods assigned a priority of 1, 2, or 3 will be contacted. If you leave a box empty, you will not be contacted at all for that event. For example, if your pager is 1, AIM is 2, e-mail is 3, and ICQ is 4, and you set account creation to 3, then you will be paged, contacted via AIM and e-mailed, but not contacted via ICQ.

The small graphics next to each item will turn grey if that contact method won't be used for this event. The first icon is for e-mail, the second for your pager, third for AIM, and fourth for ICQ.

The types of contact events are:

- Account Creation: If a new cPanel account is created by anyone on your server (a server administrator or a reseller), you will be contacted. This will contain important information about that account, including the account username, contact e-mail address, account IP address, main domain name, password, and disk quota.

- Account Removal: If a cPanel account is terminated (removed permanently) from your server, you will be contacted telling you who (a root user or a reseller) removed the account, and what the account's username and domain name were.

- Account Suspensions or Account Unsuspensions: If a cPanel account is disabled (suspended) or re-enabled (unsuspended) by a root user or reseller, you will be informed what that account is and who did the suspension. Unfortunately, you won't be told why the account was suspended. For that you need to check the **List Suspended Users** item in the **Account Information** section of WHM. See Chapter 5 for more information about suspending or unsuspending accounts.

- Account Upgrades or Account Downgrades: If a cPanel account is assigned to a different hosting package, you will be informed who that user is and what the old and new plan packages are.

- Apache Max Clients Check: WHM automatically sets a maximum number of simultaneous clients that can use Apache before additional clients are refused. If this happens, cPanel will increase the limit and inform you of the problem. If you see this sort of event often, you should check to see why so many connections are being made.

- Disk Integrity Check: WHM will attempt to check the health of your server hard drive(s) periodically. If it notices a potential problem, it will inform you of it. Hopefully, you will have time to deal with the issue before it becomes more serious. Note that cPanel may not be able to check every hard drive, and even if it doesn't find a problem, this does not mean that your hard drive(s) is(are) healthy.

- IP Address Dns Check: cPanel will check daily to make sure your server hostname properly resolves to your server. If it doesn't, you will be contacted.

- Kernel Crash: If the **kernel** (the kernel is the "heart" of the operating system) of your server crashes or has other serious problems, your server will try to contact you. Note that this sort of error is usually serious enough to cause your server to crash, so you may not get contacted or it may be after the server has come back online.

- Kernel Version Check: WHM will periodically check the version of your server's kernel and contact you if it is aware that there is a new version of the kernel available that may improve security.

- Notification of new Addon Domains: If a cPanel account uses the Add-on domain feature to serve a new domain name from your server, you will be contacted letting you know the account username and the add-on domain name.

- Recently Uploaded Cgi Script Mail: This event is a bit misnamed. cPanel will check after every update (`/scripts/upcp`) to see if there are any new CGI (Perl or Python) or PHP scripts that have the ability to send e-mail. If it finds any, you will be contacted noting where the new script is installed, and you will also be shown the relevant section of the script in question; so you can decide if it is something to worry about (a spammer or insecure script).

- Trojan horse or File Modification Check: WHM will periodically check to see if critical files have been changed in unexpected ways or if it detects dangerous processes like Trojan horses that may compromise the security of your server. This item sounds great, but it is easy to fool and not a reliable indicator of true security problems.

 Remember that your server must be functioning well enough to contact you about any event. If your server is overloaded or down, you won't be contacted until load goes down or the server comes back online.

Set Your Server's Hostname

Before you go any further, you should ensure that your server has a proper hostname set up. Your server's hostname is a **Fully Qualified Domain Name (FDQN)** in the form of *shortservername.domain.com* where the first part is anything you desire (think of it like your server's first name). The rest is a domain name that you own or control. For example, *lion.myserversarecool.com* would be a good hostname if you own the domain myserversarecool.com and you aren't already using the subdomain "lion" elsewhere. Keep in mind that you won't be able to use your server's hostname as a subdomain later (unless you change the hostname first), so choose wisely.

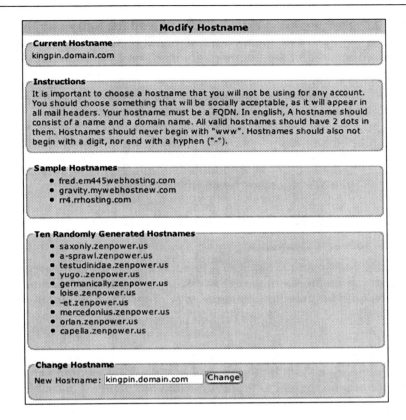

Once you've chosen a name, click **Hostname** under **Networking Setup** in WHM, and you will be presented with a screen such as the previous one. Type in your hostname, and click the **Change** button. If you've picked a proper hostname, you will be prompted to also set up DNS A records for the new hostname. You can choose to do this now or later. If you choose to add the A records later, you can either do it manually (see Chapter 7) or click on **Add an A Entry for your Hostname** from the **DNS Functions** menu in WHM and add them that way. You will see text similar to the following:

```
Found your hostname to be: server1.domain.com
Found your short hostname to be: server1
Found your domain name to be: domain.com
Found your main ip to be: 111.111.111.111
If this looks correct,
Add the Entry
```

This lists your full sever hostname, the short hostname (just the first part of the full hostname), and the domain the server hostname is in, as well as the main IP address of this server. If everything looks correct, click the **Add the Entry** button to add the A record to your server. Watch for reported errors. If there are any, you may need to enter the A record manually. See Chapter 7 for more on DNS zones and A records.

If you don't plan on hosting the domain that contains the hostname on the same server, you will need to add an A record to the DNS zone for that domain on whatever server the domain is hosted on (or wherever the DNS zone records are served from). In addition, you will also want to add A records for the server hostname to the server itself, even if you don't host the domain on that server.

You can also change your server's hostname when logged into the root shell. Just type:

```
hostname your.server's.hostname
```

(Where *your.server's.hostname* is the FQDN hostname you want the server to be called) and that will set the hostname. However, you'll need to add, remove, or modify the A records for the new hostname as appropriate. This command will not do so automatically.

Setting the Server's Clock and Date

Now you should set the current date and time on your server. Typically, the server will be set by default to whatever the date and time is wherever your server is hosted. You may find it more convenient to make the server's time match yours or the location where most of your customers are located. If so, click on **Server Time** in the **Server Configuration** section of WHM.

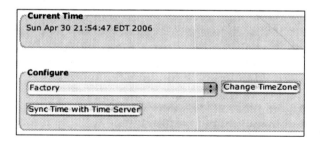

This will show you the date and time the server is currently set to, and allow you to set a new time zone, and synchronize the server's clock and date, based on the time zone you set with the nearest atomic clock (time) server on the Internet.

In the **Configure** section, you can select a new time zone from the drop-down menu. This menu will likely contain hundreds of possible choices. Note that there are just many different names for the same time zone. For example, **US/Eastern** is the same as selecting **America/New_York**. To make matters worse, nothing is alphabetized, so you may have to do some searching. Once you find one that matches your preferred time zone, select it, and click the **Change TimeZone** button. The **Current Time** item should change to match your selection.

To have the server check with the nearest Internet time server, click **Sync Time with Time Server**.

Setting Up Extra Hard Drives

If you have more than one hard drive installed in your server, you may need to set it up now. The easiest way to do this is to click on **Format/Mount a new Hard Drive** under the **Disk Drives** section of WHM. If you have any additional hard drives installed that are not yet set up and mounted, this will tell you that it detects an additional hard drive and the location of that drive.

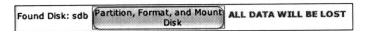

Click the button to format the hard drive. All the data on the drive (if any) will be lost if you proceed, so be sure that is what you want to do.

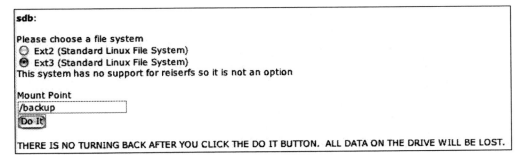

Next, you will be presented with a few options, as shown in the previous figure. First, you will have to choose what sort of format you want to use for the drive. **Ext2** and **Ext3** will certainly be options, though you may have more such as **Reiserfs**. Ext2 and Ext3 are actually the same type of format and are the most common Linux formats. Ext3 is Ext2 with the addition of **journaling**. A journaled file system allows the disk to automatically write information about what changes are made on the disk, so if there are problems later, a journal-aware disk repair program like **fsck** will be able to use that information to fix some kinds of damage. Journaling makes the disk somewhat slower, but is a more secure format. I recommend that you choose **Ext3** if you don't have another preference.

You can learn more about common Linux file systems and journaling here: `http://yolinux.com/TUTORIALS/ LinuxClustersAndFileSystems.html`

Next, select the **Mount Point**. You can think of this like the "name" of the mounted hard drive. The mount point should always begin with a forward slash (/) followed by the name. There are two typical choices here; either **/home2** so you can use the extra hard drive to store additional accounts, or **/backup** so you can use WHM to automatically back up all account and other critical data in case your main hard drive fails (all hard drives will fail eventually, and servers that are on 24/7 and writing constantly to the disks are particularly hard on them). I recommend **/backup** unless you plan on backing up your server data somewhere else (perhaps off-site).

Click **Do It** if you are sure this is what you want. You won't be able to change your mind, there are no additional warnings, so be careful! *Do not stop or click* on another link once the formatting has begun, or you may corrupt the hard drive. Let it finish. If you made a mistake with your choices, you can unmount the disk and try again later.

Choose Your Data Backup Strategy!

One thing that many new dedicated server owners overlook is what they will do in the event of a disaster. What happens if your server is hacked, and critical data is lost, or what will you do when some piece of hardware in your server dies? You need to plan for disaster from the start if you want to minimize the inconvenience to your customers later.

One thing you can and should do is set up automated backups of your critical server data right now. We'll discuss backups in more detail later, but for now let's work with WHM's built-in data backup features. Click on **Configure Backup** in WHM's **Backup** section. Here you can set up cPanel's own automated backup solution, called **cpbackup**.

Configure Backup	
Main >> Backup >> Configure Backup	
Backup Status:	◉ Enabled ○ Disabled ○ Restore Only
Backup Interval *(Note: Selecting Daily Backup with give you monthly and weekly as well unless you choose not to retain them below. Selecting Weekly backup will give you monthly as well unless you choose not to retain them below.)*	◉ Daily ○ Weekly ○ Monthly
Backup Retention	☑ Daily ☑ Weekly ☑ Monthly
Days to run backup	☑ Sunday ☑ Monday ☑ Tuesday ☑ Wednesday ☑ Thursday ☑ Friday ☑ Saturday
Remount/Unmount backup drive (requires a seperate drive/coda/nfs mount)	○ Enabled ◉ Disabled
Bail out if the backup drive cannot be mounted (recommended if you have selected the above option)	○ Enabled ◉ Disabled
Incremental backup (only backup what has changed. (**No Compression**, not compatible w/ftp backups)	○ Enabled ◉ Disabled
Backup Accounts	◉ Enabled ○ Disabled
Backup Config Files (not needed to restore specific accounts)	◉ Enabled ○ Disabled
Sql Databases (at least per accounts is needed to use the restore feature)	○ Per Accounts Only ◉ Per Accounts and Entire Mysql Dir ○ Mysql Dir Only
Backup Raw Access Logs	○ Enabled ◉ Disabled
Backup Type	○ Remote Ftp Server (Accounts Only) ◉ Standard
Ftp Backup Host (Remote Ftp Backup Only)	111.111.111.111
Ftp Backup User (Remote Ftp Backup Only)	ftpuser
Ftp Backup Pass (Remote Ftp Backup Only)	password
Ftp Backup Directory/Path [optional, a directory called cpbackup in the ftp account's directory root will be used if none specified *examples: /home/fred/cpbackup,/backup/cpbackup,/files/cpbackup*] (Remote Ftp Backup Only)	
Use Passive mode for Ftp transfers (required if you are behind a firewall or ftp backups fail)	○ Enabled ◉ Disabled
Backup Destination (this should be a dir/nfs/coda mount with at least twice the space of all your /home* partitions. Setting this to /home is a VERY BAD IDEA.):	/backup
Select Specific Users	Select >>
Save	

cpbackup isn't a perfect backup solution, but it can, if configured properly, back up the bulk of the critical data on your server. It can handle local backup to a second hard drive or remote backup via standard, unsecured **File Transfer Protocol (FTP).**

Backup Status: This is the on/off switch for cpbackup. Setting this to **restore only** will stop cpbackup from running every day but will allow you to use WHM to restore account or system data that has already been backed up. This setting is useful after a hard drive crash to restore the most recent backup without having to worry about cpbackup overwriting the backups.

Backup Interval: How often do you want cpbackup to backup files? You can choose every day, every week, or every month.

By default your chosen setting will include any other backup frequencies. So if you choose weekly, the accounts and data on the server will be backed up every week and separately once each month. If you don't want this to happen, you need to properly configure the other interval choices below. If you choose to back up files daily, weekly, and monthly, separate backups for every account and other critical data will be made in a daily, weekly and monthly directory on your chosen back up destination. This may require two to three times more disk space on the backup destination than you are backing up from.

Backup Retention: This is which types of backups will be done. The frequency you choose in the backup interval option will be selected and greyed out. You can use this to do only the type of backups (daily, weekly or monthly) you wish to do rather than all types.

Days to run backup: This is which days you wish to run the cpbackup script on. If you select a daily backup interval but only select Monday and Wednesday, then daily (and other types you specify) will only be done on those particular days of the week. By default, all days are checked. If you select a backup interval less than daily and you select multiple days to run backup, then cpbackup will run on every day you select and check to see if enough time has passed to warrant a new backup. If not, cpbackup will exit without making any backups at all.

Remount/Unmount backup drive: Set this to **enabled** if you wish to have cpbackup automatically attempt to mount and unmount the backup drive (for local backups only) as needed. If cpbackup fails to mount the backup drive, then no backups will be done. For that reason, you should leave this disabled unless you're going to watch cpbackup and make sure the drive mounts and unmounts properly.

Bail out if the backup drive cannot be mounted: If you're going to use the remount/unmount feature, then you should enable this so that cpbackup won't try to backup and store files on a non-existent backup drive (which can increase load on your server).

Incremental backups: If you enable this, only changed files will be backed up every time cpbackup runs. If you are backing up files remotely, this can cut down on the amount of bandwidth the backup takes. However, this option will not compress files that are backed up, and so you will use a great deal more disk space. Generally, leave this off unless bandwidth is a great concern.

Backup Accounts: You should leave this enabled. It will back up every cPanel account with all related data. Disable this if you want to back up critical system files only.

Backup Configuration Files: If you are doing local backups to a second hard drive, you should leave this enabled. It will back up critical system files that you can use to restore from if you make a mistake or files become corrupt. This option does not work when you are backing up files remotely via FTP. This option will automatically be deselected if you've set cpbackup to back up files via FTP.

SQL Databases: There are three options, **Per Accounts**, **Per Account and Entire MySQL Directory**, and **MySQL directory Only**.

- Per Account will only back up the databases that each account creates (in the full account backup file or directory). This can be used to restore a particular user's MySQL databases if the account needs to be restored from a full backup.

- The **MySQL Dir Only** option backs up the main MySQL directory on your server. This includes all MySQL databases, including system (root) databases and cPanel user databases. However, if you need to restore a cPanel account from a full backup, their databases will not be automatically restored by WHM. You will need to manually check the MySQL directory backup and restore the user's databases yourself.

- The **Per Account and EntireMySQL Dir** option will do both. This is the preferred option unless disk space on the backup drive is at a premium. It will allow you to restore MySQL databases automatically from a full backup file while also backing up critical system databases.

Backup Raw Access Logs: This will back up apache raw log files and logs in /var/log. None of these files are critical and so you can safely leave this item disabled unless the log files are of critical importance to your business or for security purposes.

Backup Type: This can be **standard** or **remote FTP server**. Standard will attempt to back up files onto a local hard drive or other locally mounted directory. The **remote FTP server** option will tell cpbackup to try backing up files remotely via unsecured FTP. Sadly, cpbackup cannot back up files using more secure remote methods like **SCP** (secure copy) or **SFTP** (secure FTP). cpbackup cannot back up system configuration files via FTP, so that option will be turned off if it is selected.

Ftp Backup Host/User/Password/Directory: These items will allow you to specify a valid FTP user and password on a remote system where you'd like cpbackup to store account file backups. The directory will allow you to specify a path where you want the files stored. Note that cpbackup will create a directory called cpbackup and store files in that directory (in daily, weekly, or monthly directories) if no path or directory is specified.

The FTP account password is not obscured, so be sure the password isn't one you don't want other system administrators or users with root WHM access to see.

Use Passive mode for Ftp transfers: If the server you are connecting to for remote backups doesn't work well with active FTP transfers, then enable this item to make cpbackup try to use passive mode for transfers.

Backup Destination: If you are backing up files locally (rather than via FTP), this should be set to the mount point for the hard drive or directory where you want files stored. Note that this destination must be a separate mount point on your server. The path should always start with a forward slash (/). **/backup** is the typical choice.

Select Specific Users: This will allow you to specify only certain cPanel accounts that are backed up using cpbackup. Obviously, this won't make a difference if account backups are not enabled. By default, all accounts are backed up.

Tweak Settings: Additional Configuration

The **Tweak Settings** item in the **Server Configuration** section of WHM contains a large number of miscellaneous settings that affect both the server itself, and WHM and cPanel operation.

Display and Domains

These have options to specify the quantity of accounts to be displayed on a page and to set different features related to parked/add-on domains.

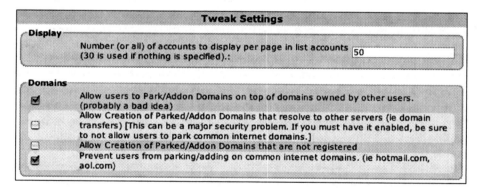

Number of accounts to display per page in list accounts: The display item will allow you to specify how many accounts appear on a single page in the **List Accounts** section of WHM. The default is 30. The word **all** will display every account on a single page.

Allow users to Park/Addon Domains on top of domains owned by others: Check this item if you want to allow cPanel users to park or add-on a domain on top of another domain owned by a user on the same server. This really isn't a smart idea unless you are the only one adding on or parking domains on this server.

Allow creation of Parked/Addon domains that resolve to other servers: This item is handy if you have trusted clients who are trying to move domains from another host or web server onto yours. However it can be a security nightmare, as users will be able to park or add-on domains that they do not own. Leave this unchecked unless you must permit this. If this is unchecked, then cPanel will check to see if an add-on or parked domain resolves to your server before permitting it to be added. The user will have to point the domain to your server's nameservers and wait for it to propagate if they want to add-on or park the domain. If you do allow this, make sure you check the item to have cPanel disallow adding or parking common Internet domains (like Yahoo.com). This doesn't stop you from adding these domains to your server, though!

Allow Addon/Parked domains that are not registered: This item, if checked will permit cPanel users to park or add-on domains that have not yet been registered by anyone. This can be handy if a user wants to prepare for a domain they will register shortly or that they have only just registered. Otherwise, cPanel will check to make sure the domain exists and points to your server before permitting it to be added or parked.

Prevent users from Adding/Parking common interest domains: This will attempt to stop users from adding on or parking common Internet domains like `hotmail.com` or `google.com`. This should be checked, especially if you permit the adding on or parking of domains that don't resolve to your server.

Mail

These are options for mail settings, like those for controlling spam.

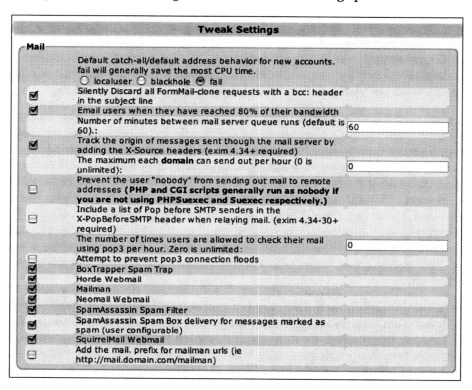

Default catch-all/default address behavior for new accounts: This allows you to set the default catch-all (default e-mail address) action for all new accounts.

- localuser will default to delivering mail addressed to accounts not defined in the domain's cPanel account to the main cPanel user e-mail address (this is the cPanel username of the account @ the user's main domain).

- blackhole will delete mail sent to accounts that do not exist in that domain without responding to it.

- fail will send a bounced message reply to any sender that tries to send mail to an account that doesn't exist in that domain.

Silently Discard all FormMail-clone requests with a bcc: header in the subject line: This is a common ploy by spammers who are trying to exploit well-documented security issues in common form mailing scripts. Check this item unless you have a special reason to want to allow this.

Note that spamming is explicitly against the Acceptable Use Policy (AUP) of most NOC's, and repeated violations may cause your server to be permanently disconnected.

Email users when they have reached 80% of their bandwidth: This will cause WHM to send an e-mail to users once they've reached 80% usage of their monthly bandwidth allotment. The e-mail address to which WHM will send the warning is the one the user sets for the contact e-mail address in their cPanel account. If the user does not set a contact e-mail address, then they will not receive the warning. The server will continue to warn them until their bandwidth usage is reset or the limit raised. This should give most users plenty of time to contact their reseller, or you to purchase more bandwidth.

Number of minutes between mail server queue runs: The mail queue stores mail that cannot be delivered for some reason (either locally or remotely). The mail server will check for stalled mail in the set number of minutes and try to deliver it again. This does not affect new mail as it comes in or leaves the server, but only those messages that cannot be delivered. The default is 60 minutes, and that is a good value for most servers.

Track the origin of messages sent through your server: This should be checked. It will add special headers to every message that gets sent from your server. These headers will make it easier to track down spammers on your server.

The headers will record the location of the script used to send the message as well as the user id of the user whose account the message was sent from. If you have phpsuexec and suexec enabled, this will make it very obvious if a script is being used to spam, since it will record the cPanel username of the user that owns the account where the spam is coming from. If you don't have phpsuexec and suexec enabled, then the user id of the sender will probably be the user "nobody" (user ID 99). However, the script path may still be listed.

Maximum number of messages a domain can send per hour: If this is set to a number other than zero, then every domain will only be permitted to send that many messages per hour. Any additional messages sent in that hour will usually get bounced back to the sender with a "this domain is unrouteable" error. This can stop large spam campaigns, but it can also interfere with legitimate mail uses like popular mailing lists. Setting this item to zero or leaving it blank will allow all domains to send as many messages as they wish per hour.

Prevent user "nobody" from sending mail: Only check this item if you are running both suexec and phpsuexec on your server, otherwise you will block legitimate mail being sent by web scripts on your server (such as forums). This item will stop mail from being sent from your server with the user set to "nobody." Scripts on servers that do not have phpsuexec and suexec installed will send mail using the standard mail functions and thus send them as the user "nobody" unless the script is sending mail using **SMTP**. This should be enabled if you are running phpsuexec and suexec on your server, as this will help stop spammers.

Include a list of POP-Before-SMTP users to sent messages: Other than password authentication, cPanel servers also permit use of another type of authentication called **POP-Before-SMTP**. This authentication method isn't as secure as password authentication, but some users prefer it. The way it works is that the mail server makes a note of every IP address that successfully authenticates to check mail via the POP3 protocol. Any IP address that has successfully logged into the mail server to check mail will be permitted to send mail through the server for the period of 30 minutes (by default) for that domain. Checking this item adds a special header to every message sent through your server using the POP-Before-SMTP authentication method showing all of the e-mail accounts that could have been authenticated to send this message. This can help track abuse, but it can also expose otherwise private e-mail addresses to public scrutiny, since anyone who receives the message can see the extra header.

Number of times users can check mail: Any number, except zero, will limit the number of times a user can check e-mail via POP3. This can help stop denial of service attacks, but if a user checks mail more than this number of times, they will receive an error telling them they may not check mail at this time. This ban will lift once the next hour starts. Zero in this field or leaving it blank will allow users to check POP3 mail as often as they like.

Attempt to stop POP3 connection floods: When checked, this will cause the mail server to keep track of the number of concurrent connections and stop additional connections if too many connections have been made. Once the number of concurrent connections drops below a critical value, more connections will be permitted. This is designed to stop denial of service attacks against the mail server.

BoxTrapper Spam Trap: Box Trapper is an anti-spam challenge-and-response system that cPanel offers. Uncheck this if you don't wish to offer this feature to any clients. Use WHM's **Feature Sets** if you want to restrict access of this feature to only certain accounts.

Horde/Neomail/Squirrelmail: These are three different webmail clients offered by cPanel. Uncheck any of these items to disable that webmail client for all users on this server. Use WHM's Feature Sets if you want to restrict access to certain accounts.

Learn more about these webmail clients here:

Horde (IMP): `http://www.horde.org/`

Squirrelmail: `http://squirrelmail.org/`

Neomail:
`http://neocodesolutions.com/software/neomail/`

Note that cPanel will be removing Neomail as an option soon, since it won't work properly with the new maildir mail storage format that will become the default on cPanel servers. It is likely they will replace neomail with another webmail client when that happens. See Appendix A (`http://www.packtpub.com/web_host_manager/book`) to learn more about the new maildir format and how to switch your server to it.

Mailman: Mailman is mailing list software that cPanel offers. Uncheck this to deny use of Mailman to all users on this server. Use Feature Sets if you want to restrict access to particular accounts.

You can learn more about Mailman here:
`http://list.org/`

Add the mail. prefix for Mailman URLs: This item is a matter of personal preference. You can check this, and all access to Mailman on this server will come from mail.domain.com instead of just domain.com.

MySQL and Notification

MySQL has option to specify the version to be used and also has an option for troubleshooting in case of authentication problems for users on MySQL 4.1. Tweak settings also offers options to warn users in case they exceed limitations made on bandwidth or diskspace.

Tweak Settings

MySQL

MySQL Version to use (you must run Software/Update Server Software (or /scripts/mysqlup) for this to take affect. You should then run buildapache/easyapache after changing this option. You may also need to run /scripts/perlinstaller --force Bundle::DBD::mysql. **Updating from a previous verion of MySQL to a later version is *not* automaticlly reversable. You should backup your databases if you think you might wish to downgrade in the future.**
　◯ 5.0　◉ 4.1

☑ Use old style (4.0) passwords with mySQL 4.1 (required if you have problems with php apps authenticating)

Notifications

☑ Mail Box Usage Warnings

☐ Disable Suspending accounts that exceed their bandwidth limit (will clear all suspensions is disabled)

☑ Disk Space Usage Warnings

MySQL version: Click on the appropriate radio button to choose which version of MySQL you wish to use on this server. You really should decide this before adding accounts to the server. Note that choosing a new version of MySQL will require you to recompile PHP so that it uses the correct MySQL support. See Chapter 4 for information about recompiling PHP. Also, if you decide later to downgrade to an older version of MySQL, you may have to restore the entire MySQL directory from a recent backup made before you upgraded MySQL. If you don't do this, you will probably cause MySQL to stop functioning properly or cause problems for users with their databases.

Use old-style MySQL passwords: This is for use with MySQL 4.1 because it debuted a new, more secure and longer password hash. This new format is incompatible with old-style 4.0 password hashes, and should be checked if you are using MySQL 4.1 and are having problems with users not being able to log into web scripts that use MySQL databases. That will force MySQL to continue to use the old-style password hashes.

Mailbox warnings: Users will be warned by cPanel with an e-mail if their e-mail account is getting close to or has gone slightly over the allotted disk space quota for that account. This will give them a chance to clear out their mailbox before mail gets held in the mail queue or bounced back to the sender.

Disable suspending accounts for going over bandwidth: If you don't want WHM to automatically suspend any account that goes over their allotted bandwidth then check this item. This will also re-enable any account that had been suspended due to bandwidth overusage.

Disk space warnings: If a cPanel account uses 80% or more of its available disk space, cPanel will send a warning e-mail to the contact e-mail address the user set in cPanel. If one is not set, then no e-mail warnings will be sent to that user. Uncheck this, and no users will ever get a warning if they get close to using all of their disk space. This won't allow users to go over their disk space allotments, though.

Software

These options let you configure add-ons to your cPanel users:

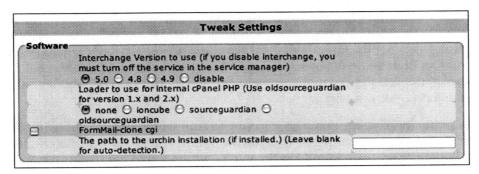

Interchange version: Interchange is an e-commerce solution. If you use Interchange, you can choose which version of the Interchange server you wish to run. Note that if you decide to offer Interchange to your clients, the creators of Interchange don't support Interchange as installed by cPanel. Also, cPanel Inc. is typically very slow about upgrading Interchange to new versions. The current version is 5.4, and cPanel currently installs up to 5.0. I recommend that you leave this software disabled in favor of smaller, lighter, better-supported e-commerce scripts.

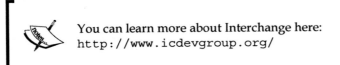

You can learn more about Interchange here:
http://www.icdevgroup.org/

Backend PHP Loader: Servers that have WHM and cPanel installed, actually run two separate copies of Apache web server (and PHP). One is the front-end (public) copy of Apache and PHP that websites use, and then there is a backend copy (private) copy that serves only WHM and cPanel. This setting controls which, if any, encoded PHP loader you wish to use with WHM and cPanel only. (You can use different loaders if you wish, with your public copy of PHP.) Some third-party WHM or cPanel add-ons may require the use of a particular type of loader. Note that you should only set this to something other than none if you are sure you need to do so. Also, you can only choose one type of loader to use, as they are not compatible with one another.

FormMail-Clone: FormMail-Clone is a custom version of the popular but very insecure **Matt's Script Archives** FormMail script (`http://www.scriptarchive.com/formmail.html`). FormMail is a web-based form processing script that turns web forms (like "contact us" forms) into something mere mortals can read and understand. The problem is that this script hasn't been updated since 2002 and there are many bugs in the script (as acknowledged by the author). These bugs can be exploited by spammers to send spam from the domain using the FormMail script. cPanel offers a custom version of this script which fixes many of the bugs present in the standard version. Unfortunately, the copy in cPanel can still be exploited to send spam. Checking the **silently discard FormMail-clone requests with a BCC: in the subject line** item will help stop some of the more obvious attempts, but I recommend that you disable this script and encourage users to find another, more secure form processing script.

Path to Urchin installation: Some NOCs offer **Urchin** web stats software with their servers. Urchin is a very powerful web statistics program. So powerful in fact, that Google bought the company and has turned the product into the free web-based Google Analytics (`http://www.google.com/analytics/`), which cPanel cannot directly integrate. If your NOC offers Urchin 5 with your server, cPanel can include this stats package with Webalizer, Analog, and AWSTATS. Unless you've installed Urchin in a special location, you should leave this item blank. cPanel will try to automatically find the installed copy of Urchin (if there is one) and allow you to offer it to customers.

Stats, Logs, and Status

These options let you enable or disable four web statistics programs, and options related to them.

Tweak Settings

Stats Programs

- ☑ Awstats Reverse Dns Resolution
- ☑ Analog Stats
- ☑ Awstats Stats
- ☑ Webalizer Stats

Stats and Logs

- ☑ Allow users to update Awstats from cPanel
- Number of days between processing log files and bandwidth usage (default 1, decimal values are ok): `1`
- ☐ Delete each domain's access logs after stats run
- The load average above the number of cpus at which logs file processing should be suspended (default 0): `10`
- ☑ Do not include password in the raw log download link in cPanel (via ftp).
- ☐ Do not reset /usr/local/apache/domlogs/ftpxferlog after it has been seperated into each domain name's ftp log
- ☐ Keep log files at the end of the month (default is off as you can run out of disk space quickly)
- ☐ Keep Stats Log (/usr/local/cpanel/logs/stats_log) between cpanel restarts (default is off)
- Chmod value for raw apache log files (0640 is the default): `0640`
- ☐ When viewing bandwidth usage in WHM, always display in Megabytes first.
- ☑ Exim Stats Daemon (required for smtp bandwidth logging; must also be modified in the service manager as well)
- Stats Log Level (default is 1, larger numbers indicate more debug information in /usr/local/cpanel/logs/stats_log) [0...10]: `1`

Status

- The load average that will cause the server status to appear red (leave blank for default): `10`

AWSTATS Reverse Dns resolution: The AWSTATS web stats program has the ability to perform a reverse DNS lookup on all IP addresses in a user's web log and display the name that the IP address resolves to. This will take some additional time during web log processing to look up this information and increase the CPU load of the backend web log processing script. If you have a fast server or one that won't have many cPanel accounts on it, you may wish to enable this, as users tend to prefer it.

Analog/AWSTATS/Webalizer: These are all web statistics programs that cPanel can offer to users. If you uncheck any of these, no accounts on this server will be able to use that stats program. If you want more fine-grained control over what web stats program you use, the **Statistics Software Configuration** feature is discussed below. Note that, if you enable a stats program that has never been used on this server before, it can take 12 to 48 hours before your users see any statistics listed in that program in cPanel. If your server is not overloaded, and you want to force the web log processor to run right now, log into your server's root shell and run /scripts/runlogsnow. This will start the bandwidth and web log processing process immediately.

You can learn more about each web stats programs at the links below:

Analog: `http://www.analog.cx/`

AWSTATS: `http://awstats.sourceforge.net/`

Webalizer: `http://www.mrunix.net/webalizer/`

Allow users to update AWSTATS from cPanel: The AWSTATS web stats script has the ability to update itself with current information if the user clicks on a link at the top of the AWSTATS display in cPanel. If you enable this, users will see and be able to use that link to update AWSTATS at any time. If it is unchecked, no such link will appear. This process can add significant load on your server, so you should only permit this if you have a fast server.

Number of days between processing log and bandwidth files: Typically, WHM will update users' bandwidth usage and their web logs once per day (usually after midnight, server time). However, if you prefer, you can increase or decrease the number of days between web log and bandwidth processing. 1 is one day, 2 is two days, and so on. If you want to process logs and bandwidth every 12 hours (twice per day), you would set this to .5. Bandwidth and web log processing takes a lot of time and adds a lot of load on the CPU of your server, so don't process this too often.

Delete each domain's access logs after stats run: This will delete the raw web log files on the server after a domain's web stats programs have been updated with the latest information. This will save some disk space on the server, but this should be left off if you want your users to be able to manually download or process their web logs at a later time.

The load average above which logs will not be processed: As stated earlier, processing web logs and bandwidth usage does take a lot of time and increases CPU load. If you set this to any number, the web stats and bandwidth processing script will suspend its work until the average CPU load falls below the number you set. Do not set this too low, or your server may never process web logs or bandwidth. Leave this item blank if you want WHM to process the logs and bandwidth regardless of how much load is currently on the server.

Do not include the account password in the raw log download in cPanel: cPanel allows domain owners to download the raw Apache web logs for their domain via FTP. Links to each of these logs are displayed in the FTP account management section in cPanel. These links are live, and clicking on them will attempt to log you in to download the chosen log immediately. If you leave this item checked, the link will include the password for the user's account so that they won't have to enter anything to download logs. However, the password is not obscured and can be viewed by anyone who can view those links. This is a security risk, so you should disable this feature. It is better to inconvenience users (making them enter their passwords to download logs) than to allow the cPanel account password to fall into the wrong hands.

Do not reset the domain's FTP transfer logs: With this unchecked, WHM automatically removes the old data from the FTP transfer log once web stats have been processed. If you leave this checked, the FTP transfer log can grow to a massive size. Unless you need to keep the raw data for some reason, it is best to leave this item unchecked.

Keep log files at the end of the month: With this unchecked, WHM automatically removes old data from the raw apache log file each month to keep the size reasonable. If you check this item, WHM won't remove old data, and the raw log will continue to grow each month. Leave this off unless you need to keep old data for some reason. Users can still choose to archive old apache web logs in their cPanel accounts if they wish. This only affects the main Apache raw log file.

Keep Stats Log between restarts: WHM automatically keeps records of web stats processing every day. This can be useful if there is a problem with web stats processing. However this file can get large. By default, WHM will automatically remove and create a new log file every time the server is restarted. Unless you need to keep the data for debugging purposes, you should leave this item unchecked.

CHMOD value for raw Apache log files: This is the default numeric permissions of the Apache raw log files. Leave this set to 0640 (user read and write, group read, and others no access) unless you need special permissions for some reason.

When viewing bandwidth usage in WHM, default to megabytes: If this item is unchecked, the bandwidth display for each account in WHM will be shown in gigabytes rather than megabytes by default. Checking this item reverses that preference.

Exim Stats Daemon: WHM can track the mail bandwidth use for each user if the exim stats daemon is active. If this is unchecked or the daemon isn't working, then mail sent and received on the server will not be tracked and deducted from the user's monthly bandwidth allotment.

Stats log level: A higher number will log more information to stats logs (at the expense of disk space and CPU load levels). Unless you need more information logged, you should leave this set to 1.

The load average that will cause the status display to be red: The service status display in cPanel and WHM displays the current average CPU load level. If that average load is more than whatever number you enter here, the status display will turn from green (good) to red (overloaded). The right number to enter here is going to depend on what sort of server you have and what your personal tastes are. Don't set this too low, or your users may panic if they constantly see the CPU load in the red. However, you do want to set it to a number above which you would personally find to be a concern. Leaving this item blank will cause the load display to change to red if CPU load is more than 1, which is too low for nearly all servers.

System

These are system related settings.

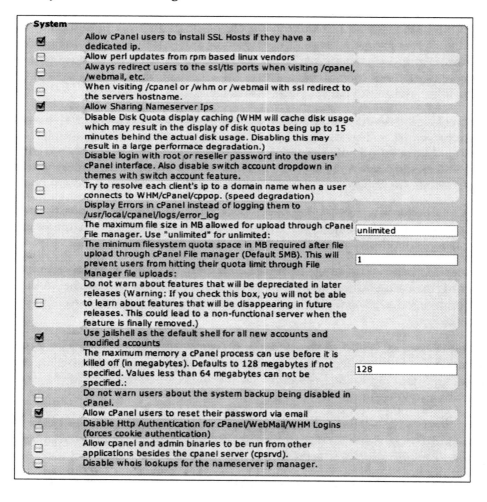

Allow users to install SSL certificates if they have a dedicated IP address: In order for a domain to have a SSL certificate for secure web transactions, that domain must be assigned a dedicated IP address. If this item is checked and a cPanel user has a dedicated IP address assigned to their account, they will be able to use features in cPanel to install their own SSL certificate without your help. If this is unchecked, then the user will have to seek your assistance to install a SSL certificate for their domain. If a user doesn't have a dedicated IP address, they won't be permitted to install an SSL certificate regardless of this setting.

Allow Perl updates: Perl is used extensively by WHM and cPanel, and changes to Perl may affect how WHM or cPanel operate. Therefore you should leave this unchecked unless you want to allow your server to install Perl updates released by your operating system vendor (rather than letting WHM handle Perl updates).

Always redirect users to SSL ports when accessing /cpanel, /whm, or /webmail: Users can typically log into cPanel, WHM, or webmail by entering their domain name followed by /cpanel, /whm, or /webmail in their web browser. If this item is checked, and if a user tries to access cPanel, WHM, or webmail insecurely, the system will automatically redirect them to the secure ports for these services. This way, you can force all users to log in securely wherever possible. If this item is unchecked, the user can choose to use insecure login methods if they choose to do so.

When visiting /cpanel, /whm, or /webmail via SSL, redirect to server's hostname: If you have a SSL certificate installed on the main shared IP address that matches your server hostname, you can automatically have login attempts changed to match the server hostname instead of the user's domain name (https://domain.com/cpanel becomes https://your.server.hostname/cpanel). This will stop the user's web browser from displaying a warning about the SSL certificate not matching the name of the domain. Note that this does not help if you are using a self-signed SSL certificate (which WHM and cPanel do by default).

Allow sharing nameserver IPs: To help reduce unneeded IP address usage, you should check this item. If this is unchecked, any nameservers assigned to this server will use a dedicated IP address that isn't being used for something else. If this is checked, then the nameservers can be assigned to IPs that are used for other purposes (like the main shared IP address).

Disable disk quota caching: To greatly speed up the display in cPanel and reduce CPU load, each account's disk space usage is cached for a while and not updated in realtime. Check this item to force WHM and cPanel to update disk usage in realtime. This is not recommended unless you have a very fast server and have many customers complaining about the lag in updating disk space usage statistics.

Disable root login to cPanel account and disable account switching menu: If this item is unchecked, then you have the ability to log into any cPanel account on the server using the server root password. Resellers can also log into any account they own using their reseller password. In both cases, a user logged into a cPanel account this way will see a special drop-down menu at the top of the cPanel interface allowing the user to quickly switch between accounts they own. If you check this item, you will stop these features from working.

Try to resolve the user's IP address when they log into WHM/cPanel/cpPOP: Whenever someone logs into cPanel, WHM, or mail via POP3, their IP address is recorded. You can see this in the "last login from" display in cPanel. If you want IP addresses to be resolved to their names, check this item. However, this will slow down access to these services.

Display errors in cPanel: cPanel normally logs any error that happens to /usr/ local/cpanel/logs/error_log, so you as the system administrator can help diagnose problems with cPanel. However, if you would rather that such errors get logged to the user's cPanel error log (which they access in cPanel), then check this item.

Maximum file size upload in cPanel file manger: If you type a number in here, no user will be able to upload a file larger than that size in megabytes using cPanel's web-based file manager. Set this to **unlimited** if you don't want to impose a limit on users. Note that this limit *does not* affect FTP quotas or available disk space.

Minimum quota to allow file transfers via cPanel file manager: Whatever number you set this to, users will not be able upload files using cPanel's file manager if they do not have at least this much available disk space (in megabytes) available to their account. If you do not specify a number, 5 MB will be used by default.

Do not warn about depreciated features: If cPanel Inc. plans on removing some feature from cPanel or WHM in the near future, you will typically be notified that the feature will be going away and that you may want to stop using it or use the feature that replaces it. This will give you time to make other arrangements or stop relying on that feature. If you check this item, you will not receive these warnings.

Use jailshell as the default shell for all new accounts and modified accounts: You can enable (or allow resellers to enable) SSH shell access for individual cPanel users. If this item is not checked, any user granted shell access will have a full shell with no special restrictions. Allowing full shell access is a serious security risk. If you must grant some users shell access, you should check this item so that the default shell for users that are granted shell access is the more restrictive and more secure jailshell. A jailshell is a chrooted shell. To learn more about chroot and how it helps protect your server, see http://en.wikipedia.org/wiki/Chroot

Although a jailshell is more secure, it is not foolproof, especially on a cPanel server. The safest thing to do is not permit shell access to any user.

Maximum memory use for cPanel processes: This item limits how much memory any cPanel or WHM processes are allowed to use on your server. The default, nothing, is specified as 128 MB. You can specify any amount from 64 to however many MB of RAM your server has installed. You probably should not modify this item unless you know you are having problems with cPanel and WHM due to memory usage.

Do not warn users about system backup being disabled in cPanel: With this unchecked, if you have cpbackup disabled completely, users will usually receive a warning in cPanel's backup area, letting them know that the system is not automatically backing up their files. However, this warning can cause confusion since users may think that they will not be able to use cPanel's backup features, which is not true. Check this item to disable that warning.

Allow cPanel users to reset their password via email: If this item is checked, then a user will be able to have their cPanel account password reset from the failed login screen. They can just follow the on-screen directions, and a new password will be mailed to the e-mail address they specified as their cPanel contact e-mail address. If this item is disabled, then a user that forgets their cPanel password will need to contact you or their reseller to have their account password reset.

Disable HTTP authentication for WHM, cPanel, webmail: Normally, cPanel uses the standard HTTP authentication method to have your web browser prompt you for your username and password. With this item enabled, cPanel, WHM, and webmail will use session cookies and a standard web-based login page to prompt users to log in. This may work better on some servers.

Allow cPanel and admin binaries to be run by other users: If you check this item, users other than cPanel's can run cPanel binary files and other administrative binaries. You should leave this item unchecked unless you are sure you need other users to be able to access these files, as allowing access to others is a security risk.

Disable whois lookups from the nameserver IP interface: When you assign new nameserver IP addresses using the Nameserver IP feature in WHM, it automatically checks the IP addresses assigned to your server to make sure everything is OK. However, this can take some time if you have lots of IP addresses, so you may wish to enable this feature. Unless the time it takes really bothers you, you should leave this item unchecked.

cPAddons

In cPanel 10.8.2, cPanel Inc. has improved the existing cPanel script add-on's features to try to make it more secure, more manageable, and more flexible. However, this new system is not compatible with the older script add-on system and, since it is new, may not be entirely bug free. At this time, cPanel is leaving both systems in place, but the old add-ons system will eventually be completely removed.

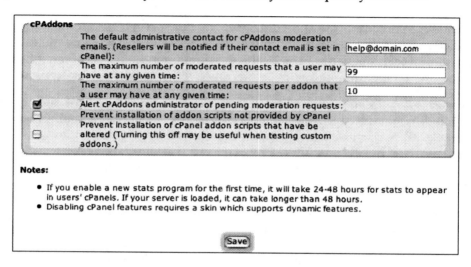

The default administrative contact email address for moderation requests: This is the e-mail address that will be contacted for moderation requests from the new script add-on system.

The maximum number of moderation requests a user may have at one time: This is the total number of moderation requests a particular user can have open at any one time. Any additional requests are ignored until existing requests are dealt with.

The maximum number of moderation requests a user can have at any one time per addon: This number is the total number of open moderation requests a single user can have for each add-on script in cPanel.

Prevent installation of addon scripts not provided by cPanel: There are third parties that have traditionally offered additional add-on scripts for cPanel's Script Library such as the **OpenInstaller** project at http://openinstaller.com/ and cpskins.com's **Autoinstaller** at http://cpskins.com/. If this item is checked, then scripts from these third-party sources will not be able to be used. This doesn't affect third-party script installers like **Fantastico Deluxe** at http://netenberg.com/ that do not use cPanel's script installer features.

Prevent the use of any modified addon scripts: This feature is mostly for debugging support. cPanel won't allow users to install scripts that have been modified in any way from what cPanel Inc. provides them. Some hosts do modify existing cPanel add-on script packages to add new features or special graphics. With this checked, those items will not work.

Do not forget to press the **Save** button if you make any changes to the **Tweak Settings** screen. Any changes you make will be noted on the next screen confirming those changes.

Statistics Software Configuration

Tweak Settings allows you to turn on or off the various web stats programs you wish to offer, but you can much more closely regulate the operation and use of the web stats programs if you wish. To do so, click on **Statistics Software Configuration** in WHM's **Server Configuration** section.

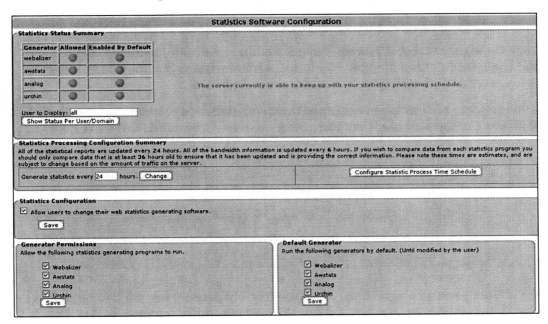

The **Statistics Status Summary** section displays which web stats programs are installed on your server, which ones cPanel users are currently allowed to access, and which ones are enabled by default when a new account is added to the server. Green dots mean the item is available or enabled by default, and red dots mean the item is not available or not enabled by default. Also you will see some green or red text next to the web stats table. If the text is green and states that your server is able to keep up with the current processing schedule, this is a good thing and what you should see in most cases. However, if the web stats update schedule you've chosen is too strenuous for the server, you may see red text letting you know that some or all of the accounts on the server are behind the processing schedule you've set. If they are behind, you will be able to click a link to see which accounts are behind and how many minutes behind they are.

If you regularly find that your server is unable to keep up with the stats processing schedule, you should check **Tweak Settings** to make sure you haven't set the *stats processing load cutoff value* too low. In addition, you may wish to disable some web stats programs so that your server can more easily process the logs each night.

The **Statistics Processing Configuration Summary** will provide you with an overview of the current schedule you have set concerning how web logs and bandwidth usage will be processed. By default, all web logs are updated every 24 hours, and bandwidth is updated every 6 hours. You can change the number of hours between processing by raising or lowering the **Generate stats every___hours** value. The summary will change to note the new schedule based on what you have entered.

Click **Configure Statistic Process Time Schedule** if you want to alter the time logs and bandwidth. This will allow you to specify a timeframe that may be less busy on your server and allow logs to be processed without delay.

If you check the **Allow users to change their web statistics generating software** in the **Statistics Configuration** section, then a new section will be added to the interface:

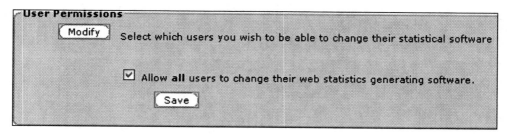

In the **User Permissions** section, you can select which users you want to be able to modify the stats programs they use by clicking the **Modify** button, and choosing which accounts you want to permit to make changes to your default settings. Users will only be able to make modifications to those stats programs that are enabled server-wide.

Alternately, you can check the **Allow all users to change their web statistics generating software** item and click the **Save** button to allow all users to change which stats programs they use.

You can change which web stats programs run on your server from here as well as from **Tweak Settings,** by checking or unchecking the appropriate web stats programs from the **Generator Permission** section and then clicking **Save** to apply the changes.

You can also allow stats programs to run, but turn them off by default (so they only run if the user specifically enables them in cPanel) by checking or unchecking the stats programs list in the **Default Generator** section and then clicking **Save** to apply the changes.

> Web statistics programs store data and graphics in each user account. This means if you have all stats packages on by default, not only are you affecting the time it takes to process the logs, but each account may lose 50-200 MB of disk space due to the data and graphics storage for the web stats programs.
>
> For these reasons, it is probably a good idea to turn off all but one web stats program by default and allow cPanel users to switch or add others if they use them. The most popular web stats package is AWSTATS, so if you pick only one, that is probably the one to choose.

Summary

In this chapter you learned how to navigate the root WHM interface, configuring how and when your server contacts you if certain events happen, choosing the best cPanel build track, and updating your server both manually and automatically each night. In addition, we learned about formatting and mounting extra hard drives, and figuring out what you might want to use them for. We explored how to Set the date, time, and time zone of your server, and how to choose a proper hostname for your server.

You learned about configuring cpbackup, and learned what the backup script is capable of and what its limitations are, setting a wide variety of WHM and cPanel settings in Tweak Settings. You now know about configuring when your server processes web stats logs and bandwidth, and also about controlling which web statistics programs you offer to clients, and whether they can make their own modifications in cPanel.

In the next chapter, you will learn how to work with Apache, MySQL, PostgreSQL, PHP, and Perl in WHM, and set them up to your liking.

4

Apache, PHP, Perl, and Databases

Before you attempt to put paying clients (or yourself) on your new server, you will want to make sure your web server (Apache), PHP, Perl, and MySQL (and PostgreSQL) are configured the way you need them. That's what we will examine in this chapter. Specifically, we will explore:

- What Apache, PHP, Perl, MySQL, and PostgreSQL are
- Updating Apache and PHP via WHM and SSH
- Apache and PHP configuration options
- PHPsuEXEC versus standard PHP module
- PHP Safe Mode
- Installing Zend Optimizer
- Updating Perl
- Adding Perl modules via WHM, Perlinstaller, or CPAN
- Installing or updating MySQL
- Resetting the local MySQL root password
- Additional MySQL Access Hosts
- Setting up a remote MySQL server
- Repairing a MySQL Database
- Change a MySQL user or database password
- MySQL Process List
- PhpMyAdmin
- Installing PostgreSQL
- Limitations to PostgreSQL on a cPanel Server

By the time you've finished this chapter, you will be able to confidently use the tools WHM provides to manage web service, programming languages, and databases even if you've never worked with any of these things before.

Before we look at how to configure and work with Apache, PHP, Perl, PostgreSQL, and MySQL, we need to understand what they are and how they relate to one another.

Apache: Web's Best Friend

In order for your server to be able to serve pages on the Internet, it needs some special software. The software cPanel uses is called **Apache**. Apache is an open source project, and one of the most popular web servers on the planet.

Apache currently has two main supported branches: the older **1.x series**, and the newer **2.x series**. The 1.x series is the one that cPanel currently uses. This branch has been in wide use for many years and is very stable. Eventually, cPanel plans to support Apache 2.x, which isn't a traditional upgrade to the existing 1.x branch. 2.x is a complete rewrite of the Apache web server to make it more modular and easier to maintain. However, not all Apache 1.x modules have been rewritten for 2.x.compatability yet. Both branches are actively maintained, but most of the development work done on Apache right now is on the 2.x branch.

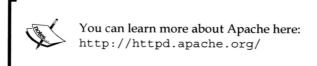

> You can learn more about Apache here:
> http://httpd.apache.org/

PHP: Hypertext Processor

PHP rather creatively stands for PHP Hypertext Processor. It is a dynamically processed scripting language that is well-suited for web development. HTML is wonderful, but it doesn't handle dynamically changing content well. PHP was designed with this sort of thing in mind. PHP is processed by the server at the time the script is accessed, and output is generated as appropriate. The person viewing the output would only see the output itself and not the PHP code that created the output (unlike viewing the source of a HTML page). The dynamically generated nature of PHP makes it a good choice for web scripts like forums, blogs, or content management systems whose content can change often.

To learn more about PHP and what it can do, visit the following links:
PHP main website: `http://php.net/`
W3 School's PHP Tutorial:
`http://www.w3schools.com/php/default.asp.`

Perl: The Programming Language that Powers cPanel

Perl is a cross-platform modular programming language. Much of cPanel and WHM are written in Perl. cPanel supports users running Perl scripts via CGI. **CGI** stands for Common Gateway Interface. The functionality of Perl can be extended through Perl modules (add-on code).

Learn more about Perl and CGI:
Perl: `http://perl.org/`
CGI: `http://hoohoo.ncsa.uiuc.edu/cgi/`

MySQL: A Database for the Masses

MySQL is a widely used open-source database. It is the default database type installed on all cPanel servers. Databases such as MySQL are often used to store data that web scripts need (like user information or forum posts), because they make storage and retrieval a simple process. Although MySQL is considered an open source database, it has a separate license for commercial use, and so some commercial products may be required to purchase a license.

For more information about MySQL and its open-source and commercial licensing terms, visit `http://mysql.com`.

PostgreSQL: The "Other" Database

PostgreSQL is a widely used open-source database. Since PostgreSQL is completely open source (covered by the BSD license) and does not have a separate commercial license, some people may prefer to use it. Web scripts may support the use of PostgreSQL databases, but you should first check with the developer to see if there is PostgreSQL support. cPanel does support use of PostgreSQL, but at this time, support is not as robust as it is for MySQL.

You can learn more about PostgreSQL from
`http://www.postgresql.org/`.

Configuring Apache on a cPanel Server

All cPanel servers actually come with two copies of Apache and PHP running on them. One copy manages cPanel and WHM, and is specially configured for them. The other copy serves public websites and can be directly configured by you to meet the needs of your clients.

PHP scripts must be dynamically interpreted by the web server each time they are accessed so that appropriate output can be generated. Hence, PHP support must be added to Apache in the form of a PHP module. If this support isn't added to Apache, PHP scripts will just be downloaded to the user's computer every time they try to access one.

When referring to the two copies in this book, we will call the cPanel and WHM copy of Apache and PHP the "back-end" copy, and the public version that serves user websites the "front-end" copy.

Configuring or Updating the Back-End Copy of Apache and PHP

WHM itself takes care of updating the back-end copy of Apache and PHP as needed (unless you have cPanel and WHM set to not automatically or manually update as discussed in Chapter 3), so you typically shouldn't need to reconfigure or update it on your own.

If you find that you are having problems with features or functions in WHM or cPanel that are related to PHP, you can log into your server via SSH as root and run:

```
/scripts/makecpphp
```

This will reinstall a clean copy of PHP, and all the needed back-end components and settings. There is no similar feature or option in WHM, so you will have to use this script if you think you need to recompile the back-end copy of PHP.

The back-end copy of PHP uses the following `php.ini` file for configuration:

```
/usr/local/cpanel/3rdparty/etc/php.ini
```

You do not need to make changes to this file. If you do, be aware that some features of cPanel or WHM may cease to work properly.

Configuring or Updating the Front-End Copy of Apache and PHP

WHM offers you the ability to manually update Apache and PHP on your server, should you want to do so. WHM will automatically update your front-end copy of Apache (though it may not do so as soon as a new version is available). To manually update Apache or PHP, click on the **Update Apache** item in the **Software** section of WHM.

Alternatively, you can update using /scripts/easyapache from a root shell. The WHM **Update Apache** feature configures and runs /scripts/easyapache, and displays the results in WHM, so it doesn't really matter which method you use.

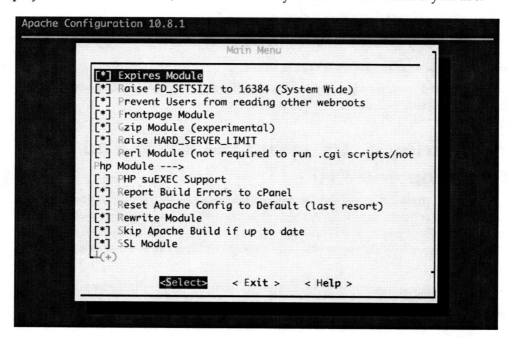

If you've never configured Apache or PHP before, you may find the options presented to you to be a bit overwhelming. Just remember, when in doubt, don't add or remove the features that Update Apache or easyapache have installed by default. You could end up breaking Apache or PHP, or cause Apache to become very slow or use a lot of CPU load. Only add those items you are sure you want or need.

If there are certain modules or features you need compiled into Apache or PHP, the time to add them is prior to placing paying customers on your server. This way, if you choose the wrong options or change your mind, you can recompile Apache and PHP without having to worry about downtime for your customers. Of course, you can still recompile Apache and PHP once your server goes into production, but you will need to be a bit more careful to avoid downtime due to misconfiguration.

Apache-Related Configuration Options - Part 1

Here are the options that easyapache and Update Apache currently offer:

Expires module: The mod_expires is module allows the server administrator and users to set HTTP cache Expires headers for files on the server. The Expires header tells the recipient's web browser (or their ISP's proxy server) that this file can be served from the cache until a specified time. This module is enabled by default on cPanel servers. Learn more about mod_expires here: http://httpd.apache.org/docs/1.3/mod/mod_expires.html.

Raise FD_SETSIZE to 16384: This will increase the maximum number of file descriptors per Apache process. This is enabled by default on cPanel servers.

Prevent Users from Reading other Webroots: This will not permit other users on the same server to access other people's web root (public_html) directory. This is a security measure, and it is enabled by default on cPanel servers.

FrontPage module: mod_frontpage is one half of the Microsoft FrontPage server-side extensions (the other half gets installed into each user's account when they enable FrontPage extensions in cPanel). This is enabled by default on all cPanel servers. You should not disable it unless you know you are never going to allow users to enable FrontPage extensions on your server. If you do disable it, be sure to disable the FrontPage installation feature in the **Feature Manager** in WHM (see Chapter 7).

Gzip module: mod_gzip compresses content on the fly on the server when a page is requested. This compression will reduce the amount of bandwidth the page uses and does not require special software to be enabled on the client's side. This item is disabled by default on cPanel servers. Note that this module can place additional load on the server for each page, since the compression is all done on the server's side before sending to the requester. If your server is already fully loaded with existing traffic, you may not want to enable this.

Raise HARD_SERVER_LIMIT: This increases the maximum number of concurrent child processes that Apache can handle before denying additional connections. This is enabled by default on cPanel servers.

Perl module: This module adds a Perl interpreter into Apache itself. You do not need to enable this to allow users to run Perl scripts on your server. You should leave this disabled, unless you know you need it. You can learn more about mod_perl and how it works here: http://perl.apache.org.

PHP Configuration Options

PHP: This should be checked unless you don't wish to offer PHP to your clients. There are a wide variety of PHP modules that you can enable, and all of the modules easyapache supports are listed in an indented row.

PHP Version: There are several versions of PHP that cPanel currently supports. Choose only one from this list. The versions offered will vary depending on which version of cPanel and the Apache install script you are using. Unless you need PHP 5 support on your server, the best choice is probably 4.4.x, as this is currently the most secure build of PHP 4.x available. PHP 5.x isn't as compatible with some popular web scripts yet. Note that by the time you read this, easyapache may support other versions, so you will have to choose appropriately.

BC Math: The **Binary Calculator (BC)** is used for precision math functions. This item is enabled by default on all cPanel servers. You should only disable it if you are sure you won't need it. You can learn more about BC math functions here: `http://www.php.net/manual/en/ref.bc.php`.

Calendar Support: This adds functions to PHP that make it easier to convert dates between different calendar formats. This is enabled by default on all cPanel servers. You can learn more about calendar functions in PHP here: `http://www.php.net/manual/en/ref.calendar.php`.

CURL: CURL (which stands for Client URL) adds functions that make it easier for PHP to communicate with other servers over a wide range of protocols. Although this isn't enabled by default, many PHP e-commerce solutions require the use of CURL. Learn more about CURL here: `http://www.php.net/manual/en/ref.curl.php`.

CURL SSL Support: This adds SSL/TLS support to CURL (HTTPS).

DOM XSLT: DOM XSLT stands for Document Object Model: Extensible Stylesheet Language Transformations. This adds functions to PHP to allow it to more easily translate one XML format into another. You can learn more about XSLT support in PHP here: `http://www.php.net/manual/en/ref.xslt.php`.

EXIF: EXIF stands for Exchangeable Image File Format. This feature allows PHP to more easily work with the EXIF data stored in many image files (typically by digital cameras or image manipulation programs). What is stored in the EXIF metadata can vary from image to image, but it often includes the time the picture was taken, how it was taken, camera settings, and so on. Learn more about EXIF support in PHP here: `http://www.php.net/manual/en/ref.exif.php`.

Flash: When this is installed, functions are added to PHP to make it easier to create and work with Flash (`.swf`) files. Learn more about the Flash functions added to PHP here: `http://www.php.net/manual/en/ref.swf.php`.

FTP: With this enabled (as it is by default on all cPanel servers), PHP gains the ability to control most aspects of FTP communications between servers. Without it, PHP does still have basic FTP support. Learn more about the extensive FTP-related functions this module adds at this site: `http://www.php.net/manual/en/ref.ftp.php`.

GD: This enables the GD2 graphics library module. This module allows PHP to work with all kinds of common image formats. Although this module isn't enabled by default, many popular PHP scripts require it (or another graphics library like **ImageMagick** or **NetPBM**), so you'll probably want to enable this. Learn more about GD here: `http://www.boutell.com/gd/`.

Gettext: The `gettext` module makes it easier to work with multiple languages (internationalization) in PHP scripts. Many PHP scripts make use of this, so it is another module that you may want to consider enabling. Learn more about GNU `gettext` here: `http://www.gnu.org/software/gettext/manual/gettext.html`.

Iconv: This PHP module provides character set conversion capabilities that make working with international character sets much simpler. You can learn more about `libiconv` here: `http://www.gnu.org/software/libiconv/`.

IMAP module: This module enables c-client support in PHP, which is a module that makes it easier to work with the **IMAP**, **POP3**, and **NNTP** protocols.

Java: Enabling this allows PHP to work with Java servelets. Working with server-side Java can put a strain on your server, so it isn't recommended unless you have very fast hardware or otherwise plan to limit its use. Enabling Java functions in PHP is not the same as enabling Tomcat or Resin.

Mb String: Multibyte string functions make it easier to work with multibyte language encodings in PHP. Learn more about multibyte string functions here: `http://www.php.net/manual/en/ref.mbstring.php`.

Mcrypt: Enabling this allows PHP scripts to more easily work with various encryption protocols like DES and Blowfish. Some e-commerce scripts may require this.

Memory limit: This implements stricter memory limits. Without some modification, you will likely find the new limits to be a bit too low for most scripts.

Mhash: This module enables a uniform interface for working with various hashing algorithms like `SHA1` and `CRC32`. To learn more about mhash, visit: `http://mhash.sourceforge.net/`.

Ming Support: This allows PHP to work with Flash (`.swf`) files. Ming is different than the "Flash" option mentioned above (which uses `libswf`), although they accomplish basically the same tasks. Depending on your needs, Ming may be a better choice than `libswf`. However, some versions of Ming are a bit flakey on cPanel servers, so be sure to test it on your server before taking the server live if you plan to offer this. Learn more about Ming here: `http://ming.sourceforge.net/`.

Magic Quotes: This automatically escapes incoming text like single and double quotes (so the input is stored properly in databases). Some scripts need this on and others need it off depending on how they are coded. (The preferred method is not to rely on magic quotes, but to use the `addslashs()` function instead.) This feature is enabled by default on all cPanel servers. Most popular scripts try to turn Magic Quotes on or off as needed, so this just affects the default setting. Learn more about Magic Auotes here: `http://www.php.net/magic_quotes`.

MM Session module: This module allows PHP to utilize the Mohawk session software (now called **MCache**), which provides for consistent session management especially designed for large web server farms. At the time this book was written, the MM Session module support in easyapache was experimental. Learn more about MCache here: `http://www.mohawksoft.org/?q=node/8`.

MySQL module: This allows PHP scripts to work with MySQL databases. This is enabled by default on all cPanel servers. Unless you don't plan on offering clients MySQL databases you should leave this enabled.

> You will have to recompile PHP with the latest MySQL
> support when you upgrade to a major new version
> of MySQL.

SNMP: SNMP stands for Simple Network Management Protocol, which is designed to allow monitoring of network appliances like routers and computers. This allows PHP to work with the Net-SNMP package to monitor network conditions and equipment. You should only enable this if you are sure you will need it. You must also install **Net-SNMP** on your server (separately) before you enable this. Learn more about Net-SNMP here: `http://www.net-snmp.org/`.

OpenSSL Support: Enabling this allows PHP to use OpenSSL to work with SSL/TLS encryption. Some e-commerce PHP scripts may require this. Learn more about OpenSSL here: `http://www.openssl.org/`.

Discard Path: This allows PHP, when compiled as a CGI binary, to be saved outside of the web tree so that users won't be able to circumvent `.htaccess` security measures. This is enabled by default on all cPanel servers.

PDFlib: This installs **PDFlib**, which allows PHP to work natively with PDF files. This library is not open-source, and if anyone on the server is going to use it for commercial purposes, it may require that you acquire a license before installing it. See `http://www.pdflib.com/products/pdflib/index.html` for more information and details on licensing.

Pear: PEAR stands for PHP Extension and Application Repository, and it serves as a framework for installing and distributing PHP components. Learn more about Pear here: `http://pear.php.net/`.

PostgreSQL: This enables **PostgreSQL** database support in PHP. It is required if you plan on using PostgreSQL on your server and want PHP scripts to be able to access the databases. If PostgreSQL isn't installed on your server yet, easyapache will run `/scripts/installpostgresql` before compiling PHP. However, you will still need to make a few modifications to the standard PostgreSQL installation before it will work in a cPanel environment. This is discussed in more detail later in this chapter.

Pspell module: This adds functions to PHP to allow it to spell-check words. You must install the **Aspell** library if you plan to use Pspell. Learn more about Aspell and its features here: `http://aspell.sourceforge.net/`.

Sablot XSLT: If you enable this, PHP will be able to use the **Sablotron XML** toolkit to work with XML files. Learn more about Sablotron here: `http://www.gingerall.org/charlie/ga/xml/p_sab.xml?s=org`.

Safe Mode: PHP Safe Mode is an imperfect method of trying to enforce security in a shared hosting environment. Safe Mode disables certain functions and limits some features of PHP in order to make it harder for a malicious PHP script to cause problems on your server. This may sound like a good thing, but it takes the "heart" out of PHP while not providing as much security as one might hope. Many popular PHP scripts do not work when Safe Mode is enabled. There are better (though perhaps not easier) ways to secure PHP scripts. Safe Mode will be completely disabled in PHP 6.0. To learn more about PHP Safe Mode, visit: `http://www.php.net/features.safe-mode`.

> For a discussion of why Safe Mode isn't as safe as it seems visit `http://ilia.ws/archives/18-PHPs-safe_mode-or-how-not-to-implement-security.html`.

Sockets: Enabling this allows PHP to work with low-level socket-based communications. Sockets are enabled on all cPanel servers by default. Learn more about PHP socket functions here: `http://www.php.net/manual/en/ref.sockets.php`.

Use system MySQL: Enabling this will allow PHP to use the version of MySQL installed in your operating system (as opposed to the separate copy cPanel typically uses). Only enable this if you know you need it.

Track Vars: This allows PHP to keep track of variables. This is enabled by default on all cPanel servers.

FreeType Support: Enabling this allows PHP to use the **FreeType** font engine. Learn more about FreeType here: `http://freetype.sourceforge.net/index2.html`.

Versioning: This enables PHP extension versioning support and is enabled by default. Depending on your server platform and installed software, versioning may not be desirable. If you encounter problems, disable it.

WDDX: WDDX stands for Web Distributed Data Exchange and is an XML-based technology designed to allow web applications on a variety of platforms to more easily exchange data. For more information about WDDX, see: `http://www.openwddx.org/`.

XML RPC: This option allows PHP to create and work with XML RPC clients. XML RPC is designed to allow scripts on a variety of platforms to make procedure calls over the Internet. Learn more about XML RPC here: `http://www.xmlrpc.com/`.

Zip: This allows PHP scripts to read the contents of Zip files. It requires Zlib to be enabled. Learn more about PHP Zip support here: `http://www.xmlrpc.com/`.

Zlib: This allows PHP to transparently work with *gzip-compressed* files. This is enabled by default on all cPanel servers. Learn more about Zlib support in PHP here: `http://us3.php.net/manual/en/ref.zlib.php`.

PHPsuEXEC Support: This compiles and runs PHP as a CGI module in a **suEXEC** environment (similar to the way Perl scripts are run). This means that all PHP scripts will be run as the user whose account they are run from. This can make finding the owner of exploited or load-intensive PHP scripts much easier. However, it does increase the amount of time it takes to run a PHP script, and it also places higher loads on the web server. On slower hardware this can be quite noticeable if your clients are using a lot of PHP scripts.

PHPsuEXEC also forces users to keep file and directory permissions at or lower than 755. Any file or directory set to anything higher than that will cause 500 (Internal Server) errors. In addition, PHP directives that would normally be added to `.htaccess` files should be added to a `php.ini` file instead. This `php.ini` file can contain only those values that the script needs to change in order to run properly.

It is *not* advisable to enable or disable PHPsuEXEC on a server that already has customers on it. Due to the restrictions and functionality changes PHPsuEXEC requires, changing will mean that your users must manually check their files and directories, and make the necessary changes, or their scripts may stop working.

Apache-Related Configuration Options - Part 2

The rest of the options in easyapache apply once again to Apache itself or the build process, and not to PHP.

Report Build errors to cPanel: If you enable this, cPanel Inc. will be notified any time easyapache runs into problems compiling Apache or PHP, so they can work on fixing any bugs.

Reset Apache Config to default: Do not enable this item unless you absolutely must do so. It will completely remove all Apache configuration setting and remove most of the data from `httpd.conf`. This will cause websites to stop working until their data is added back into the `httpd.conf` file. This should only be used for troubleshooting purposes if nothing else works.

Rewrite module: The rewrite module is very useful. It allows Apache to dynamically change or redirect URLs based on a set of rules the user adds in an `.htaccess` file. This has a wide variety of uses, including redirecting access from one URL to another and creating shorter "friendly" URLs. Learn more about what `mod_rewrite` can do here: `http://httpd.apache.org/docs/1.3/mod/mod_rewrite.html`.

Skip Apache Build if up to date: This does exactly what it says; it stops **easyapache** from recompiling Apache if it is already the latest available version. This can save you some time.

SSL module: Enable this to add SSL/TLS support to Apache. Apache will not be able to serve `https:` URLs without this.

suEXEC module: This enables the standard CGI suEXEC module (for things like Perl and Python scripts, not for PHP).

Verbose Build: If you enable this, you will see the raw output of the Apache and PHP build process. If this is disabled, easyapache will clean up the output to make it easier to read. If you are having problems with getting modules to compile properly, verbose mode will typically provide more information about exactly what the issue is.

Once you've selected the options you need in Apache and PHP, click **Build** to start the compiling process.

The display onscreen in WHM will update in real time, showing the progress of the build. If you do not have the verbose mode checked, then any serious errors will be listed onscreen in red. If you see such errors, make a note of them, as they will stop that particular module or component from being installed.

Note that not all components or options will work with every server platform or version of PHP. If you have problems compiling Apache or PHP, then you should try removing the contents of `/home/cpapachebuild` (where temporary files used for building Apache and PHP are kept). This will remove any corrupted TEMP files, and force easyapache to use clean copies. Also, you may have to scale back on which components you install via easyapache.

If Apache fails after the build process, log into your server as root, and type the following:

```
/usr/local/apache/bin/apachectl configtest
```

or

```
service httpd configtest
```

(The latter item may not work on all platforms, but the former should.)

This will test the `httpd.conf` file for the front-end copy of Apache, and make sure there are no obvious configuration errors.

The **configtest** feature may show some potential issues and still say **Config OK** at the end of the test. If so, the errors listed aren't likely to stop Apache from starting.

If you find serious errors, you will need to address them before Apache will be able to start. This may involve recompiling with fewer or different features, or manually editing your `httpd.conf` file to fix the problems.

You can find the front-end copy of the `httpd.conf` file here on cPanel servers:

```
/usr/local/apache/conf/httpd.conf
```

Once you've addressed any issues and configtest reports **Config OK**, try restarting Apache either by selecting the **Restart Apache** (httpd) item from **WHM's Restart Services** section or run the following via root shell:

```
/usr/local/apache/bin/apachectl restart
```

or

```
service httpd restart
```

If it still fails to start properly and you aren't sure what to do to fix it, contact your NOC for assistance.

Installing Zend Optimizer

The **Zend Optimizer** is a free Apache module that can improve the speed of execution of PHP scripts, and it is also required in order to run Zend encoded scripts on your server. Zend encoding protects the code in PHP files so that it cannot be examined by end users but will still execute properly on a server with PHP and Zend Optimizer installed.

Although cPanel Inc. has not included a feature in WHM to install Zend Optimizer from WHM, it does include a script that you can run from a root shell that makes installation simple. All you need to do is run:

`/scripts/installzendopt`

Accept all of the default suggestions in the installer.

To see if Zend Optimizer is installed on your server and to see what version you are running, type the following from a root shell:

`php -v`

You will see output similar to this:

```
PHP 4.4.2 (cli) (built: Apr 25 2006 16:23:11)
Copyright (c) 1997-2006 The PHP Group
Zend Engine v1.3.0, Copyright (c) 1998-2004 Zend Technologies
    with Zend Extension Manager v1.0.9, Copyright (c) 2003-2006, by Zend
Technologies
    with Zend Optimizer v2.6.2, Copyright (c) 1998-2006, by Zend
Technologies
```

So long as you see a line about the Zend Optimizer and a version number (typically the last line in the output from this command), then it is installed and running. Do not confuse the Zend Optimizer line with the php **Zend Engine** version. PHP includes some code from Zend called the Zend Engine. This is not the same as the Zend Optimizer.

 To learn more about Zend Optimizer and Zend encoding, visit: http://zend.com/.

Configuring and Working with Perl

Although WHM and cPanel can work successfully with numerous different versions of Perl, cPanel Inc. only officially supports one particular version of Perl. You can look for the current version of the cPanel approved Perl installer by going to: http://layer1.cpanel.net/.

You should use that version unless there is some specific reason you must use some other version. Using an older or newer version of Perl may cause problems with WHM and cPanel, so if you experience issues, make sure you are using the correct version of Perl. You can check this by running the following from a root shell:

```
perl -v
```

This command will show you what version of Perl is installed. If it isn't the latest approved version of Perl from cPanel, you should probably install the cPanel version. Directions for how to do this are discussed in Chapter 2.

Adding new functionality to Perl is a good deal easier than Apache or PHP. You can use several different tools to accomplish the same task. In WHM, you can use the **Install Perl Module** feature under the **Software** section. If you are logged into your server via SSH as root, then you can also use the `/scripts/perlinstaller` script or CPAN.

However, just as with Apache and PHP, you should not install additional Perl modules unless you are sure you will need them.

Installing Perl Modules in WHM

WHM makes installing new Perl modules very easy. Click on **Install Perl Modules** from the **Software** section of WHM, type in all or part of the name of the module you would like to install, and click **Search**.

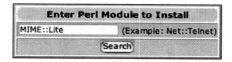

This will bring up a list of modules that match the text you've entered. Click on the name of the module you would like to install, and WHM will install it for you. If the module is already installed, WHM will look for and install any new updates. WHM will also automatically install any other required Perl modules in order to get the one you've selected to install properly.

Installing Perl Modules Using the Perlinstaller Script

You can also install Perl modules from the root shell by using a script that cPanel includes called `perlinstaller`. Using it is fairly simple:

```
/scripts/perlinstaller [--force] Module::Name
```

`/scripts/perlinstaller` is the path to the `perlinstaller` script. `--force` is optional. If you include it, it will make the system reinstall a fresh copy, even if that module is already installed. After that is a list of the exact names of the Perl modules you want to install, separated by spaces. Capitalization of the Perl module name matters, so make sure you type everything correctly.

Installing Perl Modules Using CPAN

There is another way you can install or upgrade Perl modules from a root shell. You can use **CPAN** (Comprehensive Perl Archive Network). To start working in CPAN, just type cpan at the root shell prompt.

Once in CPAN, you can install any module by typing:

```
[force] install Module::Name
```

force is optional and, if included, will force CPAN to reinstall a fresh copy of the named Perl module, even if the latest version is already installed. install is the command used to install Perl modules, and that is followed by the exact name of the Perl module to be installed. Capitalization matters in the name of the Perl module, so be careful.

Once you've finished installing the Perl modules you need, type exit on a separate line to leave the CPAN interface.

Checking Perl Scripts and Automatically Installing the Needed Modules

WHM offers a handy, if not foolproof, feature called **Check/Repair a Perl Script**, which is located in the **Software** section.

Perl Script Checker
This feature will check a perl script for modules that are missing from the server and attempt to install them as needed.
Enter the full path to the perl script (ex. /home/user/public_html/me.cgi): /home/domain/public_html/cgi-bin/perlscript.pl
Check

It doesn't really repair Perl scripts, but it does look inside the script that the user is having problems running and attempts to figure out which Perl modules the script requires in order to run properly. It will then install any modules that it determines are needed and that aren't currently installed.

All you have to do is type in the absolute path to the script you want to check, and then click the **Check** button. WHM will do the rest. If modules need to be installed to support that script, you will be informed of this and will see the installation process for those modules.

 If this still doesn't allow the Perl script to run properly, check the user's cPanel **Error Log** as this will usually contain useful information about why the script won't run. Sometimes it is as simple as changing the permissions on the script.

Upgrading and Working with MySQL

WHM includes a number of tools that help you work with MySQL databases on your server. Most of these features can be found in the **SQL Services** section of WHM.

Upgrading MySQL

To upgrade MySQL, the first thing you need to do is make sure you've chosen the correct version that you wish to use. You do this in **Tweak Settings** by selecting the version of MySQL you want to use (5.0 or 4.1) and saving changes. (See Chapter 2 for more on **Tweak Settings** and selecting the appropriate MySQL version.)

To make sure the latest version of MySQL that you've chosen is installed, you can click on **Update Server Software** in the **Software** section of WHM or by running `/scripts/mysqlup` from a root shell. If you use `/scripts/mysqlup`, you can also append `--force` to reinstall MySQL, regardless of whether the current version is already installed or not.

If you are upgrading to a major new version (such as the upgrade from 4.0.x to 4.1.x, or 4.1.x to 5.0.x), you will also need to recompile PHP with the correct version of the MySQL module, or else PHP scripts won't be able to access the upgraded databases. How to recompile Apache and PHP was discussed earlier in this chapter. You may also want to force the reinstallation of `Bundle::DBD::mysql`, which allows Perl scripts (and cPanel and WHM) to access the upgraded databases. Modern versions of WHM should automatically upgrade `Bundle::DBD::mysql`, but if you run into any problems, you can do it manually by logging into your server via SSH as root and typing the following at the root shell prompt:

```
/scripts/perlinstaller --force Bundle::DBD::mysql
```

or by using CPAN:

```
cpan
force install Bundle::DBD::mysql
exit
```

If you are just upgrading to a new minor version (such as 4.1.13 to 4.1.18, or 5.0.1 to 5.0.2), you shouldn't need to recompile PHP or reinstall the Perl module.

You cannot easily downgrade to an older version of MySQL once you have upgraded, so you may want to backup /var/lib/mysql and perhaps /etc/my.cnf, before upgrading so that, if something goes wrong with the upgrade, you can downgrade to the previous version, and then restore the MySQL database data and settings from your backup.

Adding MySQL Remote Hosts in WHM

Users can use the MySQL area of their cPanel account to add IP addresses that can remotely access the MySQL databases (so long as they have the correct database username and password to access those databases). However, you can add IPs that will be able to remotely access MySQL databases on your server directly from WHM. Click on **Additional MySQL Access Hosts** in WHM to add remote IPs. On the screen that appears, enter one IP address on each line (as many as you need), and then click **Save** to commit the changes.

Any IP addresses you add here, won't immediately be able to access all databases on the server remotely (with the proper authentication). In order for the changes to apply to a particular customer, they must go into their cPanel and click on **MySQL**. This will update the allowed remote hosts.

Alternately, you can force the update on all clients *immediately* by clicking the words **Click Here!** on the **Additional MySQL Access Hosts** screen in WHM. You can also access this directly in your web browser by going to the following link:
`https://hostname.domain.com:2087/scripts2/mysqlupdateall`

where *hostname.domain.com* is your server's hostname or main IP address.

If you choose to allow remote MySQL access, then you need to make sure that port 3306 is open on your server. This may require editing your firewall settings if you use one.

 Be careful if you need to add a dynamically assigned IP address as a remote access host. Since this IP address will eventually be passed on to other users, you should make sure you remove dynamically assigned IPs once the intended user has finished with it.

Changing a MySQL User or Database Password

If your clients are having problems changing MySQL user passwords, then you can step in and do it for them. Click on **Change a User or Database Password**, and you will be shown a list of all the databases and MySQL set up on your server.

Click on the database or database user from the displayed list that you want to change the password for, and then type the new password at the top of the display (below where it says **New Password**). This password will not be obscured, so be mindful of who is around you while you are changing the password. Then click on the **Change Password** button to commit the change.

Resetting MySQL's Root Password

The MySQL service comes with its own master (root) password that will allow you to perform administrative tasks, and add and remove databases. Even if you never need to access MySQL as root, you still need to set a secure password. If you don't set a secure root MySQL password, users on your server may be able to access databases for other users and delete or change them. This is a clear security risk.

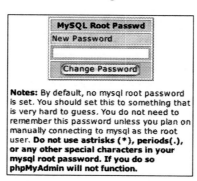

Type your new MySQL root password in the box on this screen. You should make it long, random, and hard to guess. However, due to limitations in some versions of phpMyAdmin, you should avoid special characters in your password. Also, don't make the root password for your server and the root password for MySQL the same. Unless you plan on using the MySQL root interface, you will never need to remember this password. If you need to use the root MySQL interface later, you can always go back into WHM and change the MySQL root password again.

Repairing MySQL Databases in WHM

You can also repair MySQL databases that may have become somewhat corrupted (perhaps when they were transferred from another server). Click on **Repair a Database** in WHM, and you will be presented with an unsorted list of all of the database users and databases on the server. Note that client databases will be prefixed with their cPanel usernames.

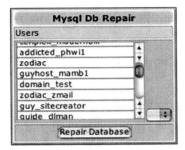

Select the database you want to try to repair from the list, and click **Repair Database**. The results of the attempt will be displayed on the screen shortly thereafter. This feature uses MySQL's own database repair function. If the repair attempt fails, you may need to restore the database from a known good backup.

 See http://dev.mysql.com/doc/refman/4.1/en/ repair.html for more information on the MySQL repair function.

Resetting the Local MySQL Root Password

If you try to reset the root MySQL password using the feature mentioned above and it fails, you can try this alternate method to reset the MySQL root password. However, you should only do so if the other method fails. Click on **Reset Local MySQL Root Password** to try this.

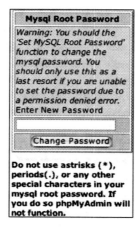

Enter the MySQL root password you want to use, and then click **Change Password**. WHM will then do several things that should hopefully get the MySQL root password set successfully so that you can reset it later using the standard MySQL root password feature mentioned earlier.

If this doesn't work, then you should contact your NOC for assistance.

Setting Up a Remote MySQL Server in WHM

We've already covered what to do if you want to allow others to remotely access MySQL running on this server, but what do you do if you want your clients on this server to use MySQL running on a separate server? You click on **Setup Remote MySQL Server** in this server's WHM.

By default, WHM and cPanel use MySQL set up locally (referred to as "localhost"). However, this doesn't mean you can't use a remote MySQL server if you prefer. All you have to do is have a remote MySQL server set up and accessible on the Internet, and it should allow SSH connections from your main (WHM/cPanel) server. Then you enter the appropriate information on the previous screen, which includes the remote server hostname or IP address (removing the word localhost and entering the correct information), the remote server's SSH port (which is typically 22 unless you've changed the SSH port), the remote server's root password (which is not the MySQL server root password), the user with su (wheel group) access (if you don't permit direct root logins), and the su user password. Click **Setup** to begin the process. If all goes well, your WHM/cPanel server will now be able to use the remote MySQL server rather than the one installed locally.

Showing MySQL Processes

If you find that MySQL is putting a strain on your server, and you want to see what is going on, click **Show MySQL Processes** in root WHM. This will display all currently running processes in MySQL along with some critical information that will help you track down what processes are doing and who they belong to. This is only a list, so in order to act on any one MySQL process, you will need to log into MySQL as root via SSH and take care of the issue. Alternately, you can try restarting MySQL to see if that clears out any stuck processes.

phpMyAdmin

Clicking on the phpMyAdmin link in root WHM will start phpMyAdmin in a new window with root MySQL access. **phpMyAdmin** is a script that allows you to edit MySQL databases without having to resort to a command line. It is also the same version of phpMyAdmin that your users can access in WHM (although they won't be accessing MySQL as root, and they won't be able to create databases in MySQL).

So what does root MySQL access get you in phpMyAdmin?

- Full access to all databases on the server
- The ability to create or delete all databases in phpMyAdmin
- Full administrative access to all features and functions that phpMyAdmin offers

Therefore if you need to access, repair, or edit databases, you don't need to log into the user's cPanel or know the database user password. Do be careful though, because you can delete or ruin a perfectly good MySQL database if you aren't careful.

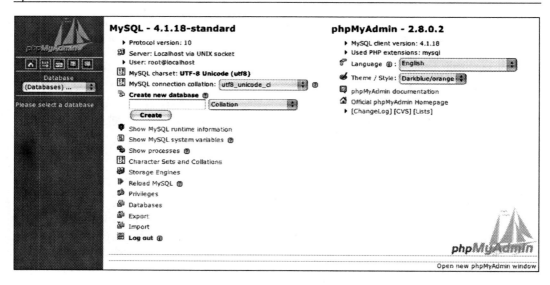

Unfortunately, phpMyAdmin is too complex a piece of software to discuss in this book. Thankfully, there is an excellent book that has it covered if you're interested in phpMyAdmin—*Mastering phpMyAdmin for Effective MySQL Management* from Packt Publishing (Second Edition ISBN 1-847191-60-6).

Restarting MySQL

There may come a time when you need to restart MySQL. If so, then you can click on **SQL Server (MySQL)** in the **Restart Services** section of root WHM. You will be asked if you are certain you wish to restart this service, and if you click **Yes**, MySQL will be stopped and restarted, and the results displayed. If you are unable to restart MySQL, you should check to see if MySQL is installed properly (and perhaps run /scripts/mysqlup -force to be sure). If nothing you try works, please contact your NOC for assistance.

Installing and Working with PostgreSQL

PostgreSQL doesn't enjoy as robust support in WHM and cPanel as MySQL does. In WHM, other than installing PostgreSQL and configuring it for use with cPanel, you're on your own. Unfortunately, discussing the root shell interface for PostgreSQL is beyond the scope of this book. If you'd like to learn more about PostgreSQL and how to use it, please visit the following link: http://www.postgresql.org/docs/.

Installing PostgreSQL

If you choose to offer PostgreSQL as an option for your customers, you must first install it, since it is not installed by default on cPanel servers. To do this, you have two choices, use `/scripts/installpostgres` when logged into your server as root via SSH, or select the PostgreSQL option in Update Apache discussed earlier in this chapter. If you install PostgreSQL via the `installpostgres` script, then you will still need to use easyapache (and enable PostgreSQL support in PHP). If you enable PostgreSQL in Update Apache in WHM or in easyapache, then `/scripts/installpostgres` will automatically run at the appropriate time.

Once finished, there is still more work to be done. Log into WHM as root if you haven't already, and select **Postgres Config** from the **SQL Services** section of WHM.

If this is the first time you've installed PostgreSQL on this server, be sure to click the **Install Config** button at the top of this screen. It makes changes to the default PostgreSQL configuration so that it works properly with cPanel. When finished, you should navigate back to this screen and set a PostgreSQL root password (just as you set one earlier for MySQL). Do not forget either of these steps.

Once you've finished, a new PostgreSQL option will appear in the user's cPanel accounts where they can manage PostgreSQL databases.

If you have any problems, contact your NOC for assistance.

Restarting PostgreSQL

As with MySQL, there may come a time when you feel the need to restart PostgreSQL. If so, you can do this in a similar fashion to restarting MySQL. Click on **SQL Server (PgSQL)** in root WHM, and click **Yes** when prompted if you want to stop and restart the server. The results will be displayed on screen. If you have any problems restarting PostgreSQL that you are unable to fix, contact your NOC for assistance.

Summary

We've come to the end of another chapter. So what did you learn? You now know what Apache, PHP, Perl, MySQL, and PostgreSQL are, and what they are used for. You know how to correctly configure, install, or update Apache and PHP. You understand the various configuration options available in easyapache, and know what Safe Mode and phpsuEXEC do, and why you might want to use them. You can install Zend Optimizer if required to and know how to check to see if it is enabled on your server. You know how to restart Apache and use `configtest` to check for serious configuration problem. You also know how to work with Perl, and install or reinstall Perl modules.

You've learned how to upgrade or reinstall MySQL and even install PostgreSQL. You know what features WHM offers us to work with MySQL databases, and can use them to track issues with databases and even fix some of those problems. If all else fails, you now know how to restart MySQL and PostgreSQL in root WHM.

In the next chapter, we discuss all the features that WHM gives us to work with standard (non-reseller) customers. These features are something you will likely spend a lot of time using, so don't miss it!

5

Working with User Accounts

We've finally prepared the server enough to be able to place some paying customers on it. WHM offers a wealth of features that help you manage user accounts. In this chapter, we will discuss how to create and manage accounts on your server, including:

- Transferring all accounts from a WHM/cPanel, Plesk, Webportal, or Ensim dedicated server to your new server
- Transferring multiple accounts from an Alabanza server to your new server
- Transferring a single account from your old server to your new one using root password or superuser password
- Transferring a single account using the username and password for the account (WHM/cPanel servers only)
- Alternate methods of transferring accounts or files from one server to another
- Creating and editing hosting packages and feature sets
- Creating new user accounts
- Modifying an account or multiple accounts at once
- Upgrading/downgrading an account
- Changing a user's password
- Changing a site's IP address or changing several at once
- Managing shell access
- Quota modification
- Viewing bandwidth usage
- Limiting bandwidth on an account
- Suspending or unsuspending an account
- Listing suspended accounts
- Showing active (not suspended) and inactive (suspended) accounts

- Modifying the suspension page
- Resetting user accounts with custom bandwidth back to package limits
- Unsuspending all bandwidth exceeders
- Listing subdomains
- Listing accounts
- Terminating an account
- Terminating multiple accounts
- Changing ownership of an account
- Rearranging accounts
- Sending e-mail to all users on your server at once
- Customizing your user's accounts with skeleton files and branding

When you've finished this chapter, you will be able to manage user accounts like a pro. Since these functions are something you will be using regularly, don't rush through this chapter, and feel free to come back at any time to re-read sections as needed.

Transferring User Accounts from Other Servers

You may be moving up from a cPanel Reseller account to a dedicated or VPS server, or you may have used a competing hosting control panel prior to this, or perhaps you've only had a shared hosting account with another provider up to now. You may also want to help move some of your clients over from other servers to yours. If so, WHM has the ability to help you automate copying accounts in several ways.

Copying accounts from other servers is not foolproof. Not only are some bits of information lost (such as manually added/edited items in a domain's DNS zone), but sometimes an account may not copy over properly. If you have problems, or if the account can't be copied automatically, you will have to move data manually, which could be a lot of work. Make sure you (or your clients) have complete, recent backups of any data you are trying to move in case the automated moves do not go well.

Transferring Multiple Accounts from another Server Using the Root or Administrator Password

To copy multiple accounts to your new server is greatly simplified if you have root (on Linux servers) or administrator (on some other servers) access. WHM is capable of copying user accounts (multiple or single) from cPanel servers, as well as a variety of competing hosting control panels if you have that sort of access.

```
Main >> Transfers >> Copy multiple accounts from another server
Server to copy from (ip or FQDN): [                    ]
Server root password:              [                    ]
Remote Server is: ⦿ WHM 4.5+ ○ Pre WHM 4.5 ○ WebPanel ○ enXim ○ pXa (Pl*sk) 1.x, 2.x, 5.x, 6.x ○ ZerXex's dXm
[Grab Account List]

Remote SSH port: [22      ]
User with su access (only if root ssh login is disabled): [              ]
User with su access password: [              ]
Use Ftp to transfer cpmove files (requires a user with su and ftp access): ☐

For this to work, you must be running WebHost Manager 4.5+, pl*sk, or enXim on the remote server!
```

1. Type in the name (old.servername.com) or IP address of the server to copy from.
2. Type in the old server's root password.
3. Select the type of web administration software the old server is running. (They replace some letters with X's in the name of competing web administration software, for example, enXim is Ensim.)
4. If your server does not permit the root user (the server administrator account) to use SSH, then you will need the username and password of a superuser (someone in the wheel group).
5. Click on **Grab Account List**.

WHM will attempt to connect to the server and start copying off accounts. If you receive an error telling you that WHM could not log in or could not find the server, make sure you've typed the information above correctly, and try again. It is also best to make sure if you are transferring from another cPanel host, that both servers have the same version of cPanel.

The bar at the bottom of the screen will slowly progress to 100% as it copies accounts off the old server, and eventually tell you that it has finished. It will list every account it manages to copy off the old server successfully in a sidebar on the left.

Transferring a Single Account from another Server Using the Root or Administrator Password

To copy a single account to your new server is greatly simplified if you have root (on Linux servers) or administrator (on some other servers) access. WHM is capable of copying user accounts from cPanel servers, as well as a variety of competing hosting control panels if you have that sort of access.

Enter an account to copy
Server to copy from (ip or FQDN):
Server root password:
Username to copy:
Give new account an ip address: ☐
Skip Copying Reseller Privs: ☐
Remote Server is: ◉ WHM 4.5+ ○ Pre WHM 4.5 ○ WebPanel ○ pXa (Pl*sk) 1.x, 2.x, 5.x, 6.x ○ ZerXex's dXm ○ enXim 3.x ○ Alab*nza ○ CIH0st/Spectr0
[Setup]
Remote SSH port: 22
User with su access (only if root ssh login is disabled):
User with su access password:
Use Ftp to transfer cpmove files (requires a user with su and ftp access): ☐
Note: You must be able to connect via ssh from this server's ip address for this to work properly

1. Type in the hostname (old.servername.com) or IP address of the server to copy from in the first box.

2. Type in the old server's root password.

3. Type the username of the account you are trying to copy.

4. Select the type of web administration software the old server is running. (They replace some letters with X's in the name of competing web administration software, for example, enXim is Ensim.)

5. If your server does not permit the root user or administrative account to use SSH, then you will need the username and password of a superuser (wheel group) account.

6. Click on **Setup**.

WHM will attempt to connect to the server and start copying off the account. If you receive an error telling you that WHM could not log in or could not find the server, make sure you've typed the information above correctly and try again.

While WHM is transferring the account(s), do not close the browser window, click the back or stop buttons, or do anything else to interrupt this process until WHM tells you it has finished. If you quit the browser or do anything to interrupt the transfer, then the account may be corrupted. You may need to delete it in WHM and try again or clean out temporary account files. This process may take a long time, and you will need to wait through the process. It is also best to make sure if you are transferring from another cPanel host that both servers have the same version of cPanel.

Once this process finishes successfully, you will probably want to check the account and make sure that it is assigned to an appropriate package and cPanel skin.

No custom DNS zone settings are copied from other servers, so you may need to manually add the additional DNS zone information. (See Chapter 7 for more on managing DNS.)

Transferring Multiple Accounts from an Alabanza Server

The process to transfer accounts from an Alabanza server to your new server is almost identical to transferring accounts from other kinds of server.

ALA Account Copier

Main >> Transfers >> Copy multiple accounts from an Alab*nza server

Server to copy from (ip or FQDN):
Server root password:
Access username:
Access user's password:
Grab Account List

For this to work, you must be running ala-cp on the remote server, the access user must have su access to root, and the server must accept ssh connections from

0%

1. Click **Copy multiple accounts from an Alab*nza server** to bring up a separate account transfer window.

2. Enter the name (old.server.com) or the IP address of the Alabanza server you want to copy accounts from.

3. Enter the server root password.

4. Enter the Alabanza server access username (one with su access to root)

5. Enter the password of that user.

6. Click **Grab Account List** to begin the process.

Make a special note of the warning on this screen if you get any errors. Your old server must accept SSH connections from the IP address of your new server, or the account copy will fail. If you get an error, check all the information you entered above to make sure everything is set correctly.

 Again, don't use your browser to stop or navigate away from the page during the copy process while it is in progress. If you want to skip copying an account, click the appropriate button on screen.

The bar at the bottom of the screen will slowly progress to 100% as it copies accounts off the old server and eventually tell you that it has finished. It will list every account as progress is made on copying it (or if it fails for some reason).

 Once this process finishes successfully, you will probably want to check each account and make sure that it is assigned to an appropriate package and cPanel skin.

Transferring a Single Account Using the Username and Password for the Account (cPanel Servers Only)

If you don't have root access to the cPanel server where the accounts are coming from, WHM may still be able to copy over most of the user's data so long as you know the user's old cPanel username and password.

This process requires that both your server and the other server have recent versions of cPanel installed, and that both are working optimally. Even so, this sort of copy may fail. Be prepared to help move the user data manually if needed.

Enter an account to copy

This feature REQUIRES ideal conditions on the remote server. The remote server must have ftp running, a working copy of perl, cgi enabled, and a STANDARD unmodified cPanel configuration. The remote server admin can easily prevent this type of copy from working if they choose since this does not require any type of privileged access. If any of these are requirements are not met this will fail. This feature is not recommended for copying account over 250 megabytes. It should only be used as a last resort when you do not have the root password to the remote server.

Server to copy from (ip or FQDN): [ ]

Domain Name (only required if web root protection is enabled on the remote server): [ ]

Username to copy: [ ]

User's password: [ ]

Give new account an ip address: ▢

The Remote Server must be cPanel3 or later.

[Setup]

---

1. Enter the name (old.server.com) or the IP address of the server you are copying the account from.

2. Enter the main domain name for the user whose account you are about to copy (optional, but a good idea anyway).

3. Enter the cPanel username of the account you wish to copy.

4. Enter the user's cPanel password.

5. Click the checkbox next to **Give New Account an IP Address** if you want to assign the new account a static IP address on your new server.

6. Click **Setup** to begin the process of copying the account.

WHM will attempt to connect to the server and start copying off the account. If you receive an error telling you that WHM could not log in or could not find the server make sure you've typed the information above correctly and try again.

While WHM is transferring the account, do not close the browser window, click the back or stop buttons, or do anything else to interrupt this process until WHM tells you it has finished. If you quit the browser or do anything to interrupt the transfer, then the account may be corrupted. You may need to delete it in WHM and try again or clean out temporary account files. This process may take a long time, and you will need to wait through the process. It is also best to make sure if you are transferring from another cPanel host that both servers have the same recent version of cPanel if possible.

Once this process finishes successfully, you will probably want to check the account and make sure that it is assigned to an appropriate package and cPanel skin. You may also have to manually edit the account's DNS zone if they had any special customizations.

Alternative Methods of Moving User Accounts from Other Servers

If none of the above methods work for transferring account information and files off your old server, you do have other options:

- Create an account for each user you want to transfer to your new server. Log into the user's cPanel account on the other cPanel server, and use cPanel's backup area to make backups of the home directory, MySQL databases, and e-mail aliases and filters. Then log into the same user's account on the new server, and use cPanel's restore features in the backup area to upload the user's data. (Doing so does not count towards the user's bandwidth limitations.) You can find more information on cPanel's backup features by reading: *cPanel User Guide and Tutorial* from Packt Publishing (ISBN-1-904811-92-2), or visit http://www.packtpub.com/cPanel/book.

- If the other server isn't a cPanel server, and you have root or administrator access then you can always access the other server and compress the data in the user's account, and then transfer the data to the new server, and decompress the file, and move data where it needs to go in the user's new cPanel account (you will need to create the account in advance on the new server).

- If you don't have shell/command line access on the other server, then use FTP to download as much data as you can, and manually move it into place in the new account on your current server.

- If nothing else works, contact your NOC and ask for help transferring accounts. There may be an additional charge for this service.

Now that you have your user account information transferred, don't forget to copy over other server scripts or special software from the old server (if you are moving from another dedicated server) before you bid your old host and server farewell.

Review Copy Accounts Log

WHM keeps track of the accounts that have been copied to the server recently. You can review this log to see if there were any problems with the copy process. Click on **Review Copied Accounts** in the **Transfers** section of WHM.

Account Transfers in the Last 30 Days				
Source	**Destination**	**Time**	**Id**	
@	⟹	Sat Apr 29 20:09:41 2006	oyxFcURfe3r9cesz	View Log

This will tell you the source account (account username@server) and the destination account on your server as well as the time and unique transfer ID. Click on **View Log,** and you will see all of the information on the account copy process, just as you saw on-screen when the copy was in progress, including any errors.

Working with Packages and Feature Lists

Before you add brand new accounts to your server, you need to take time to set up hosting packages and feature lists. This will make it easier for you when you create new accounts, and also will enable third-party hosting management software (like **WHM Autopilot** http://whmautopilot.com/, or **ModernBill** http://modernbill.com/, or **Account Lab Plus** http://netenberg.com/accountlabplus.php).

Creating a New Feature List

The **Feature Manager** allows you to create feature sets; these sets control access to cPanel features, so you can have certain sets that allow full access to all features, and some that only permit users to access a limited set of features.

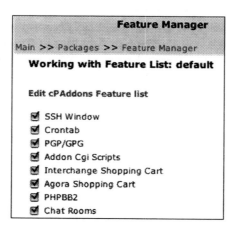

Feature Manager

The feature manager allows you to disable/enable features inside of each users cPanel. Once you build a feature list you should edit the package you wish to assign it to and add the feature list.

The feature lists for cPAddons (user installable scripts) can be found by following the link in the feature list editor

Two special feature lists called "default" and "disabled" will affect all users.

- If you disable a feature in the "default" feature it will be disabled in every users' cPanel, unless another feature list grants them the feature.
- If you disable a feature in the "disabled" feature it will be disabled in every users' cPanel. Unlike the "default" feature list no other feature list will be able to override this and grant the feature. If you don't want anyone to be able to turn this feature on at all, disable it in this list.

Add a New Feature List

Feature List Name: [   ] [Add]

Edit a Feature List

[default ⬍] [Edit]

Delete a Feature List

[disabled ⬍] [Delete]

1. Click on **Feature Manager** in the **Packages** section of WHM, and type in a new name for the feature list you wish to create where it asks for a feature list name.

2. Click on **Add**.

3. Deselect those items that you do not want your users to have access to.

4. Click on **Save**.

Feature Manager

Main >> Packages >> Feature Manager

Working with Feature List: default

Edit cPAddons Feature list

☑ SSH Window
☑ Crontab
☑ PGP/GPG
☑ Addon Cgi Scripts
☑ Interchange Shopping Cart
☑ Agora Shopping Cart
☑ PHPBB2
☑ Chat Rooms

If you want to only offer certain automatically installable scripts in your user's cPanel Script Library area, then click on the **Edit cPAddons Feature List** item at the top of the feature list display. Deselect items you don't want to offer with this package and save changes.

You will be able to assign feature lists to hosting packages later.

Editing an Existing Feature List

To edit an existing feature list:

1. Click on **Feature Manager** in WHM.
2. Select the package name you want to edit from the drop-down list under the **Edit Feature List** heading on this screen.
3. Click on the **Edit** button.
4. Edit the feature list as desired. Unchecked items will not be offered in this feature list checked items will be offered.
5. Click **Save** to save your changes.

Any package that uses the edited feature list will immediately reflect these changes.

> The default feature list is just that, the default set of features new accounts will have access to unless you assign them a different feature list. The default list automatically has all features and scripts enabled unless you edit it. The disabled feature list controls which features no other feature sets can offer (created by you or by resellers). Any items unchecked in the disabled feature list will be off-limits on all feature lists (including the default list) and to resellers. You should make sure that you disable permanently any features that you don't want resellers to offer.

Deleting an Existing Feature List

To remove an existing feature list:

1. Click on **Feature Manager** in WHM.
2. Select the package name you want to edit from the drop-down list under the **Delete a Feature List** heading on this screen.
3. Click on the **Delete** button.
4. Confirm the deletion.

You cannot delete the default feature list.

Creating a New Package

A package in WHM is a collection of server resource limits that control disk space, bandwidth, e-mail accounts, subdomains, FTP accounts, and so on. You can assign as many users (or resellers) to a package as you want. Packages make it easy to change the amount of resources and features an account is allowed to use without having to manually edit every account individually. Further, if you make changes to an existing package they will affect every user assigned to that package.

To create a new package, click on **Add Package** under the **Packages** section in WHM.

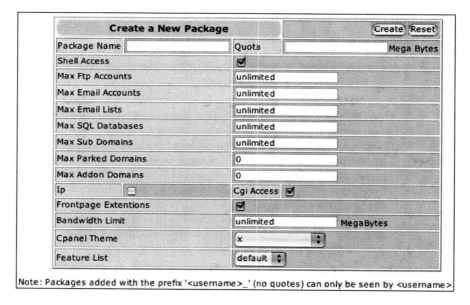

Most of the settings are fairly obvious, but let's walk through them one by one.

The **Package Name** is whatever you want to call the new package. If you add a particular reseller's cPanel username and an underscore "_" before the package name (**reseller_package1**), that reseller will have access to that package (if you permit it).

WHM does support package names with spaces in them, but you should probably still avoid using spaces since some third-party tools and older versions of cPanel don't work properly with them.

Quota is the maximum amount of disk space in megabytes that you want to assign to this account. Typically, WHM allows users to go slightly over this maximum amount if there is space available before suspending their account.

Shell Access is a checkbox because it is either on or off. On a shared server, SSH access can be a serious security risk. You may want to enable a jailed shell option if your users need it (jailed and regular shell options are discussed later). Keep in mind that almost all users don't need shell access, so you really shouldn't give this out indiscriminately.

Max Ftp Accounts is where you can set a maximum number of FTP accounts for this package type. This option typically defaults to unlimited. Typing "0" (zero) turns off the ability of the user to create any additional FTP accounts. They will still have the main FTP account (that matches their cPanel username and password), but they won't be able to create any more accounts.

Max Email Accounts is where you set the maximum number of POP3/IMAP e-mail addresses for this account. This is initially set to "unlimited". Type a number to set how many accounts can be created. Keep in mind that e-mail accounts do count towards disk space and bandwidth limits that you set, so even if this option is set to unlimited, you, the user, will actually have some practical limit. The user will always have one e-mail address (that matches their cPanel username and password) even if you type zero in this area, but they won't be able to create any on their own. For some reason, there isn't a separate option to set the number of e-mail forwarding addresses allowed, and the number permitted is controlled by whatever you put into this area. This means that e-mail accounts and number of forwarding addresses will match. Hopefully this will be fixed in a future version of WHM.

Max Email Lists is where you can set the maximum number of Mailman (http://list.org/) mailing lists users in this package have access to. This is initially set to "unlimited". Type a number to set how many lists can be created.

Max MySQL Databases is where you set the maximum number of MySQL databases to which users in this package will have access. This is initially set to "unlimited". Type a number to set how many databases can be created.

If you have PostgreSQL installed and compiled into PHP, then this number appears to grant them the same number of PostgreSQL databases. Perhaps, a future version of WHM will add a separate option for PostgreSQL.

Max Subdomains is where you can set the maximum number of subdomains (subdomain.domain.com) that users in that package can create. This is initially set to unlimited. Type a number to set how many subdomains can be created.

Max Parked Domains is where you can set the maximum number of parked domains that users will be able to add. Parked domains are additional domains (seconddomain.com) that point to the same content as your main domain (domain.com). The user only has a single cPanel account to control all of his or her parked domains.

Max Addon Domains is where you can set the maximum number of add-on domains that users will be able to add. This is another feature that many resellers choose not to give their clients, but that decision does make some sense in this case. Add-on domains differ from parked domains in that the additional domain (seconddomain.com) points to a different directory in the main user's `public_html` directory so that the additional domain can have totally different content. End users visiting an add-on domain don't know that the domain is actually hosted from the same cPanel account. Of course, the end user only receives one cPanel account to manage all the domains they add-on, and it also counts against their disk space and bandwidth limits.

IP: Check this box to assign one of your several static IP addresses (if your server comes with any) to this domain. Generally, you will leave this unchecked, in which case the main shared IP address will be used.

Cgi Access: Leave this checked if you want accounts in this package to have CGI/Perl scripting access. This will also add a special `cgi-bin` directory into the user's `public_html` directory.

Frontpage Extensions: If you leave this checked, then the server-side Microsoft FrontPage extensions will be installed by default in all new accounts that use that package. We typically recommend that you leave this unchecked because if the user isn't going to use the extensions, they can interfere with the normal operation of the account. The user can still install the FrontPage extensions at any time in their cPanel if they need it.

Bandwidth Limit: Enter a whole number here (no decimals) to specify how much bandwidth (in MB) you want to assign to accounts in this package. As long as you have, **Email users when they have reached 80% of their bandwidth** in **Tweak Settings** enabled, your users will automatically receive an e-mail when their site reaches 80% of their assigned bandwidth for the month, giving them time to contact you and buy more bandwidth. This will happen only if they have a contact e-mail address set in cPanel.

Bandwidth limits are reset at the beginning of each calendar month, regardless of when the user paid for their account. Also, if a user gets suspended for being over bandwidth, it could take WHM a while to unsuspend the account (depending on your settings in the **Tweak Settings** feature in WHM). Therefore, it would be good for you to make sure, your users are aware that they should take bandwidth limits very seriously.

cPanel Theme: Here you can select what installed cPanel theme you'd like to give to users of this package. You can choose whatever theme you prefer, but remember than not all cPanel themes offer all available cPanel features. (See Chapter 9 in this book, or Chapter 12 in *cPanel: User Guide and Tutorial* from Packt Publishing (ISBN-1-904811-92-2) for more on cPanel themes.)

Feature List: Assign the package a feature list, or leave it set to default. This controls the features that the users assigned to this package are permitted to use.

Once you are sure you have all the features the way you want them, click on **Create** at the top of this window. If you want to start over with a default set of options, click on **Reset**.

Continue this process for every package you'd like to create. All packages must have a unique name on your server. To allow resellers some leeway with naming packages, their packages are created with their main account usernames prefixed to the package name they select (reseller_package1). Reseller clients will only see "package1" if their cPanel theme displays the hosting package name.

Deleting Packages

To delete a package, click on **Delete Package** in WHM, select the package you want to delete, and click on the **Kill** button.

Any user accounts assigned to a package that you delete will still have the same restrictions they had before you deleted the package. WHM treats the user's account as a custom package. If you want to change the features and resources the account has access to, then you need to assign that user to a different package.

Editing an Existing Package

If you decide later that you need to change what a package offers, just click on **Edit Package** in WHM, select the package you want to edit, and you will find yourself at a screen similar to the **Add Package** feature discussed earlier. Make any changes that you feel you need to, and then save the changes.

WHM will display the progress as it makes those changes to every user account assigned to that package. Do not click back, close your browser window, or visit another link, while WHM is showing you the changes made to user's accounts, or the changes may not be applied to all users assigned to that package.

Upgrading or Downgrading a User's Account: Changing the Assigned Package

If you want to change the package that a user's account is assigned to, click on **Upgrade/Downgrade an Account** in the **Account Functions** section of WHM.

1. Select the user's domain name or cPanel username to upgrade or downgrade, and click on **Modify**.
2. Select the new package from the list, and click on **Change**.

The new package (and the feature list assigned to that package) will be applied immediately, and you will be shown the differences between the two plans.

 If the new plan offers less disk space or bandwidth than the user has used thus far, their account will be suspended the next time bandwidth checks are done by the server.

Working with User Accounts

Now that you've set up some packages and feature lists, you are ready to start adding new accounts and working with those that you may have already transferred over.

Creating New User Accounts

Click on **Create a New Account** if you want to add a brand new account to your server.

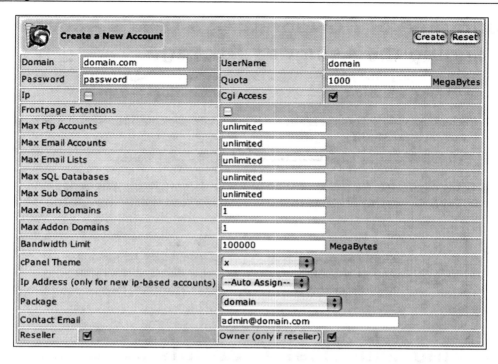

If you've set up packages, then you will probably want to skip down to the bottom of this screen where you can select a package out of a drop-down list. Once you select a package, it will automatically change the different settings on this screen to match the settings of the package.

The only five things you will need to edit if you've selected a package are:

- You must enter the FQDN (domain name without www.) where it says **Domain**.

- A username will automatically be selected in the **UserName** field (though you may change it to something else). Usernames must have eight characters or less and should generally avoid non-alphanumeric characters (+, %, &) and definitely not include a space, (WHM shouldn't allow you to add a space, so this should be a non-issue.) The username must also be unique on your server. It is also best to avoid usernames that start with a number.

- The **Contact Email** field at the bottom of this screen is for the e-mail address of the owner whose account you are creating. Fill it in if you know it (and you really should). If not, leave it blank, and let the user enter their contact e-mail address into cPanel later. The user can always change this contact e-mail address from the main screen of their cPanel depending on the cPanel theme you are using. Every account should have a contact e-mail address that is valid (and preferably not part of the domain being hosted on this server).

You can use it to send mass e-mails to your customers; it is the e-mail address WHM will contact automatically if the user nears their resource usage limits, and your customer can use it to reset their cPanel password if they forget it (and if you've turned on those options in **Tweak Settings**).

- The **Reseller** checkbox allows you to set up basic reseller account privileges for this account. You will still need to edit those privileges in the **Reseller Center** (discussed in Chapter 6).

- The **Owner** checkbox allows the new reseller to own his or main reseller account. If this is not checked, then the reseller won't see this account in WHM, and the resources this account uses won't affect the resource limits (if any) you place on the reseller.

Even if you do assign the user a package, you can still make changes to any values listed on this screen (which match those on the package creation screen discussed earlier). If you do this, the revised limits will apply to the user, but they will still be assigned to the chosen package. This means that if you later edit the package this user belongs to, their customized settings will be changed to match the edited package.

Modifying an Account

If you need to make changes to the basic feature set, domain name, username (for non-resellers) of a user, and do not want to upgrade or downgrade them to a particular package, then you should click on **Modify an Account**.

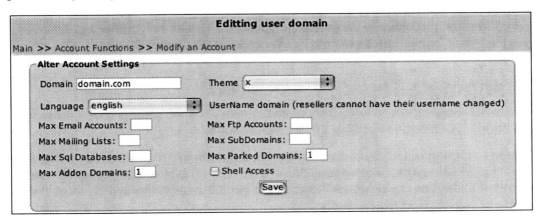

Select the username or domain name you want to modify, and then you will see the current account settings as in the previous figure. Here you can make any changes you need to. Keep in mind—a blank box with no numbers means "unlimited" and "0" (zero) means none allowed. If you want to grant shell access, click on the checkbox. When you are done, click on **Save**, and the changes will be made immediately.

You cannot change a reseller's cPanel username. If you must do so you will have to remove their reseller privileges in the **Reseller Center** (discussed in Chapter 6) first, then come back and edit their username, and go back to the **Reseller Center** to make them resellers again. This also means you will need to reassign them any accounts they had owned before.

Modifying Multiple Accounts

You can also modify multiple accounts at once. Click on **Modify/Upgrade Multiple Accounts** in the **Multi-Account Functions** section of WHM.

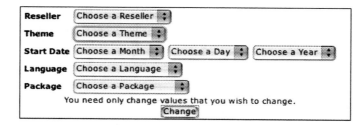

You can select any account on the server, and then choose the new values from the series of drop-down boxes at the bottom of this screen. You don't have to change every item, just those you want to change. Leave the rest at the **Choose a...** selection, then click the **Change** button to modify the accounts you've selected.

Changing a User's Password

Sometimes a user needs to have their main cPanel password reset perhaps because they forgot it or the password file got corrupted somehow.

To assign a new password to an account, click on **Password Modification**, and then select the domain name or username of the user. After this type a new password at the top of the screen, and click on either of the two **Change Password** buttons. The change will take effect immediately.

Changing the cPanel account password also changes the password for the main e-mail and FTP accounts (the ones that match the cPanel account username).

Changing Site's IP Address

If for some reason you need to change the IP address to which a site is assigned (perhaps you want to use an SSL certificate), you can make that change by choosing **Change Site's IP Address** from WHM and then selecting the username or domain name of the site whose IP address you need to change. This will display the IP address that the user's main domain (and any additional domains) is set to. You can choose a different IP address from the drop-down list for each domain.

 Keep in mind that doing this may cause the domain(s) to become unavailable to some people until the DNS changes get reflected on all DNS servers.

Changing Multiple IP Addresses

You can also modify the IP addresses for multiple accounts at once. Click on **Change Multiple Sites' IP Addresses** in the **Multi-Account Functions** section of WHM.

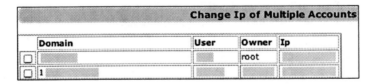

Check all of the domains you want to change IP addresses of and click on the **Change Ips of Selected Accounts** button, and you will be taken to a screen very much like the one pictured for the **Change Site's IP Address** feature. Choose the new IP addresses from the drop-down boxes, and click the **Change** button to commit the change.

[127]

As with the single account's IP address change feature, it may take some time before the sites whose IP addresses you've changed are visible on the Internet again.

Managing Shell Access

The "shell" is the command line interface that your Linux server uses. (Your users may refer to this as SSH or Telnet access.) SSH is actually a method of communicating between two computers securely, but many people seem to think of them as one and the same. Clicking on **Manage Shell Access** will allow you to see all user accounts on your server and what (if any) shell (SSH) access they are permitted.

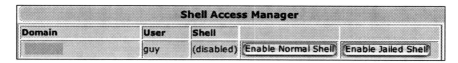

Shell Access Manager				
Domain	**User**	**Shell**		
	guy	(disabled)	Enable Normal Shell	Enable Jailed Shell

Shell access can be a security risk; so you should be very careful as to whom you grant such access. From the table that appears on screen, you can click a button to give users access to a standard shell or to a jailed shell. A jailed shell greatly restricts the access the user has and what he or she can do. It is more secure. If you are going to grant shell access to users, it is probably a good idea to give out jail shell access. Just click the appropriate button to grant access to a standard shell or a jailed shell (or revoke shell access altogether).

Moving an Account to a Different Partition

If you have more than one /home partition, WHM will typically put new accounts on the partition with the most amount of space available, but if you want to move an account from /home to /home2 or vice versa, you can do so by clicking on **Rearrange Accounts** in WHM.

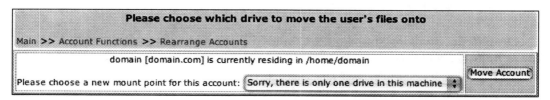

Please choose which drive to move the user's files onto
Main >> Account Functions >> Rearrange Accounts
domain [domain.com] is currently residing in /home/domain
Please choose a new mount point for this account: Sorry, there is only one drive in this machine ▲▼   Move Account

Select the domain name or the username of the account you'd like to move and click on either **Rearrange** button. If you have space available and two or more /home partitions, you will be able to select another location from the drop-down menu. If you don't have enough space or another partition, you will be informed of this.

> Be careful when moving accounts. Some scripts or cron jobs that your customers use, may use the absolute path to the file (like /home/USERNAME/public_html/gallery/script.php). If you move the account to /home2, then that user's script or cron job may stop functioning until they edit it to reflect the new location.
>
> Also, if you move an account it could take a few minutes for the domain to be accessible on the Internet due to DNS and Apache changes.

Quota Modification

If you want to change the disk space an account is permitted to use without upgrading or downgrading a user's account, you can do so by selecting **Quota Modification**.

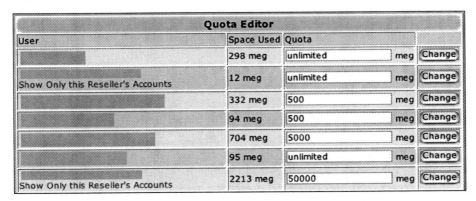

A list of all the users on your server will appear in a table in the main pane of WHM. Here you can see how much disk space they are using and how much they are permitted to use. The accounts that are over or close to their disk quota will be color coded, yellow for over 80% usage, red for over the defined limit. You can change this maximum number ("unlimited" means the account is permitted to use as much as they want until they use up all available disk space on your server).

If the quota for all accounts is set to zero, then your quota files are probably corrupted. You have two choices—click on the link to repair the quota files at the bottom of this screen in WHM or log into your server as root via SSH and run the following command:

`/scripts/fixquotas`

Perhaps better yet, fix that and several other common problems at the same time by running:

`/scripts/fixeverything`

Warning! This can take a while.

Viewing Bandwidth Usage

You can view how much bandwidth each account (and domain and subdomain) are using by clicking on **View Bandwidth Usage**.

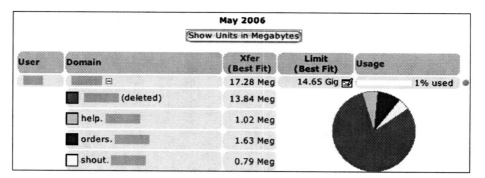

In a short time, a table will be displayed showing the bandwidth usage for each domain, subdomain, and account on the server in both MB and GB. You can see how much bandwidth is assigned to each account, and if an account has gone over bandwidth limits (or has come close to doing so), the account will be marked with either yellow or red.

There will also be a pie graph and separate statistics for each subdomain that has any bandwidth used this month. Clicking the + next to the main domain name will display the subdomain stats and pie chart.

Limit Bandwidth on an Account

If you wish to change the bandwidth limit on an account without changing packages, you can click on **Limit Bandwidth Usage,** and choose an account or domain to edit.

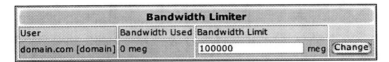

Bandwidth Limiter			
User	Bandwidth Used	Bandwidth Limit	
domain.com [domain]	0 meg	100000	meg (Change)

The table that appears will display the domain [username], the amount of bandwidth used to date, the current bandwidth limit (which you can edit). The limit is listed in MB, so 2000 is 2,000 MB or 2 GB in typical hosting parlance. Click on **Change** when you have finished editing the bandwidth limit. Note that this will not immediately unsuspend an account that has gone over bandwidth; you need to unsuspend the account or wait for WHM to do so.

Suspending or Unsuspending an Account

There comes a time when you may need to suspend an account for a variety of reasons. Perhaps the account violated your terms of service or acceptable use policy, or maybe they've forgotten to pay for the account. In any case, you can instantly suspend or unsuspend an account by using the **Suspend/Unsuspend an Account** feature in WHM.

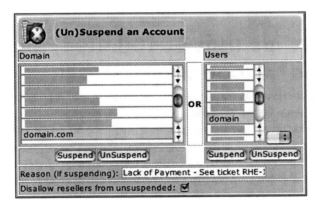

Select the username or domain name you wish to suspend, and write a short reason in the provided box (so later you can remember why you did it, and so that resellers and other administrators can see why it was done).

Despite the poor grammar, the checkbox below the **Reason** box will stop a reseller (if it is one of their accounts) from unsuspending the account. Leave it unchecked if you want the reseller to be able to unsuspend the account, and then click on either **Suspend** button. To unsuspend an account, just select the domain or user, and click on either **UnSuspend** button. If you are unsuspending an account for bandwidth overusage, make sure the account has more bandwidth assigned to it (via **Limit Bandwidth Usage** or an account package upgrade) else the account will be suspended again soon.

Listing Suspended Accounts

If you want to see what accounts (if any) are suspended on your server, click on **List Suspended Accounts**.

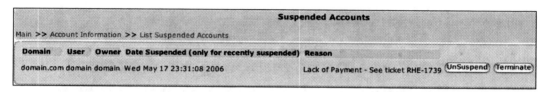

All suspended accounts will be listed with the domain name, username, owner (reseller username or root for server owner), the date suspended, and the reason for suspension. You will also be able to click on a button next to each suspended account to either unsuspend it or terminate it.

Showing Active (not Suspended) and Inactive (Suspended) Accounts

Show Active and Inactive Accounts is similar to the **List Suspended Accounts** feature, but this command shows both suspended accounts and accounts that are not suspended separated out so you can see at a glance all accounts on your server and whether they are active. In addition, you can also make all accounts that are currently suspended active again by clicking on the **Make Inactive Accounts Active** link at the bottom of the list of accounts in the main pane of WHM.

Modifying the Suspension Page

WHM comes with a default page that is automatically displayed whenever a suspended account is accessed via the web.

Modifing Suspension Page

Main >> Account Functions >> Modify Suspended Account Page

Please note: If you have redirected your hostname so that it does not go to the default cPanel page, your suspended clients will not see this page. You will have to copy the /usr/local/apache/htdocs/suspended.page/ directory as well as everything inside the directory to the /home/username/public_html/ directory of the account that your hostname is being redirected to.

```
                        <html>

                <head>
                <style>
                    a:link { font-family: arial, verdana; font-sizw: 11px; color: #000000;
text-decoration: none; }
a:visited { font-family: arial, verdana; font-sizw: 11px; color: #000000; text-decoration:
none; }
a:active { font-family: arial, verdana; font-sizw: 11px; color: #000000; text-decoration:
none; }
a:hover { font-family: arial, verdana; font-sizw: 11px; color: #000000; text-decoration:
underline; }

  font { font-family: arial, verdana; font-sizw: 11px; color: #000000; text-decoration:
none; }

  td{ font-family: arial, verdana; font-sizw: 10px; text-decoration: none; }
  table{ font-family: arial, verdana; font-sizw: 11px; text-decoration: none; }
  body { background-color: #F0F0F0; scrollbar-face-color: #6E788C;
scrollbar-shadow-color: #696969; scrollbar-highlight-color: #cfcfcf; scrollbar-3dlight-color:
#cccccc; scrollbar-darkshadow-color: #808080; scrollbar-track-color: #9B9FA7;
scrollbar-arrow-color: #000000 }

  .title { font-family: arial, verdana; font-size: 9pt; font-weight: normal; }
  .distributers { font-family: arial, verdana; font-size: 11pt; font-weight: normal; }
  .info { font-family: arial, verdana; font-size: 8pt; font-weight: normal; }
  .design { font-family: arial, verdana; font-size: 8pt; font-weight: normal; }

  .menu { border-top: 1px #374646 solid; border-left: 1px #374646 solid; border-right:
1px #374646 solid; border-bottom: 1px #374646 solid; font-family: verdana, arial;
font-size: 8pt; font-weight: normal; }
  .cellheader { border-top: 1px #374646 solid; border-left: 1px #374646 solid;
border-right: 1px #374646 solid; border-bottom: 1px #374646 solid; font-family:
verdana, arial; font-size: 20pt; font-weight: normal; color: #F1F1F1; }
  .scellheader { border-top: 1px #374646 solid; border-left: 1px #374646 solid;
border-right: 1px #374646 solid; border-bottom: 1px #374646 solid; font-family:
verdana, arial; font-size: 15pt; font-weight: normal; color: #F1F1F1; }
  .bigcellheader { border-top: 1px #374646 solid; border-left: 1px #374646 solid;
border-right: 1px #374646 solid; border-bottom: 1px #374646 solid;  font-family:
verdana, arial; font-size: 30pt; font-weight: normal; color: #F1F1F1; link: #F1F1F1; vlink:
```

Save

However, it's not all that good looking; so you may prefer to jazz it up a bit or make it fit the look of your hosting company. To do this, just click on **Modify Suspended Account Page** on the WHM sidebar. A box will be displayed with the raw HTML code for the default page. You can edit this directly or copy and paste in new HTML code.

Resetting User Accounts with Custom Bandwidth Back to Package Limits

If you want to see a table listing all users, their bandwidth usage limits, and what bandwidth limits the account is actually set to right now, then click on **Reset Package Bandwidth**, and you will see a table with that information.

Reset Accounts to Package Bandwidth			
This function will show every account where the bandwidth limit has been changed from the package default and will let you easily reset it to the limit that the package has.			
Domain	User	Current Bandwidth Limit	Package Bandwidth Limit
	addicted	15000 Meg(s)	unknown Meg(s)
	aeon	15000 Meg(s)	unknown Meg(s)

In addition, if a user's bandwidth limits are different from those of the package they are in, you will be able to reset the limit to that of the package. This is useful if users purchase bandwidth from you for a month, and after the month is over, you want to find those users so that you can reset them to "normal" limits.

Unsuspending All Bandwidth Exceeders

This will cause all accounts that have been suspended because of lack of bandwidth to be reset to active status. It will last until the next time the accounts are checked for bandwidth overusage (usually 12-24 hours, though it may be as little as a few minutes) unless more bandwidth is granted to those accounts. Simply click on **Unsuspend Bandwidth Exceeders,** read the advisory, and click on **Ok**. This takes effect immediately.

Listing Subdomains

Clicking on **List Subdomains** will display a table with all the domains on the server that currently have subdomains set up, and list what add-on or parked domains they also have. This makes it easier to see how everything breaks down.

List Accounts

Clicking on **List Accounts** at the top of the Account Functions area of the WHM sidebar will list every single domain on your server with lots of vital information. Furthermore, you can search the server for domains or accounts that meet certain criteria. This can be a real boon if you own several servers and are looking for a single domain out of thousands. Even better, you can download a **Comma Separated Values** (.csv) file that your spreadsheet program (like Microsoft® Excel, for example) can turn into a spreadsheet automatically.

The accounts get listed in a table that gives you the following information:

- Domain name
- IP address
- Username of account
- Contact e-mail address
- Setup date
- Partition (/home, /home2, etc.)
- Quota (maximum disk space permitted for this account.)
- Disk space used
- Package assigned to account
- cPanel theme
- Reseller (who "owns" this account, the reseller account name or "root" for you)

There are 30 rows in each page of the table by default (which you can change in **Tweak Settings** or by entering a new number in the **Accounts Per Page** section). If you want to switch to a different page, you can do so by clicking the appropriate page number listed under the table.

If you have a lot of sites, navigating the table by page number looking for the site(s) you are interested in would be a real pain. Thankfully, there is a search box below the table that allows you to search for sites based on a wide variety of criteria. The search box is set up by default with an expression that will filter the list and display all ".net" domains on your server. If you are interested in finding all sites using another **Top Level Domain (TLD)**, just change "net" to "com", or "org", or "edu", or whatever.

At the top right corner of this screen above the table is a link to download a CSV file that you can open with your favorite spreadsheet program, so that you can work there if you find that easier. To download the file, just click on the **Download CSV File** link. Depending on your browser and settings, you may want to right-click on this link and download the linked file to the disk that way.

Many of the items (like **Partition, Quota,** and **Owner**) have small edit icons. These take you directly to the feature that will allow you to edit that particular item for that account.

The small cPanel icon near the domain name in **List Accounts** will open a new window and log you directly into that user's account (so you don't need to know their account password). There are a few limitations to this administrative login though. You won't be able to create databases, install scripts, or read webmail for any user (except the main account).

 Resellers can also use this to log into accounts that they own (or they can use their reseller cPanel account password to log into their client's cPanel accounts).

Changing Ownership of an Account

In WHM, there are two kinds of accounts that can "own" user accounts, the server administrator (called "root") or a reseller (any account you specify in the **Reseller Center**). All accounts can always be edited or changed by you as the server administrator but resellers only have permission to edit their "owned" accounts (for example, those customers that they have resold accounts to). Someone must own every account.

There are times when you may need to change who "owns" an account. The most typical reason for wanting to do this is if you transfer an account from another server and want to assign control of it to a reseller. If you need to do this for any reason, just click on the edit icon next to the **Owner** name in **List Accounts**, and this will allow you to select the domain name or user account that you want to assign to either yourself or a reseller. Simply select the domain or account, and then select which reseller (or "root") to switch the account to.

Terminating an Account

Terminating an account totally removes all traces of the account from your server. It deletes all of the user's files, all domains, e-mail, and so on. This command cannot be undone (unless you have a backup of the account, of course).

Click on **Terminate Account** in WHM, and select the account or domain you want to terminate. Check **Keep DNS Zone** if you want to keep the DNS information for the site you are deleting (typically done if you plan on moving the site elsewhere, and want to keep the DNS zone in the current location and edit it to point to the new location, so that downtime due to DNS propagation is minimized). Now click on **Terminate** if you are sure you want to do this. There is no second chance!

Terminating Multiple Accounts

Use this option if you would like to delete multiple accounts from your server. As with terminating a single, doing so is *permanent,* so be sure you very carefully select accounts to delete.

```
To complete this action you must type the following phrase in the box below
"I understand this will irrevocably remove all the accounts that have been checked"
I understand
Destroy Selected Accounts
```

Just check the boxes next to the accounts you wish to delete. In this case, you need to actually type into the box provided:

I understand this will irrevocably remove all the accounts that have been checked

Then click **Destroy Selected Accounts** to delete the accounts selected.

Rearranging Accounts

The **Rearrange Accounts** feature is designed for server administrators who own multiple servers. If you have set up your servers in a cluster, you can move accounts from one server to another just by selecting the accounts and specifying the server you want to move the account(s) to.

E-mailing All Users on Your Server at Once

If you want to send every user on your server an e-mail to inform them of important changes or information, you can do so by selecting **Email All Users** from WHM.

```
Main >> Account Functions >> Email all Users
            Click here to attempt to guess emails for customers who have not entered an address
From Name    Spr Host Support
From Email   support@sprhost.cp
Subject      Updates

      Send Email to Reseller's Customers as well.
                           Send
```

Enter the name and e-mail address you want the e-mail to come from. Type in a subject, and then enter the text of your e-mail. Clicking on the checkbox at the bottom of the screen "send e-mail to reseller's customers as well" will send the e-mail to your reseller's customers as well. When you are ready to send, click on **Send**. Keep in mind that this e-mail will only be sent to those customers that have a contact e-mail address set up in cPanel.

There is an option to try and guess e-mail addresses for customers who haven't entered an address in cPanel's contact area, but it generally doesn't do a very good job (at most setting the contact address to the account's main cPanel e-mail address), so it's probably best to skip it. However, if you prefer to try it, click on the link at the top of the page, and it will attempt to guess. You will need to navigate back to the message using your browser, since it doesn't automatically take you back there.

Modifying cPanel and WHM News

There is another way for you to contact customers. Click on **Modify cPanel/WHM News** in the **cPanel** section of WHM.

```
Please use html tags in news. Make sure to use a <br> to break lines.

Global cPanel News (displayed in all cPanels [including resellers' customer]):
```

In this area you can enter HTML text that will appear in all cPanel accounts (even reseller's customers), only those customers owned by "root" (you), your reseller's cPanel or WHM account, or just your reseller's customer's cPanel accounts.

All you have to do is paste in some HTML code, and it will be displayed in the appropriate location. For most themes this means that the news will appear somewhere near the top of the cPanel or WHM account.

This is a good place to put information or links that you want all customers to see in their cPanel or WHM accounts without having to e-mail them directly.

Resellers will be able to use this feature to put their own custom news in their customer's cPanel accounts if you permit them to do so.

Customizing Accounts

You may want to customize every new account created on your server, or display your own hosting company logo or some information in your customer's cPanel accounts. If so, WHM offers some special features that will allow you (and your resellers) to do those things.

Customizing Accounts Using the Skeleton Directory Feature

You might want to be able to put a "this website is coming soon" page on all new accounts, or perhaps you'd like to include some custom error message files. If so, you and your resellers can use the **Skeleton Directory** feature in the **Account Functions** section of WHM.

If this is the first time you've ever used this feature, click on that link in WHM. A special directory will be created, and you will be told where that directory is. For you, that location is typically /root/cpanel3-skel. For your resellers, the skeleton directory is typically created in their home directory. Once the directory is created, you can place files inside that directory and they will automatically be copied into all new accounts that are created (in the same location in that user's account).

For example, if you put a simple placeholder file in /root/cpanel3-skel/public_html/index.html, all new accounts that get created by you (root) will have that special index.html file in their public_html directory (until they remove it, of course). Your reseller's accounts will have your reseller's own custom files (if they've activated the **Skeleton Directory** feature by clicking on it one time) instead of yours.

Customizing the Look of Your Customer's cPanel Account

You and your resellers can customize the graphics of any cPanel theme that supports cPanel branding. To do that, click on **Branding** in the **cPanel** section in WHM.

```
xmail bluelagoon monsoon x2 iCandy x 7dana
```

We are working with the x theme.

Image/Text	Name
	top_01_bg
	top_01_1

Click on the name of a theme listed here, and the graphics you can customize will be displayed along with their filenames, descriptions, and a field to upload customized graphics or return the displayed graphics to their cPanel theme defaults.

You can download the graphics and change them as you see fit (though the size, shape, format, and filename of the custom files should match their default counterparts). You can then upload the custom graphics on this screen, and they will be displayed in your customers' cPanel accounts (if they are assigned that theme). Your resellers can do the same for their customers if you permit them. Clicking on the **Make Default** button next to each graphic will revert the graphics back to their default version.

Summary

Guess what? You've finished yet another chapter! It's time to pat yourself on the back, as you've learned a lot in this chapter. You've learned how to copy accounts from other servers to your server. You know how to create new accounts and use WHM's many account features to control access to features, modify accounts in a variety of different ways, and even customize your customer's accounts with your own files and graphics.

In the next chapter, we'll look at the **Reseller Center**, and all of the various features you can grant your resellers. If you never plan on offering reseller accounts, then you can safely skip the next chapter.

6

Working with Reseller Accounts

Now that we've covered how to use WHM to manage our own customers, it is time to focus on customers who would like to be able to resell some of the cPanel accounts you give them or simply have the freedom to manage several of their own accounts themselves. These customers are referred to as **resellers** in WHM, regardless of whether they actually resell accounts. In this chapter we will discuss:

- What are reseller accounts and what are they good for
- Things to consider before offering reseller accounts
- Setting up reseller accounts
- Managing resellers with the **Reseller Center**

When you've finished this chapter you will be able to set up and manage reseller accounts with ease.

Who Exactly are Resellers?

Often, users who are new to hosting get intimidated by the term "reseller". Any customer of yours who also has the ability to access WHM and create or manage separate cPanel accounts is considered to be a reseller in WHM and cPanel. A reseller account does not have to actually sell anything, though. A reseller could use the account to manage several of his own domains with separate cPanel accounts.

What are Reseller Accounts Good for?

From the perspective of the server owner (you), reseller accounts offer another potential revenue stream with fewer support costs (since you only have to support the reseller themselves, and you aren't obligated to provide direct support to their customers). It will also allow you to keep some customers who need more flexibility and that have outgrown the shared hosting plans you offer.

For your clients, having the ability to upgrade to a reseller account from a standard shared hosting account can be a big plus. The customer can use a reseller account to manage numerous personal accounts, each account with its own separate cPanel account (rather than using add-on domains in a single cPanel account). Perhaps more importantly, being a reseller allows your customer to start their own web hosting business without the major expenses and learning curve of buying their own dedicated server or VPS. Plus, they will continue to get support from you, whom they are probably used to working with by now.

Things to Consider before Adding Reseller Accounts

There are several things that you should consider before you decide to offer reseller plans to your customers.

Where will You Put the Resellers, and How many Reseller Accounts will You Place on the Server?

Since resellers can often add many accounts to your server, it is important to think about where you will put them. If this is your first dedicated server or VPS, then you may not have the money right now to invest in yet another new server or VPS just for reseller accounts. However, keep in mind that, for every reseller you add to your server, your server will have to support many cPanel accounts. For example, if you put 10 reseller accounts on your server, and they each get 10 customers of their own, your server will be supporting 110 accounts. If you aren't careful, that number could grow to several thousand cPanel accounts.

Ideally, it is probably best to place reseller accounts on a separate server. If you do that and have problems with your own shared hosting clients, it won't affect your resellers (who are presumably paying you more and expecting a certain level of service). Also, it will be much easier for you to keep track of reseller accounts if they are on a different server.

What if Your Reseller Clients Have Violated Your Acceptable Use Policy?

You may have very strict hosting policies in place for your customers in order to keep your customer accounts and server or VPS safe and running smoothly. You may also carefully screen every account that you host to make sure that the accounts are legitimate. However, your resellers may not have the resources or knowledge to be able to carefully screen their clients. This means you will need to monitor your reseller's clients for violations of your acceptable use policy.

If you do find a violation on your server, and the user is a client of one of your resellers, you clearly need to do something. However, you need to be cognizant that your reseller's clients may have no idea that they are being hosted by a reseller on your server and may react with shock if you tried to contact them directly.

You should have a clear policy in place for dealing with this sort of issue. Resellers need to understand what will happen if you discover a problem—will you contact them about the problem first and let them deal with it, or will you suspend the user's account first if it is overloading your server, and then try to contact the reseller?

With shared hosting it is possible for a single customer to overload a server and cause slowdowns or other issues for all of the other accounts on the server. Therefore, you may not want to wait hours for resellers to deal with a serious problem on their own, but you do need to make it clear in advance what action(s) you will take and how you will communicate the issue to the resellers so that they can work with the customer. (We will explore some ways of monitoring your server in Chapter 8.)

Can You Handle the More Complex Support Issues that Resellers Often have?

Although the number of support requests will probably be fewer than your standard shared hosting accounts, resellers have more complex needs than a standard shared hosting customer. Resellers have access to a subset of WHM features in addition to standard cPanel features and may expect more robust service. If you aren't familiar with WHM and cPanel, you may want to focus on standard shared hosting until you feel you can handle the sorts of issues resellers may throw at you.

If you are certain you are ready, read on to learn how to work with reseller accounts.

Working with Reseller Accounts

Reseller accounts are hybrid accounts. They have a main cPanel account just like standard shared hosting customers, but they also have access to WHM to help them manage their accounts. What features they have access to depend on what you choose to permit them.

Setting Up a Reseller Account that isn't Already a Customer of Yours

Initial setup of a reseller's account, if they aren't already a customer of yours, follows the same account creation process that we learned about in Chapter 5. The first thing you will probably want to do is create a package that you can use for reseller accounts.

Creating a Package for the Reseller's Main cPanel Account

Creating a special package for the reseller's main cPanel accounts isn't required, but is generally a good idea. It will make initial setup easier for you, and also some third-party hosting business management tools may require a special reseller package.

If you plan on assigning ownership of the reseller's main account to them (rather than assigning the account to you), then you will want to make sure the initial package you use for the account isn't going to use up all of the reseller's assigned resources. For example, if your smallest reseller plan allows the reseller to use 5 GB of disk space and 500 GB of bandwidth, and you assign the main reseller account a package that allows the main account to use 4 GB of disk space and 400 GB of bandwidth, then the reseller will only have 1 GB of disk space and 100 GB of bandwidth to resell to his customers. Of course, if the account is owned by the reseller, then he can change the assigned package (if you permit them to do so), but you still don't want to make the main account use all of those resources.

If you plan on not allowing the resellers to own their main cPanel account, then you will want to assign it a reasonable package, since they will be able to use even more of your server's resources. For example, if the resellers resource limits are 5 GB of disk space and 500 GB of bandwidth, and you assign 4 GB of disk space and 400 GB of bandwidth to the reseller's main account, the resellers will be able to resell the entire 5 GB of disk space and 500 GB of bandwidth assigned to them while being able to use another 4 GB of disk space and 400 GB of bandwidth for their main reseller cPanel account. This means that, if the resellers use all the resources available to them, they will use a total of 9 GB of disk space and 900 GB of bandwidth. However, if the main account isn't owned by the resellers, then the resellers won't be able to change the resources assigned to their main cPanel account.

To create the package, just click on **Add Package** in the **Feature Manager** section of root WHM, create the package, and save it. Then you can actually create the reseller's main cPanel account.

...

Creating a New Reseller's Main cPanel Account

The username and password assigned to a reseller's main account will also be the username and password that they will use to access WHM.

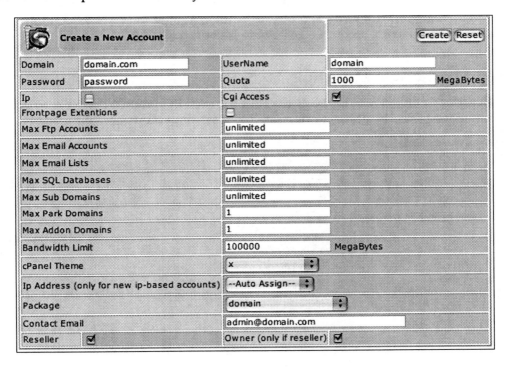

You fill in this information just as you did in Chapter 5 when creating a standard cPanel account. The only thing you need to pay special attention to are the **Reseller** and **Owner** checkboxes at the bottom of this screen. If you check **Reseller**, then this new account will automatically be designated as a reseller. You will still want to edit permissions in the **Reseller Center** before sending the account information to your customer. Check the **Owner** box if you want the reseller to own their main account (so they can modify it, and so it will count against the reseller resource usage limits that you set in the **Reseller Center**). If you don't check **Owner**, then the reseller's main account will be owned by you (root). The reseller will be able to access it as a cPanel account, but it will not appear in the reseller's list of accounts nor will it count against their resource usage.

Upgrading an Existing Standard cPanel Account to a Reseller Plan

You can also upgrade any existing cPanel account and make it into a reseller. In order to do that you will need to access the **Reseller Center** in WHM, and assign reseller privileges to the account you want to become a reseller.

The Reseller Center

The **Reseller Center** can be found in the **Reseller** section of root WHM. It is where you can manage nearly all functions related to reseller accounts on your server.

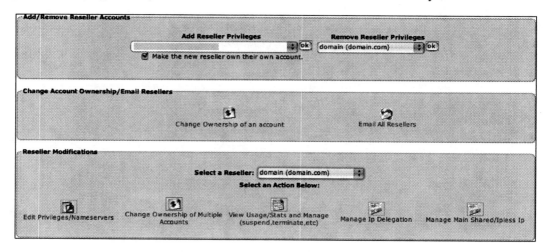

There are three main sections to the **Reseller Center** interface — **Add/Remove Reseller Accounts, Change Account Ownership/Email Resellers,** and **Reseller Modifications.**

Adding and Removing Reseller Privileges

To add reseller privileges to an account, select the standard cPanel account from the drop-down list under the **Add Reseller Privileges** heading, then check or uncheck the **Make the new reseller own their own account** checkbox as you prefer. (Checking these items are the same as checking the **Reseller** and **Owner** items when you create a new account.) Click the **ok** button when finished. The user will be able to access WHM using their cPanel username and password right away, but they won't have access to any features in WHM or be able to create accounts until you edit their reseller privileges.

To remove reseller privileges, select the reseller account from the drop-down list under the **Remove Reseller Privileges** heading, and click **ok** to remove the privileges. Be sure this is what you want to do, as there is no confirmation.

Accounts previously owned by a reseller will continue to be owned by the ex-reseller even after you delete that reseller's privileges. However, that user will no longer be able to manage accounts or access WHM. If you want to reassign the reseller's accounts to someone else (or to yourself), you should use the **Change Ownership of Multiple Accounts** feature in the **Reseller Center**.

Changing Single Account Ownership

If you want to move ownership of a single account from one account (or root) to another account (or root), click the **Change Ownership of an Account** icon in the second section of the **Reseller Center**. Here you can select an account by the domain name or cPanel username, and click **Change**. From the new screen select the new owner for this account from the drop-down list of choices (either a reseller or root), and submit changes.

You can also access this feature from the **List Accounts** feature in the **Account Functions** section of WHM. Click the small edit icon next to the name of the owner of the account you want to switch.

E-mailing All Resellers (Only)

Clicking on **Email All Resellers** in the second section of the **Reseller Center** will bring you to an interface much like the **Email All Users** feature discussed in the previous chapter. However, this feature will only e-mail your resellers. It won't e-mail your customers or your reseller's customers. Just fill in the name you want people to see in the **From** field of the message followed by your preferred e-mail address, subject, and body of the message. Click the **send** button to immediately send the e-mail to your resellers.

This feature will only work if your resellers have entered a valid contact e-mail address into their main cPanel account.

Changing Ownership of Multiple Accounts

In the final section of the **Reseller Center** interface you can assign multiple cPanel accounts to a reseller. Select the reseller to whom you want to reassign accounts from the drop-down list near the **Select a Reseller** header, and then click on the **Change Ownership of Multiple Accounts** icon. This will display all accounts not currently owned by the selected reseller, and who owns the accounts right now. Click the checkbox next to each account you want to reassign (being careful not to select the wrong accounts), and then click the **Change Owner of the Selected Accounts** button, and the accounts will immediately be switched to the new owner.

Monitoring and Managing Resellers

If you select a reseller account from the drop-down list next to the **Select a Reseller** header, and then click on the **View Usage/Stats and Manage (suspend, terminate, etc.,)** icon, you will be taken to a screen where you can get an overview of that reseller's accounts and resource usage.

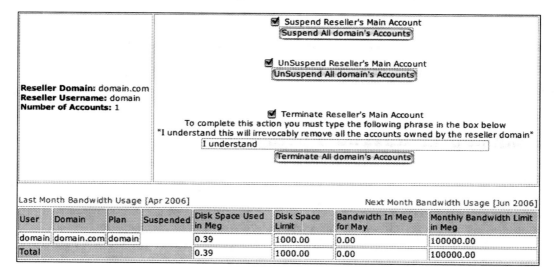

In the top section, you can see the reseller's main domain, cPanel username, and total number of accounts that he owns. Next to that information are buttons that will allow you to do a number of things to all of that reseller's accounts (and optionally to the reseller account itself).

The first item is a button that will allow you to suspend all of the reseller's accounts. If you also want to suspend the reseller's main account, check the box just above this button before clicking it.

The next button allows you to unsuspend all of a reseller's accounts. To also unsuspend the reseller's main cPanel account at the same time, click the checkbox above this button before you click on it.

The last button will terminate (delete) all of the reseller's accounts, including the reseller's main account if you check the box above this button. To make sure you understand what you are doing and really want to do it, you will have to type in the phrase **I understand this will irrevocably remove all the accounts owned by the reseller domain** into the text box provided before clicking on the terminate button.

At the bottom of this screen, you can see some vital statistics about the selected reseller's status, accounts, and resource usage. This display includes information on whether the reseller or any of their accounts are currently suspended or not, disk space used by each account, total disk space available to each account, bandwidth usage for the current month to date, and the total bandwidth the account is permitted this month. Just above the table to the left is a link that will allow you to view the previous month's bandwidth statistics. To the right is a link to view the next month's bandwidth statistics (if available).

Managing Reseller IP Address Delegation

If you want a reseller to be able to assign dedicated IP addresses to their accounts, select the reseller from the drop-down list next to the **Select a Reseller** header in the **Reseller Center**, and click the **Manage IP Delegation** icon.

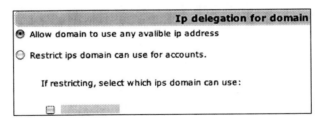

If you'd like the reseller to be able to choose any IP address assigned to your server that isn't being used by another account, leave the first radio button selected. If you prefer to restrict this reseller to certain IP addresses, you can click on the radio button next to **Restrict ips the reseller can use for accounts**. Below that, is a list of all IP addresses on the server. Check the IPs you want the reseller to use. Any IPs already in use by other accounts will be noted. You may not assign the main shared IP address of the server to resellers, so it won't appear in the list. Click the **Save** button to save the new settings.

This feature will not deallocate an IP address that the reseller is already actively using. Also, this feature will not affect anything if the reseller is not permitted to assign accounts dedicated IP addresses in the reseller privileges settings.

Assigning a Reseller a New Shared IP Address

If you would like a reseller to use a different IP address as their main (shared) IP address, then select the reseller from the drop-down list next to the **Select a Reseller** header in the **Reseller Center**, and click the awkwardly titled **Manage Main Shared/Ipless Ip** icon.

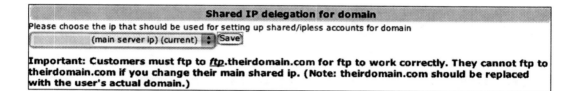

By default, all resellers and their accounts use the server's main shared IP address. If you want to change it, select the new IP address from the drop-down list on this screen, and click the **Save** button. Any of the reseller's accounts that do not have a dedicated IP address assigned to them will use this newly selected IP address.

 After switching the reseller's shared IP address, it may take a few minutes for the resellers and their accounts to become accessible again as this new information propagates. In addition, the resellers should make sure that when they FTP to their accounts, they do so to `ftp.domain.com` rather than just `domain.com`, where domain.com is their domain name.

Managing Reseller Privileges and Assigning Custom Nameservers

As mentioned earlier, granting a cPanel account "reseller status" doesn't automatically give them the ability to do much of anything. They can log into WHM using their cPanel username and password, but they won't be able to do anything in WHM unless you also grant them some privileges to use some or all of WHM's features, and permit them to create resold accounts. That is what you can do when you select a reseller from the drop-down list next to the **Select a Reseller** header, and click on **Manage Reseller Privileges and Assign Custom Nameservers** icon. There are a lot of options on this screen, so we will break the items into functional sections.

Reseller Privileges: Account Creation Limits

In this first section, you can define what limits (if any) the reseller will have when creating resold accounts.

```
Account Creation Limits

  Limit the amount of accounts domain can create by number to [      ] accounts.
  Limit account creation to pre-assigned packages (all new reseller created packages must be approved in this interface before they can be used by the reseller.)
  Limit the amount of each package that domain can create. (This implies the option above.)
  Limit Accounts that domain can create by Resource Usage. (Access to packages the user creates is automatically granted unless account creation has been limited to pre-assigned packages above. Access is not automaticlly granted to system/root created packages unless specifically defined below.)
```

If you check the first checkbox, you can specify a maximum number of resold accounts that this reseller can create by typing a number into the text box. The reseller won't be able to create more accounts than the number you specify. You can enable this feature in addition to other types of limits listed in this section.

The second checkbox allows you to limit account creation to only certain packages that you have already created in the **Add Package** feature of WHM, or that your resellers create. With this item checked, the resellers can't use any packages, even if they created them, until you approve the use of that package in this area under **Account Limits**.

The third checkbox allows you to not only limit the reseller to certain packages, but it also limits the reseller to a certain number of each approved package. Checking this option will automatically turn on the **limit account creation to pre-assigned packages** option (the second checkbox) even if it isn't currently selected. You specify the number of each package under **Account Limits**.

The final checkbox at the top allows you to limit resellers by resource usage. Many hosts use this method of limiting resellers. The reseller can create packages and use them unless they go over the resource limits set in the **Resource Limits** box. Also, if you create packages that start with the reseller's cPanel username and an underscore ("_"), the reseller will be able to use that package also. Other packages you create must be specifically approved for use by you for each reseller.

If you select more than one type of account limit, each limit will be enforced even if that means that other limits cannot be reached. For example, if you enable resource usage limits of 1 GB of disk space and 100 GB of bandwidth, and you also limit the number of accounts the reseller can create to five, the reseller will be able to use 1 GB of disk space and 100 GB of bandwidth total between five resold accounts. If the reseller creates five accounts without using all of the available resources, the reseller won't be able to create more accounts, and the extra resources may go to waste unless the reseller changes the disk space and bandwidth assigned to those five packages to fully utilize the assigned resources. Alternately, if the reseller assigns a total of 1 GB of disk space and 100 GB of bandwidth to two accounts, he will not be permitted to create more accounts (unless overselling is enabled in **Resource Limits**).

Reseller Privileges: Account Package Limits

In this section, you define which packages a reseller is permitted to use and how many of each package he can create (if you enable the "number of allowed packages" limit in the **Account Creation Limits** section).

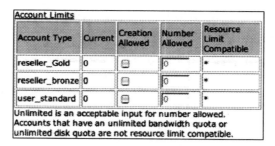

Account Limits				
Account Type	Current	Creation Allowed	Number Allowed	Resource Limit Compatible
reseller_Gold	0	☐	0	*
reseller_bronze	0	☐	0	*
user_standard	0	☐	0	*
Unlimited is an acceptable input for number allowed. Accounts that have an unlimited bandwidth quota or unlimited disk quota are not resource limit compatible.				

The table lists all packages currently created on your server. Next to each one, you can see how many accounts are using each package. The **Creation Allowed** checkbox specifies if this reseller can use this package or not. You won't be permitted to enter a number into the **Number Allowed** box unless you've got the **limit reseller to a certain number of packages** checkbox checked in the **Account Creation Limit** section. Enter the word **unlimited** if you want the resellers to be able to create as many of these packages as they want (subject to any other limits you may have imposed). The asterisk notes if this package is compatible with resource limits. If a package has unlimited bandwidth or disk space set, then it won't be compatible with resource limits, so you shouldn't permit resource limited resellers to access this package.

Reseller Privileges: Resource Limits

The **Resource Usage Limits** table allows you to set resource usage limits if you have the **Resource Usage Limits** checkbox checked in the **Account Limits** section.

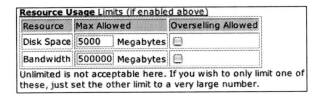

Resource Usage Limits (if enabled above)		
Resource	Max Allowed	Overselling Allowed
Disk Space	5000 Megabytes	☐
Bandwidth	500000 Megabytes	☐
Unlimited is not acceptable here. If you wish to only limit one of these, just set the other limit to a very large number.		

If you have enabled **resource usage limits**, you must enter a number into the **Max Allowed** column for both **Disk Space** and **Bandwidth**. If you prefer not to limit one of these items, just enter a very large number for that resource.

A few words about the overselling allowed feature:

Normally, resellers must have enough disk space or bandwidth to cover the creation of a new account with all of the resources they assign to it. If they don't, then WHM will not permit them to add the new account. This ensures that there are always enough resources to actually cover every single user (unless you've personally oversold the resources of your server).

Turning on overselling means you are willing to allow resellers to gamble with those resources. Users rarely use all of the resources granted to them. For example, a user might have 1,000 MB of disk space and only use 100 MB of it. Without overselling enabled, this unused resource that the reseller is paying for will go unused. However, if you permit overselling, then the reseller can create as many packages as permitted by any other limits you may have placed on them, even if full utilization of those packages by the resold accounts would cause the reseller to go over their resource limits.

The reseller's total amount of used resources still cannot go over the limits you set. If the reseller's accounts go over those limits, the reseller won't be able to create additional accounts, and the resold accounts may be prevented from uploading more (in the case of disk space overage) or suspended (in the case of bandwidth overage) until the reseller contacts you to get additional resources.

With overselling, the reseller must watch the actual resource usage and contact you to pay for additional resources as needed before their customers hit the resource limits imposed on the reseller.

If you allow all of your resellers to oversell, you are going to run into problems yourself. Getting additional bandwidth or disk drives for your server may not be quick; so you have to be very careful or all of users on your server could be prevented from uploading anything or be suspended.

I do not recommend the overselling of resources unless you are sure that resellers will carefully monitor usage and that you will have enough time to add additional resources when needed.

Reseller Privileges: Feature Limits

In the **Feature Limits** section, you will choose which features the selected reseller can use when logged into WHM. In this section, there are a lot of features that you can control access to. Thankfully, you can save a selected set of feature limits as an Access Control List (ACL) that you can apply later to other resellers. If you already have an ACL saved, you can choose it from the drop-down list next to the **Load an ACL List** heading. This will automatically check or uncheck features in this section to match the saved ACL settings.

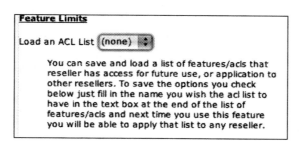

Here are the options you can choose to offer your resellers (unless otherwise noted, these items allow access to the feature in WHM with the same name).

Account Information

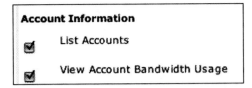

- **List Accounts**: The reseller will only see the accounts that they own in the list.
- **View Account Bandwidth Usage**: The reseller can keep track of bandwidth usage for their accounts.

Account Management

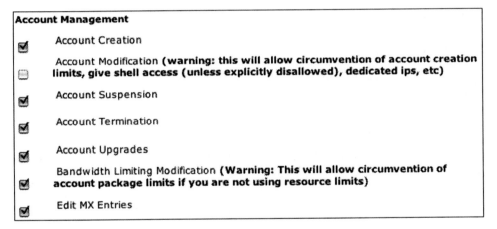

- **Account Creation**: If you don't permit the reseller to access this feature, they will only be able to manage existing accounts you assign to them.
- **Account Modification**: Resellers with access to the account modification feature may be able to grant resold accounts features you don't want them to have access to (like dedicated IP addresses). However, if you don't give a reseller access to this feature, the only way for them to change the resources they allow resold accounts to use will be to create separate packages for each change, and use the upgrade and downgrade account feature in WHM to assign them to the new package.

- **Account Suspension**: Even if the reseller does not have access to this feature, WHM may still automatically suspend accounts for going over their resource usage limits. The reseller won't be able to unsuspend accounts either if they don't have access to this feature.

- **Account Termination**: Resellers may not delete accounts that they do not own.

- **Account Upgrades**: This allows the reseller to change the package that one of their resold accounts is assigned to. If this feature and the account modification feature are both disabled, the only way a reseller will be able to change account resource limits and features is to terminate the account and recreate it from scratch (if permitted).

- **Bandwidth Limiting Modification**: This will allow the reseller to modify the bandwidth limit of users without changing their package. If you aren't using resource limits for this reseller account, you should not grant access to this feature, as they will be able to bypass the account package limits you set on them.

- **Edit MX Entries**: This will allow the reseller to edit the mail server DNS entries for accounts they own (see Chapter 7 for more on MX records and DNS zones).

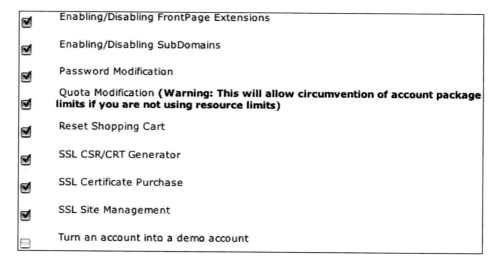

- **Enabling/Disabling FrontPage extensions**: This will allow the reseller to control the adding or removing of FrontPage server-side extensions for their account.

- **Enabling/Disabling SubDomains**: You can enable this or not as you see fit, because this feature was depreciated long ago. There is no enable or disable subdomains feature in WHM any more because it is handled automatically.

- **Password Modification**: The reseller will only be able to change passwords for accounts they own.

- **Quota Modification**: This feature allows the reseller to modify the disk space quota for accounts they own independently of the quota assigned in the account package. You should only allow this if you are using resource limits for this reseller. Otherwise they will be able to override the other limits you've placed on them.

- **Reset Shopping Cart**: If you have the Interchange e-commerce script enabled on your server, then this will allow your resellers to reset the administrative password on the chosen installation (for their clients only).

- **SSL CRT/CSR Generator**: In order for a reseller to get an SSL/TLS certificate for one of their accounts, they need a dedicated IP address, and they have to be able to generate the **Certificate Signing Request (CSR)**. If this feature is disabled, the reseller will have to ask you for assistance. Of course if you don't allow resellers to use dedicated IP addresses, then this feature is useless to them.

- **SSL Certificate Purchase**: WHM has the ability to simplify the purchasing and installation of SSL/TLS certificates from approved partners. Don't bother enabling this if you don't allow resellers access to dedicated IP addresses.

- **SSL Site Management**: These are additional tools for working with SSL/TLS certificates.

- **Turn an account into a demo account**: The reseller can show potential users what cPanel looks like using a demo cPanel account (that has many features disabled for security reasons). Demo account security has increased over the years, but demo accounts can still be a security risk, so I do not recommend you allow access to this feature.

Advanced Account Management

Advanced Account Management

☐   Rearrange Accounts (used to free up disk space)

- **Rearrange Accounts**: This will allow the reseller to move their accounts from one home directory to another, if there is one.

Clustering

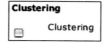

- **Clustering**: This will allow the reseller access to DNS clustering features. There is really no need for a reseller to have access to this.

DNS

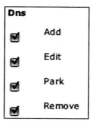

- **Add**: Allows the reseller to add custom DNS zones for domains that do not have an account on your server. It is probably best not to allow other people access to this particular feature.
- **Edit**: Allows the reseller to edit existing DNS zones for accounts that they manage.
- **Park**: Allows the reseller to park a domain on top of another domain from within WHM.
- **Remove**: Allows the reseller to delete DNS zones for accounts they own.

Packages

- **Add/Remove**: Allows the reseller to create or delete packages. All packages that resellers create are appended with the reseller's main cPanel domain name automatically.
- **Edit**: Allows resellers to edit packages that they have created.

Privileges

Privileges

☐ Allow Creation of Packages with Shell Access

☐ Allow Creation of Packages with Unlimited Diskspace

☑ Allow Creation of Packages with Unlimited Features (ie. unlimited pop accounts)

☐ Allow Creation of Packages with a Dedicated IP

☑ Allow creation of packages with Addon Domains

☑ Allow creation of packages with Parked Domains

☑ Disallow creation of accounts with packages that are not global or not owned by this user

☑ Never allow creation of accounts with shell access

- **Allow creation of Packages with Shell Access**: If this is enabled and the **Never allow creation of accounts with shell access** option is off, then the reseller will be able to grant shell (SSH) access to their customers.

- **Allow creation of Packages with Unlimited Diskspace**: If you enable this feature, you will permit resellers to create packages that could fill up the hard drive(s) on your server. This probably isn't a good idea.

- **Allow creation of Packages with Unlimited Features**: This will allow the reseller to create packages that have unlimited features, like e-mail and FTP accounts.

- **Allow creation of Packages with a Dedicated IP**: If you enable this, resellers will be able to set up accounts with dedicated IP addresses.

- **Allow creation of packages with Addon Domains**: This allows resellers to create accounts with add-on domain allowances.

- **Allow creation of packages with Parked Domains**: This allows resellers to create accounts with parked domain allowances.

- **Disallow creation of accounts with packages that are not global or not owned by this user**: This should be checked, or the reseller can use any packages created on the server by anyone so long as it doesn't put them over their reseller limits that you've defined. This is a bad idea, as it allows the reseller to see what sort of packages other resellers are offering to their clients.

- **Never allow creation of accounts with shell access**: Enabling this will make sure that no reseller can ever enable shell access on any of their accounts. This will stop the reseller from using a feature like **Modify Account** to enable shell access.

Root Access

- **All Features**: This will allow the reseller to access nearly all of the features available to you in root WHM including features like resetting the root server password and other sensitive features. If you enable this, it doesn't matter what other features you have checked, since they will have access to all of them. However, some add-on modules may not be available to the reseller. Enabling this is *not* a good idea.

Server Information

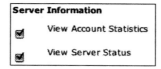

- **View Account Statistics**: This will allow the reseller to access account statistics information for their accounts in WHM.
- **View Server Status**: The same server status display is available in cPanel, but this feature will permit the reseller to see this from within WHM itself.

Services

- **Restart Services**: This will permit the reseller to restart all the services on the server like FTP, MySQL, and others from WHM.

Troubleshooting

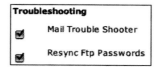

- **Mail Troubleshooter**: This feature runs a graphical display of the route that mail takes from your server to a particular e-mail account. This is used to try and identify where mail delivery problems occur.

- **Resync FTP Passwords**: This allows the reseller to resynchronize FTP passwords in case one or more of their clients have problems logging into their FTP account(s).

cPanel Management

cPanel Management
☑   News Modification
Save as ACL List (optional, leave blank to not save): [   ] (none) ↕

- **News Modification**: This allows the reseller to add news that will be displayed in all of his customers' cPanel accounts.

Once you've selected the features you want this reseller to access, you can type in a name in the text box next to the words **Save as ACL List**. When you click on the button to save this reseller's privileges, it will also save an ACL with the same features that you can use later with other resellers.

Reseller Privileges: Custom Nameservers

If you want to allow the reseller custom nameservers, then you can use the nameserver entry boxes on this screen.

Primary Nameserver:	[ ]		Assign Ip Address	Add an A entry for this nameserver
Secondary Nameserver:	[ ]		Assign Ip Address	Add an A entry for this nameserver
Secondary Nameserver:	[ ]	(optional)	Assign Ip Address	Add an A entry for this nameserver
Secondary Nameserver:	[ ]	(optional)	Assign Ip Address	Add an A entry for this nameserver
Save				

Specify the FQDN (for example, `ns1.domain.com`) in the appropriate box for the nameservers you want to set up for the reseller. This will allow the reseller to use nameservers that match whatever domain they own, so they don't have to use the ones you've set up for your business. You need to click **Assign IP Address** first, then when that is finished, click **Add an A entry for this nameserver**. Do this for each nameserver (you really should create at least two, since all domains must have at least that many).

Once everything is the way you like it, click **Save** to commit all of these changes.

Listing All Reseller Accounts and Their Clients

If you would like to display a list of all reseller accounts and their clients, you will find this feature by clicking on **Display Reseller Accounts** in the **Reseller** section of WHM.

domain	Total: 1 account	domain.com	
domain		domain.com	domain

The list will display the cPanel username, total resold accounts, and main domain of the reseller at the top, followed by a list of the cPanel username, main domain, and owner of each resold account. This list is a good way to keep track of resold accounts on your server.

Summary

In this chapter, you've learned how to create new reseller accounts, and how to add reseller privileges to existing standard cPanel accounts. You've found out how to control what your resellers can do, and how many resources they can use or accounts they can create. You can create, edit, or delete collections of functions that resellers can access using access control lists. You know how to view a list of all reseller accounts and their resold accounts, and can reassign ownership of any account to a reseller or to yourself (root).

You've mastered many things that you will use regularly, and now it is time to move on to something more advanced. In the next chapter, we'll delve into the exciting world of DNS, IP address, and SSL/TLS management. These are topics that you may not need to access every day, but they are extremely powerful and important to understand in order to use your server to its fullest.

7

IP Address, SSL/TLS, and DNS Management

You've already learned most of the basic features available to you in WHM. Now you're ready to tackle some of the more advanced features in WHM. In this chapter, you will learn how to:

- Show or delete server IP addresses
- Add an IP address
- Rebuild the IP address pool
- Show or edit reserved IPs
- Show IP address usage
- The IP migration wizard
- Change the WHM/cPanel SSL certificate
- Reset (Generate) the cPanel/WHM SSL certificate
- Use the SSL manager
- Purchase and install SSL certificates
- Delete a SSL host
- Generate a SSL certificate and signing request
- Install a SSL certificate and set up domain
- Park or point a domain
- Setup or edit domain forwarding
- List parked domains
- Add a DNS zone
- Edit an MX entry
- Edit DNS zones

- Delete a DNS zone
- Perform a DNS cleanup
- Establish a trust relationship with a primary nameserver
- Synchronize DNS records with a primary nameserver

When you've finished this chapter, you will be able to work with IP addresses, apply for and install SSL/TLS certificates, and edit DNS zones with confidence.

IP Address Management

Managing IP address usage is an important feature of WHM. Most NOCs will provide you with a few *free* IP addresses that you may use on your server as you see fit. Additional IP addresses will usually cost you more money, and you will probably be asked to justify your usage of additional IP addresses. One of the only valid reasons most NOCs will accept is the need to use them for SSL certificates (the installation and management of which we will discuss later in this chapter).

Most of the IP management functions in WHM can be found in the **IP Functions** section.

Add an IP Address

You can add IP addresses that are assigned to your server here. Click on **Add An IP Address** to do this.

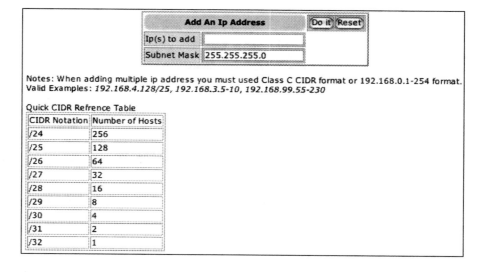

Type in the IP address or address range to be added, and then edit the **Subnet Mask** if needed. Your NOC will tell you what IP addresses you are assigned as well as what net mask to use.

Show or Delete Server IP Addresses

Clicking on **Show or Delete Server IP Address** shows a list of all IP addresses assigned to your server. You can also remove an IP address (except for your server's main IP address) from your server by clicking on **Remove** next to it.

All IPs in this list are color-coded:
Blue: Main shared IP address. This address cannot be removed.
Green: IP addresses properly added to your server. These you can remove, but you should make sure they aren't in use before doing so.
Red: IP address added to your server, but not properly bound to it. It should be definitely removed as it will not properly resolve to your server anyway.

Rebuild the IP Address Pool

Clicking on this option will instantly check for all the IP addresses assigned to your server and will make sure that they are reflected in WHM. You will be told the total number of available (unused) IP addresses that are properly bound to your server.

Show and Edit Reserved IPs

This will permit you to reserve an IP (which will stop that IP from being used by accounts or nameservers on your server).

Just check the box next to each IP you want to reserve, and then input a reason for reserving this IP so you can remember why you reserved it. This is handy if you are using software on your server that needs to be bound to a particular IP address and cannot share that address with others.

Show IP Address Usage

Click on **Show IP Address Usage** if you'd like to see how IP addresses are being used on your server. Here you can see a table that displays every IP address assigned to your server, and exactly what services or domains those addresses are being used by.

The IP Migration Wizard

This feature will help you make the transition from one set of IP addresses to another set. Click the **IP Migration Wizard** to begin the process.

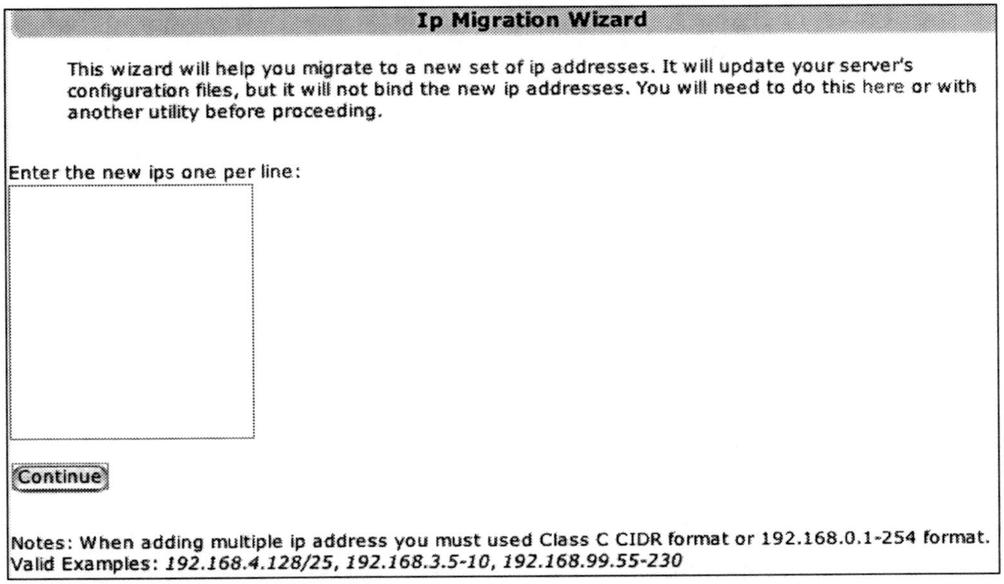

Ip Migration Wizard

This wizard will help you migrate to a new set of ip addresses. It will update your server's configuration files, but it will not bind the new ip addresses. You will need to do this here or with another utility before proceeding.

Enter the new ips one per line:

Continue

Notes: When adding multiple ip address you must used Class C CIDR format or 192.168.0.1-254 format.
Valid Examples: *192.168.4.128/25, 192.168.3.5-10, 192.168.99.55-230*

Enter each new IP address on a separate line in the text box on this page. You can also specify ranges of IPs if you prefer. Click **Continue** to have WHM update your server configuration files with the new information. You should be sure to add the new IP addresses to your server, as this feature will not do that automatically. If you click **here** in the text that appears above the text box on this page, it will take you directly to the **Add An IP Address** feature in WHM discussed earlier.

Change a Domain's IP Address

If you want to change the IP address that a domain is bound to on your server (perhaps to give it a dedicated IP address so that you can add an SSL/TLS certificate to the domain), then click on **Change Site's IP Address** in WHM.

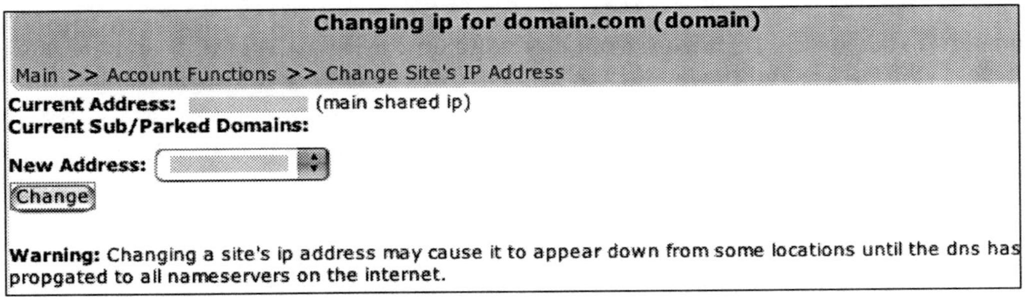

Changing ip for domain.com (domain)

Main >> Account Functions >> Change Site's IP Address

Current Address: (main shared ip)
Current Sub/Parked Domains:

New Address:
Change

Warning: Changing a site's ip address may cause it to appear down from some locations until the dns has propgated to all nameservers on the internet.

Select the domain or cPanel username of the account whose IP you want to change. This will display the IP address that the domain is assigned to and also any parked, add-on, or subdomains that this account controls. All of these will be changed to the new IP address you select from the drop-down list of IPs next to the **New Address:** header. Click the **Change** button to switch the domain(s) to the new IP address.

 Using this feature may cause the domain(s) to appear to be down for a short time as the new information propagates. Typically this isn't more than 15 minutes, though how long it takes will depend on local conditions.

SSL/TLS Management

Secure Socket Layer (SSL) also referred to as **Transport Layer Security (TLS)** certificates allow secure end-to-end communication between your server and a remote client. Most often that client is a user's web browser. SSL certificates can be added to your server through WHM, but you will need to purchase one from an SSL certificate provider (like Thawte). WHM can handle almost any kind of SSL certificate, but you should understand what you are buying and how it works before you do so. We don't have the room in this book to fully discuss the process of how SSL certificates work or get issued. The site, http://www.whichssl.com/, may help you figure out how SSL works, what kind of SSL certificate will meet your needs, and where you can get one. However, if you have any questions about how the process works, you should probably contact the signing authority from which you will be purchasing your SSL certificate.

You will find all the SSL-related features listed under the **Web SSL/TLS** and **SSL/TLS** headings in WHM.

Purchase and Install an SSL Certificate

You can install an SSL certificate from any valid authority via WHM. If you are new to SSL, WHM offers **Purchase and Install SSL Certificate**; not only will it offer to help you with the installation process, but also offer a recommendation of a couple of companies where you can buy a certificate. Click on the appropriate link to get started.

The companies listed here have a partnership with cPanel so that WHM can handle most of the work of buying and installing a SSL certificate for you. You can order, track, install, and manage your certificate orders right from this screen. When ordering, just enter the information requested for the domain you want to buy a certificate for. You will be able to securely purchase a certificate and then track the progress of the order while the information you've entered is validated and a certificate issued. Once the certificate is issued, WHM will manage installing the new certificate for you.

If you are new to the SSL/TLS certificate order and installation process, this feature may be the easiest for you to use. However, there are many other companies that offer other types of certificates, some of which may be less expensive or offer better features to meet your needs. You are encouraged to shop around before deciding.

Generate an SSL Certificate and Signing Request

If you want to install a SSL certificate for a particular domain (rather than a server-wide certificate), you will want to use **Generate a SSL Certificate and Signing Request** to generate the information that your signing authority will need to actually issue the valid signed SSL certificate.

Create a New Cert			Create Reset
Contact Info			
Email Address the Cert will be sent to.			
Cert Info (this will be displayed when a user connects)			
Host to make cert for		Country (2 letter Abbrivation)	
State		City	
Company Name		Company Division	
Email			
Password			

Enter the certificate's contact information as requested. Be sure to fill in the hostname (`domain.com`), and choose a secret password that will be hard to guess. Do not forget this password, as you will need it later. Then click on **Create**. You will need to provide the generated request (CSR) and information to your signing authority in order to obtain the certificate you need. If you have any questions about this process, please contact the company who will be issuing the certificate.

You can find a list of two letter country codes here: http://www.iso.org/iso/en/prods-services/ iso3166ma/02iso-3166-code-lists/ list-en1.html.

Install an SSL Certificate and Set Up the Domain

Once you (or one of your users) receive a domain SSL certificate, you can enter the information on the **Install an SSL Certificate and Setup Domain** screen to activate it.

The first thing to do is to fill in **Domain** (the domain name) and **User** (the cPanel username), and specify the dedicated IP address assigned to the domain. If you enter information for which you've already generated a **Certificate Signing Request** (CSR), then WHM will automatically fill in additional information. If not, try clicking on the **Fetch** button.

If no other information is filled in on this screen that is fine. Just paste the blocks of information you received from the company issuing the certificate into the appropriate boxes. Also make sure the domain name, username, and IP address exactly match the domain for which you are installing this certificate. Some certificates may require a Certificate Authority (CA) bundle to work on your server. If you need one, typically the company you received the certificate from will provide it to you.

When finished, click **Do It**. If you receive any errors, check the information you entered and try again. If you continue to receive errors, contact your certificate issuer first to make sure you have all the correct information, and then contact your NOC if necessary.

> Remember that if a user wants to add an SSL/TLS certificate to their site, they will need to have a dedicated IP address assigned to their account first.

Reset or Generate a Self-Signed Server SSL Certificate

When you select **Reset Server Certificates**, and then click on **cPanel/WHM Server**, WHM generates a self-signed SSL certificate specifically used to secure your WHM, cPanel, or webmail access. Typically, WHM creates one automatically the first time it is installed, but if you find you are unable to log into your server securely or that the certificate has expired, you may need to use this feature.

> You can log into services securely by accessing your domain or server like this:
>
> WHM: `https://domain.com:2087/` (where `domain.com` is one of the domains on your server, your server hostname, or one of the IP addresses assigned to your server).
> cPanel: `https://domain.com:2083/`
> Webmail: `https://domain.com:2096/`
>
> This kind of certificate cannot be used for shared SSL or dedicated SSL (for e-commerce), but it is free and WHM takes care of generating everything you need. Just select this option, click **Generate Certificate** and WHM will create the certificate in a few seconds. You shouldn't use this if you already have a regular SSL certificate assigned to the server.

Change the WHM/cPanel SSL Certificate

If you need to change the SSL certificate assigned to your server (if you'd prefer to use a real SSL certificate or need to regenerate the self-signed certificate your server usually uses), you can use the **Change Server Certificates** feature to do so. Click on **cPanel/WHM Server** and you will be presented with a screen just like the **Install an**

SSL Certificate and Setup Domain feature. Paste the appropriate blocks that you received from the SSL certificate authority into the appropriate section of this screen. Be very careful when pasting the information. If you receive an error, double-check your entries.

Don't forget to generate a CSR by using the **Generate a SSL Certificate and Signing Request** feature first!

The SSL Manager

You can view or manage any parts of the SSL certificate that you have installed on the server by clicking on **SSL Manager** in WHM.

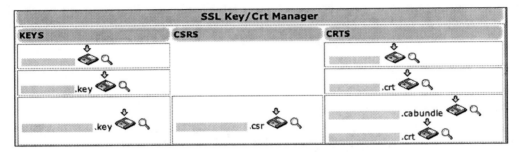

Click on the picture of a disk with an arrow above it to view on-screen the block of information you are interested in. Click on the magnifying glass icon to view extended information about that file.

Delete an SSL Host

If you want to remove an SSL certificate from your server, click on **Delete a SSL Host**, select the certificate from the list and it will be removed.

DNS Management

DNS stands for Domain Name Services. The complexity of DNS helps to make working on the Internet much easier because most of the work of translating IP addresses and services into meaningful (and working) names is handled "in the background" by DNS servers. Their job is to know that when you type `http://google.com/` you really are going to `http://72.14.207.99/`.

> The basics of DNS and how it works on the Internet is
> covered by the article at this site:
> `http://computer.howstuffworks.com/`
> `internet-infrastructure.htm`

The majority of DNS creation and edition features are listed under the heading **DNS Functions** in WHM.

Add an A Entry for your Hostname

This will add an A record to the DNS zone for your server hostname if it has not already been done (although you should have done this when setting up the server as instructed in Chapter 2). Just click this and examine the displayed information. If it is correct, click the **Add the Entry** button to complete the addition. If the information displayed is incorrect, check your **Hostname** and **Edit Settings** entries to make sure the server name and other information is listed correctly.

Add a DNS Zone

If you would like to add a DNS Zone to your server without creating a cPanel account for it, just click on **Add a DNS Zone**.

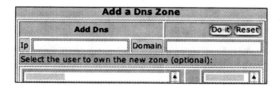

Enter the IP address and domain name for the zone, and optionally select an existing domain or cPanel account to own the new DNS zone, and click on the **Do It** button. Then you can edit this new zone if you want to (and you probably do if you took the time to set it up).

Edit an MX Entry

To change the primary MX (mail exchange) entry for one of the domains on the server, click on **Edit an MX Entry**, select the domain you want to edit, and enter the new FQDN (`domain.com`) of the main mail server for the domain. If you want to add redundant MX entries for a domain, then you will want to use **Edit DNS Zone**.

Edit DNS Zone

WHM typically takes care of most of the heavy lifting when creating or adding to a DNS zone, so it is rare that you will need to worry about editing a DNS zone, but the key to smooth and efficient operation of a domain is the DNS zone information. Nothing will cripple a site faster than incorrect or corrupt DNS zone information (other than your server being down, of course).

You can manually edit any DNS zone by clicking on **Edit DNS Zone** and selecting the domain name you wish to edit the DNS zone for.

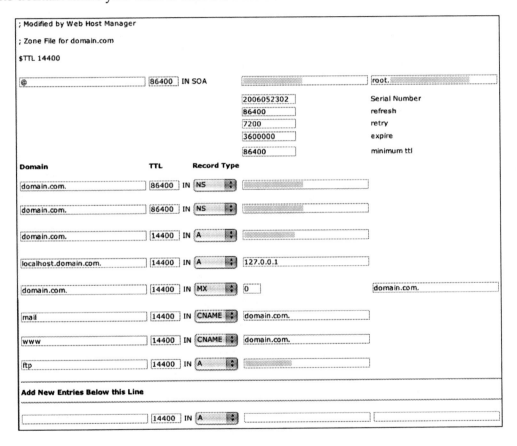

To edit the DNS zone, make changes to the appropriate text boxes. If you want to add new DNS zone entries, use the blank boxes in the **Add New Entries Below this Line** section. Enter one value in each text box, and leave any boxes you don't need empty. You can select the type of record you are adding in the drop-down list on that line. Click **Save** to save changes. If WHM notices an error, the edit will not be made, and you will be informed of the area where the problem was detected so that you can go back and fix it.

A valuable tool when working with DNS zones is `http://dnsreport.com/`.

Just enter the domain name you want to work on and click the button to pull up a report. DNS report will "walk through" the various entries in the domain's DNS record, and notify you if there are any issues that need to be reviewed or corrected. Keep in mind that not every warning or error really is a problem. However, as you will see, WHM doesn't always follow RFC guidelines by default. Most issues are minor, though, and easy to fix.

The Anatomy of a DNS Zone

Let's look at the anatomy of the DNS record.

This discussion is *not* meant to be an exhaustive look at DNS zones or how they work.

The first record in the DNS zone is the **SOA**, and you need to be especially careful with this part of the DNS zone. SOA stands for Start Of Authority and denotes that this zone is the main source of information about the domain listed. The first box will probably contain the text "@", and you should leave that as it is. The second box is the Time To Live (TTL), which is the time (in seconds, 14400 = 4 hours) that is allowed to pass on the DNS server before the record is queried again to make sure it is still valid.

The next box lists the primary nameserver for this domain. Note that there is a final period ("."), which needs to be there. The final period tells the DNS server that it is the full entry. If you forget the period, the DNS server will append the current domain name to the end of that entry. This is the main nameserver that other DNS servers will look to for information about this domain.

Following that is a valid e-mail address for this domain name. Note that instead of `user@domain.com`, the e-mail address is listed as `user.domain.com`. This is the way it should be listed so do not change it.

Under this is a column of numbers. The first number is a date code called the serial number, and it should denote the last time the domain's DNS zone was edited. It follows this format: four-digit year, two-digit month, two-digit day, two digit revision numbers. Thus, 2006012802 means that this DNS zone was last edited on January (01) 28, 2006, and that the last edit was the second edit made that day. Every time you make even a minor change, you must update the serial number, and add +1 to the revision number if you've edited more than one time that day. In the past, WHM did not create this number to follow RFC guidelines, so you may want to edit it to match the expected value if you notice they don't match. You are not likely to have problems if this serial number is in the wrong format, especially since WHM will typically correct this itself now when it makes a change to the DNS zone, but it is still worth noting.

Under that number is the "refresh" value. This is a number denoting time (in seconds) when secondary name (DNS) servers should check back with the primary nameserver to see if the serial number has changed. If the serial number changes, then the secondary nameservers will refresh their copy of the DNS zone record. This will probably be set to a number between 3600 and 7200 (1–2 hours).

Next comes the retry value in seconds. This is how long the nameserver waits before checking in for updated information if the refresh fails for some reason.

After that is the expiry time (in seconds). This is the amount of time that a nameserver holds on to its cached copy of the DNS record if it is unable to contact the master nameserver for updated information. A number between 1209600 and 2419200 (1–2 weeks) is an acceptable value.

The last number in this column is the minimum time. This value is now used for negative caching (but it was used to determine the minimum TTL value, hence the name). 86400 (24 hours) is a good value.

Some other record types that you will typically find in a DNS zone:

- **A (Address) Records**: A records map the name of a service or domain to an IP address. The domain name if used, must end with a "." (for example, domain.com.). The TTL value is typically set to 14400 (4 hours), which is an acceptable value.

- **CNAME (Canonical NAME) Records**: CNAME records allow a server to go by different "names" (domain names, and so on). Both "sides" of the CNAME record (if they include the FQDN) should have the "." at the end (for example, domain.com). You should have a corresponding A record for every CNAME record you have in your DNS zone.

- **MX (Mail eXchange) Records**: MX records specify where mail for the given domain should be routed. On your server, there is probably only one MX record, which looks something like this: **domain.com. 14400 in MX 0**

By this point, every entry above should be familiar except the last. That number is the MX record priority. Lower numbers are more important than higher numbers. What this allows you to do is have several backup mail servers, so if your primary "0" mailserver goes down, mail will be routed to the next lowest numbered MX record mailserver.

- **NS (NameServer) Records**: You should be familiar with nameservers by now. NS records are how you define what nameservers are the authoritative ones for the domain. For example: **domain.com. 14400 IN NS ns1.domain.com.**

  There really needs to be at least two NS records for every domain, but there can be more as appropriate.

There are quite a few other record types but these are the most common and most critical ones.

DNS Zone Templates

When creating DNS zones for new domains, WHM uses special templates that tell it how the zones should be set up initially. You can edit these templates by clicking on **Edit Zone Templates** in WHM.

Zone Template Editor

The Zone Template Editor will allow you to edit the default zones that are used when creating dns entries. Unless you have a custom setup, you do not need to edit these.

standard - used for creating a the default zone on a new account and parked/addon domains
simple - used for creating a zone with only an A entry for the domain.
standardvirtualftp - used for creating a the default zone on a new account with a virtual ftp ip

---

Click on the type of zone template you wish to edit, and you will be taken to a screen that will allow you to make changes to the template.

Be very careful while editing, and only do this if you are sure you need to, since an improperly set up zone template can cause problems when you try to create new domains on the server.

Normally, you should not need to edit the zone templates, as the defaults work fine in almost all situations.

Delete a DNS Zone

Click on **Delete a DNS Zone**, select the domain for which you want to delete the zone, click on **Delete**, and the site will basically drop off the Internet if the site's domain name is pointed to your nameservers. Be very careful when using this feature.

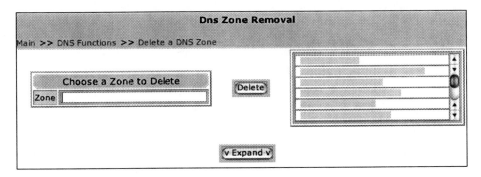

You can also delete multiple DNS zones at once by clicking the **Expand** button. This will display a list of all the domains hosted on the server with a checkbox next to each one. At the bottom of the list will be a text box and a number of buttons allowing you to select certain domains based on what you type into the text box, select all domains or reverse the selection. Clicking the **Delete** button will remove all of the selected domains.

Perform a DNS Clean-up

Use this feature every so often to clean out old or unused DNS zones. However, you need to make sure that no one is currently editing a DNS zone or doing any other DNS-related work before commencing the clean-up. WHM will inform you how many DNS zones it scanned trying to clean up the records.

Park a Domain

This feature permits you to park a domain on another domain so that when a user goes to `http://domain2.com/`, they see the content of `http://domain.com/`. This is the same sort of feature users have available in cPanel (if you permit it).

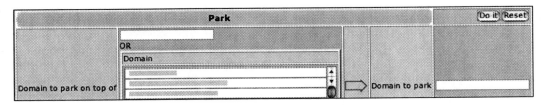

All you need to do is to click on **Park a Domain,** and then choose a domain on your server from the list displayed (or if you prefer, type in the name of the domain on your server), and then type in the name of the domain to park. So in our example, you would select domain.com (the domain already on your server) and park domain2.com on it (using the **Domain to park** text box on the right).

Set Up and Edit Domain Forwarding

If you would like to set up a domain to forward to another web address anywhere on the Internet automatically, just create a DNS Zone (or small dummy account) for the domain you want to forward (domain.com), and then click on **Setup/Edit Domain Forwarding**.

The domain forwarder is currently using the ip address. All domain that you want to be forwarded should be pointing at this ip.
Click to remove domain forwarder

Redirection Map
Domain (*.cpanel.net is acceptable) Redirection URL

	http://
	http://
	http://
	http://
	http://

Save Map

If domain forwarding isn't yet set up, click on the **Click to Create** button to set it up. You will then be told what IP address is being used for domain forwarding. You need to make sure that any domain you want to automatically forward uses this IP address. Then come back to this feature, specify the domain you want to forward and the full URL (without the http://...) that you want the domain to forward to and click on **Save Map**. The forwarding will then be set up.

You can forward all subdomains by entering an asterisk (*) followed by the rest of the domain name like this: *.domain.com.

Establish a Trust Relationship with a Primary Nameserver

This is a leftover from a legacy feature in WHM, allowing you to use another DNS server to manage the DNS zones on this (and other) server. This feature is no longer needed as the nameserver cluster feature has taken its place.

Setting Up and Managing a Nameserver Cluster

If you own several servers, you may want to designate one special server to manage all of the DNS zones on all servers and to serve as the primary nameservers for all domains on all of your servers. Having one machine manage all DNS zones makes it easier for you if you want to move domains to other servers that you manage, with very little downtime (since users will not have to change the nameservers that their domain points to if you move them to another one of your servers). Alternatively, you can mirror all DNS zones on all of your servers.

This setup is called **nameserver clustering,** and cPanel Inc. provides special server software if you want to have a single primary nameserver server here:

```
http://layer1.cpanel.net/cpanel-universal-dnsonly-install.sea
```

At the time this book was written, the software was free but required a clean supported server in order to install the nameserver-only version of WHM on it.

 The management and set-up of a primary cluster nameserver will not be discussed in this book.

If you want to set up nameserver clustering without a single master nameserver or manage an existing cluster relationship, you can click on the **Configure Cluster** item in the **Cluster/Remote Access** section of WHM.

Cluster Management

Dns Clustering

Dns Clustering allows you to get keep records synchronized across multiple servers. This system replaces the old Dns Master system used in previous versions.

⊙ Enable Dns Clustering
⦿ **(current setting)** Disable Dns Clustering
(Change)

Servers in Cluster

Hostname	Ip Address	Username	Status	Dns Role

Add a new server to the cluster

Server Ip Address: [   ] (Configure)

Dns Peers

There are currently no dns peers.

Dns Path

First, turn on the DNS clustering feature, if it isn't on already, by clicking the appropriate radio button and clicking the **Change** button. After that, you can start adding servers by typing the IP address of the server in the **Add a new server to the cluster** text box, and click on **Configure**. You will need to have the appropriate WHM remote access key or access to the other server (so you can retrieve the key) in order to add it to the cluster. Paste the key into the text box, and click on the **Do It** button. If all goes well, the server will then be added to the nameserver cluster.

You can then specify how the server behaves in the cluster. Your choices are **Standalone** or **Synchronize Changes**. If a server is set to **Standalone** in the cluster, then changes made on that server will not propagate to the other servers. However, changes made on other servers will propagate to the standalone server. If you set the server to **Synchronize Changes**, changes to zones on any server will synchronize in both directions (both to and from the server).

On the cluster management screen, you can also see any servers that are DNS peers of this one, and you can even see a graphical map showing you the relationship between the various servers in the cluster.

The WHM Remote Access Key

The **Setup Remote Access Key** feature can be found in the **Cluster/Remote Access** section of WHM. You will find it here because it is used in part to make the nameserver cluster feature possible. However, many third-party programs that want to create accounts or manage features on your server also use it. It is a public key that will allow other servers or programs to securely exchange information with your server. You should just copy the displayed block of text between the ------BEGIN WHM ACCESS KEY------ and ------END WHM ACCESS KEY------ lines and paste it into the appropriate area so the remote server or program can use it.

Click on the **Generate New Key** button if you want to create a new key (if this one has become corrupt). Don't forget to update the key on the clustered nameservers, or they won't be able to synchronize changes.

Synchronizing DNS Records

This is used when you have set up a nameserver cluster as discussed above. Click on **Synchronize DNS Records** in the **DNS Functions** section of WHM to use this feature.

On this screen you can synchronize one DNS zone to the other server(s) in the cluster by typing the domain name of the zone and clicking on the **Sync One** button. You can synchronize one remote DNS zone to this local server by entering the name of the domain and clicking on the **Sync One Local** button. If you want to synchronize all zones between all clustered servers, click on the **Sync All** button. Finally, to synchronize all remote DNS zones to this server, click on the **Sync All Local** button.

Summary

In this chapter, you've learned how to manage IP addresses, SSL/TLS certificates, and DNS entries. You can add, remove, and assign IP addresses. You can also request, install, and remove SSL/TLS security certificates as needed. Finally, you've learned how to manage DNS zone entries and handle the various features that DNS management allows such as parked and forwarded domains.

In Chapter 8 we will look at all the tools WHM gives you to be able to manage your server and keep track of how people are using your server. We'll also examine some of the security features WHM offers to help keep your server and clients safe.

8

Ongoing Server Management

Now that you have active accounts on your server and have everything set up to your liking, how do you keep track of what is happening on your server? In this chapter, we'll look at the many tools WHM provides to help you keep tabs on your server and take action if necessary, including:

- Server status
- Basic server information
- Apache status
- CPU/memory/MySQL usage
- Keeping track of disk usage
- Showing current CPU usage
- The background process killer
- Showing running processes
- Mail troubleshooting
- Managing mail queue
- Viewing mail statistics
- Rebuilding/fixing mail
- Restarting services via WHM and SSH
- Rebooting your server
- What to do if rebooting doesn't work
- Managing security

When you've finished this chapter, you will know how to keep an eye on your server using WHM, and you will also know how to deal with some issues when they arise.

General Server Information

If you want to learn more about your server itself, or if you need to see how resources such as disk space and bandwidth are being used on your server, WHM includes a number of features to make this easier for you.

Viewing General Server Information

If you click on the **Server Information** link in the **Server Status** section in WHM, you will be presented with a screen that provides a lot of information about your server.

 The exact information displayed will vary with the operating system and kernel installed as well as the configuration of your server.

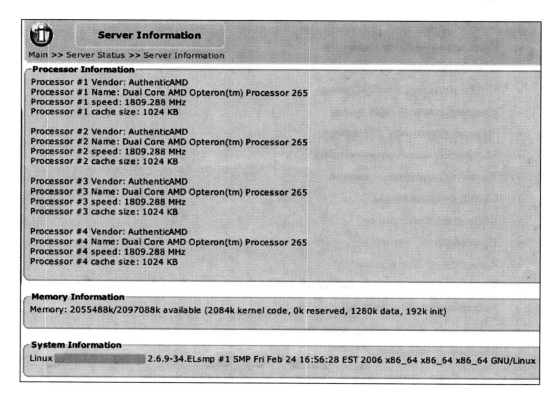

In the **Processor Information** section, you will find the information that your server operating system reports about your server CPU(s). How this information is calculated and displayed depends on your operating system and kernel. In the previous picture, the system has two dual-core AMD Opteron 265 processors. Each core is displayed as a separate processor in the list.

In the **Memory Information** section, you will see how much memory you have installed in your server and how much is currently in use. In the previous figure, the server has 2 GB of RAM.

> If you'd like to quickly convert any value to any other value (like KB to GB) or do other types of math, you can quickly do so using Google's natural language calculator in the standard Google web search field. See:
> `http://www.google.com/help/features.`
> `html#calculator`

The **System Information** section displays the server's operating system, the server's hostname, the kernel currently in use, when it was built, and the server architecture. In the previous figure, the server has Red Hat Enterprise Linux 4 installed and is using a **Symmetric Multi-Processor** enabled 2.6.x build of the Linux kernel. The server has a x86 (Intel-compatible) 64-bit architecture.

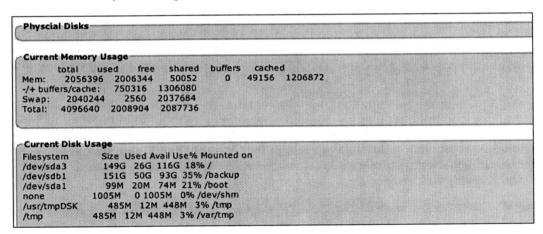

The **Physical Disks** section will display information about hard drives, CD-ROM drives, and so on that are installed on your system only if your operating system can determine that information. This typically includes the make and model of the drives as well as the size of the hard drives and what interface they are installed on.

The **Current Memory Usage** section shows you more in-depth information about memory usage on your server (including virtual memory).

Finally, the **Current Disk Usage** section shows the size and usage of every partition on your server's hard drives. This includes the file system location the total space available, the total space used, the total free space remaining, the percentage of the total available space currently being used, and the current mount point.

Viewing Disk Space Utilization and I/O Statistics

To view more in-depth and graphical information about disk space utilization, click on **Show Current Disk Usage** in the **System Health** section of WHM.

Disk Usage / Graphs

Current Disk Usage Information

	Device	Total Space	Space Used	Space Available	Percentage Used	Mounted On
	/dev/sda1	99M	20M	74M	21%	/boot
	/dev/sda3	149G	26G	116G	18%	/
	/dev/sdb1	151G	50G	93G	35%	/backup
	/tmp	485M	12M	448M	3%	/var/tmp
	/usr/tmpDSK	485M	12M	448M	3%	/tmp

IO Statistics

Device	Trans./Sec	Blocks Read/sec	Blocks Written/Sec	Total Blocks Read	Total Blocks Written
sda	16.94	419.71	245.41	228472256	133590188
sdb	6.47	556.49	707.35	302926380	385046936

In the **Current Disk Usage Information** section, you will see the same information (formatted nicely in a table) that you saw in the **Current Disk Usage** section of the **Server Information** feature mentioned earlier with the addition of simple 2D pie charts showing disk usage.

The **IO Statistics** section will display all of the hard drives installed in your server as well as some Input/Output (I/O) information including transfer, read and write speeds, and the total amount of blocks read and written.

The **IO Statistics** section will only appear if you have a compatible version of **iostat** installed on your server. Iostat is part of the **sysstat** package that you can find here: http://perso.wanadoo.fr/sebastien.godard/

Monitoring Your Server's Entire Bandwidth Usage with Bandmin

As you have learned in Chapter 5, you can keep track of an individual's bandwidth use fairly easily in WHM, but what if you want to keep an eye on a more complete picture of your server's total bandwidth usage? This is important, since most NOCs will offer you only a limited amount of bandwidth per month for use with your server. If you go over that amount, it can be quite expensive. That's why it is best to keep an eye on things regularly.

One tool WHM provides to do this is called **Bandmin**, and the link to this tool is somewhat hidden in WHM. To set up Bandmin with an administrator username and password (which you need to do before you can access it), click on the **Bandmin Password** feature in the **Service Configuration** section of WHM.

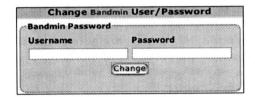

Here you can specify an administrator username and password, and click **Change** to set up the new administrator access information.

Once that is done, you can access the link to Bandmin by clicking on the word **Bandmin** in the title of the **Bandmin Password** screen. You can also link to it directly—http://your.domain.com/bandwidth/. Here your.domain.com is the server hostname or IP address.

Enter your administrator username and password, and you will be taken to the Bandmin interface. On the main screen, select a month that you want to view bandwidth logs for. This will display your server's bandwidth usage by IP address, bandwidth usage direction (incoming or outgoing), usage by day, and which domains and subdomains use each IP address. You can view bandwidth totals in megabytes, megabits, gigabytes, kilobytes, and kilobits.

Although Bandmin does not track every possible byte that could be considered for bandwidth usage by your NOC (check with them), it should be close. Note that if your NOC provides their own bandwidth monitoring tool, you should use that, as no two bandwidth monitoring tools measure what constitutes bandwidth in the same way, and this can lead to discrepancies. It is always best to use your NOCs tools, as this will provide the most accurate assessment of the bandwidth you will be charged for. If you have any questions about bandwidth usage, contact your NOC.

Make sure your clients are aware of the potential discrepancy between different bandwidth measuring tools, since the bandwidth usage reported by the various web statistics programs in cPanel will all report different values (sometimes significantly different). Your clients should watch the separate cPanel bandwidth monitoring tool also available in cPanel's web statistics processing sections if they want to know how much bandwidth they are currently using. This value is the one WHM considers when determining if a user is over his bandwidth limit or not.

Managing Services

Every cPanel server comes with a number of different services installed and running. They provide your server with the ability to serve web pages (Apache), mail (Exim and others), a name service or DNS (BIND), and other critical features needed for a public web server. Sometimes these services can misbehave, crash, or be overloaded by your users. You need a way to keep track of what is going on, and restart services or even your server itself if necessary. Thankfully, WHM is capable of watching services for you and can even automatically restart a service if it goes down.

Viewing Service Status

You can view a table full of information about the state of the various services running on your server as well as the disk space being used on your hard drive(s) by clicking on **Server Status** in the **Server Status** section of WHM. This display is the same one that your users see if they click on **Server Status** in cPanel (depending on your user's assigned cPanel theme).

cpsrvd	up	●
postgresql	up	●
named (9.2.4)	up	●
antirelayd	up	●
mailscanner	up	●
mysql (4.1.19-standard)	up	●
interchange	up	●
pop	up	●
httpd (1.3.36 (Unix))	up	●
exim (exim-4.52-7_cpanel_smtpctl_av_rewrite_mm2_mmmtrap_exiscan_md5pass)	up	●
exim-26	up	●
eximstats	up	●
syslogd	up	●
imap	up	●
ftpd	up	●
entropychat	up	●
Server Load	0.02 (4 cpus)	●
Memory Used	36.5 %	●
Swap Used	0.13 %	●
Disk sda3 (/)	18 %	●
Disk sdb1 (/backup)	35 %	●
Disk sda1 (/boot)	21 %	●

This will display every service that you've asked WHM to monitor as well as its current status and a small graphic status icon. Green means the service or usage is OK. Yellow means that the service is overloaded or nearly full. Red means that the service is down, almost completely full, or overloaded.

Server Load notes how much the CPUs are being utilized. Higher numbers mean more usage, but the scale is not a percentage. Low-end servers may become unresponsive with load levels as low as 4 to 5, while faster servers may be able to sustain load levels of 10 to 12 without slowing down noticeably. You set the load number, at which the load icon turns red, in the **Tweak Settings** area in WHM.

Each disk partition or mount point will show how much disk space is currently being used out of the total available. These are percentages. Anything between 80% and 89% will cause the disk space icon to turn yellow, and at 90% or more this icon will turn red.

Not all services and usage displays are updated in real
time. Disk space usage and service availability are cached,
and so they may not reflect the actual state of the service
or disk at that moment. It typically updates every few
minutes. It does this to reduce the load on the server from
lots of people accessing the server status. Server load is
always updated in near-real time.

Viewing Apache Status

If you want to know what the Apache web server is doing, click on **Apache Status** in
the **Server Status** section of WHM.

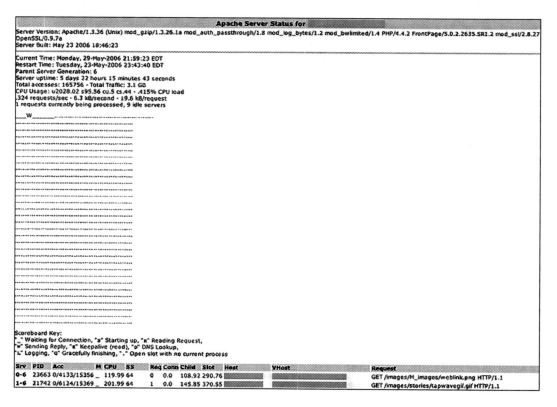

This screen provides a wealth of information about Apache and is handy to consult if
Apache is placing a heavy load on your server and you want to find out why.

At the top of this screen, you see information on the version of Apache that is running and what options were enabled when it was compiled. You can also see the date on which the server was built. Under that you see some additional information about Apache such as the last time Apache was started, how long it has been up, and how much load it is placing on your server.

The block of text under that information is known as the scoreboard. It provides a visual status of what Apache is working on at the moment. The **Scoreboard Key** at the bottom of the scoreboard lets you know what each character represents in the scoreboard. This is a great way to see how busy Apache is at a glance.

Under the scoreboard there is information on the latest 50 processes that Apache is handling. Of particular interest are the **PID, Host, Virtual Host**, and **Request**. The process ID (PID) will let you know what ID to use with the `kill` command (via root shell) if the process is hung (example: `kill -9` *processid*). The host information will let you know what IP address is making a request, the virtual host will let you know for what website on your server the request is being made, and the request information will let you know exactly what file is being requested. The path starts from the virtual host's web root (`public_html` directory).

If Apache is overloading your server and you see lots of connections to a single website on your server, you know where to focus your attentions.

The Service Manager

You can control which services appear in the **Server Status** list and you can control which services are active in the **Service Manager** in the **Service Configuration** section of WHM.

Each entry in the **Service Manager** lists the name of the service and usually a short description of most services. There are two checkboxes next to each service listed in the **Service Manager**. The first checkbox, **Enabled**, allows you to turn the service off completely by unchecking it. The second checkbox, **Monitor**, controls whether WHM and cPanel report the service as being down and send you a notice (depending on your preferences in the **Contact Manager** in WHM) when it goes down and WHM attempts to restart it automatically. If you uncheck **Monitor**, the service will still be restarted if it goes down (assuming it is enabled), but you won't be notified, and that service will not appear in the **Server Status** list. Click the **Save** button to save changes and restart **chkservd**, the cPanel service checking daemon that watches services to see if they go down and restarts them if needed.

If you enable Exim on another port, be sure to enter which port you want to use in the text box. This will allow users whose ISPs block port 25 to still be able to send mail (using the alternative SMTP port). Don't forget to also open this port in your firewall if you are using one on your server.

Not all services are listed in the **Service Manager** only those that cPanel and WHM require as well as a few third-party add-ons that add themselves to the list.

Restarting Services Manually

There will come a time when you may need to restart a service, perhaps because you've made a configuration change and you want to make sure the service starts using it right away, or because WHM is unable to restart a service that is down.

You can restart most common services from WHM's **Restart Services** section. It contains links to restart Apache, DNS (BIND), FTP (ProFTP or PureFTP), Apache, Interchange, Tomcat (if you have it installed), Exim (SMTP), POP3 (cppop), IMAP (uwimap or Courier), MySQL, PostgreSQL (if installed), and SSH (OpenSSH). Select the service you wish to restart, confirm your choice by clicking on the **Yes** button, and WHM will immediately try to shutdown and restart the service. The results will be displayed on screen. If it restarts fine, you will see confirmation of that. If the service cannot be restarted, you will be told that the service has failed to restart. If so, then you will need to investigate why the service won't restart and fix the problem.

If you'd rather restart the services from the root shell, then you can always execute the `restartsrv` script that WHM provides for that purpose. See Appendix A (http://www.packtpub.com/web_host_manager/book) for information about /scripts/restartsrv and how to use it to restart various services.

If you have any problems getting services to restart, contact your NOC for assistance.

Restarting Your Server

There may also come a time when you need to restart your entire server. Hopefully this is a rare occasion (perhaps you've installed a new kernel and need to restart the server to load it).

 Remember that whenever possible, you should give users plenty of warning before restarting your server, and you should try to schedule the restart during a period when your server isn't being used as much (perhaps late night over a weekend). Every restart will result in downtime. If there is a problem during the restart process and your server doesn't come back up, you will need to contact your NOC for assistance, as only they physically have access to your server and can check it to see what the issue is. This can take time, so do your best to minimize restarts.

If you can access WHM, it offers two different methods of restarting your server; a normal "graceful" method (similar to you telling your own computer to restart), and a "forceful" restart (similar to you turning your computer off and back on again). The graceful restart method allows your server time to shut down all processes normally before restarting. The forceful method immediately kills all processes and forces the server to restart. You risk file corruption or other problems if you forcefully restart your server; so you should choose the graceful method over the forceful method.

As with restarting services, click the type of server restart you want from WHM's **Restart Server** section, and then confirm your choice. The screen will clear, the page will stop loading, and your server should restart itself shortly thereafter. WHM will not respond to requests until the server is back online, and cPanel and WHM have restarted themselves. How long this takes depends on your server and the number of services that need to start. You should expect downtime to be at least five minutes and in some cases as much as 20 minutes. If your server does not come back online and you can't get in via SSH, then contact your NOC for assistance.

Managing Processes

You're not just limited to monitoring basic information about the services running on your server; you can also watch and manage the individual processes that are running on your server.

Displaying Current Running Processes

WHM has the ability to generate a simple text list of all of the currently running processes. To view it, click on **Show Current Running Processes** in the **System Health** section of WHM.

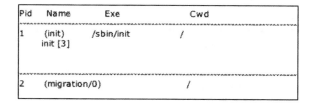

The display will show you the process ID (PID) and system name for the process that is running as well as what executable file is being run for this process and the Current Working Directory (CWD) that the process is working in. Most of the time, the CWD will be / (the root of your server). This display is only for information purposes. You cannot work with the processes listed directly from this feature.

Working with Processes on the Server

If you want to be able to trace or kill processes in WHM, you need to access **Show Current CPU Usage** in WHM.

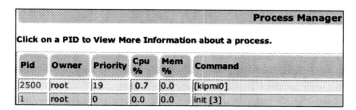

The list of processes might take some time to generate, so be patient. Once the list is displayed on screen, you will be able to see the process ID (PID) of the running process, which user owns that process, the priority the process is running at, the amount of CPU and memory resources the process is using, and the actual command being run. The list is sorted by the amount of resources each process uses. What makes this list different from the **Show Current Running Processes** feature is that you can click on the process ID number to get more information about the process, and take certain actions on it.

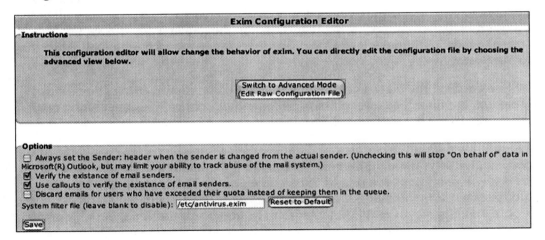

Process	entropychat
Owner	nobody
PID	4707
CPU %	0.
MEM %	0
Trace Process	Trace
Kill Process	Kill
Kill All Processes owned by nobody	Kill

If you click **Trace** the trace will be displayed in a new window in near-real time. The display will continue until the process ends or you close the window.

You can also kill the process itself, every process owned by the same user or all processes of this type. Be careful what processes you kill, or you may cause stability issues for your server.

Managing Mail

Since every cPanel server also handles mail for the domains on that server (unless you've set up a custom solution), WHM includes a number of tools that help you manage mail.

Exim Configuration Editor

Instructions

This configuration editor will allow change the behavior of exim. You can directly edit the configuration file by choosing the advanced view below.

Switch to Advanced Mode
(Edit Raw Configuration File)

Options

☐ Always set the Sender: header when the sender is changed from the actual sender. (Unchecking this will stop "On behalf of" data in Microsoft(R) Outlook, but may limit your ability to track abuse of the mail system.)
☑ Verify the existance of email senders.
☑ Use callouts to verify the existance of email senders.
☐ Discard emails for users who have exceeded their quota instead of keeping them in the queue.

System filter file (leave blank to disable): /etc/antivirus.exim [Reset to Default]

[Save]

Managing Exim Configuration

Click on the **Exim Configuration Editor** in the **Server Configuration** section of WHM to manage the settings of Exim. Exim is a **Message Transfer Agent (MTA)** that handles all incoming and outgoing mail as well as manages SMTP service.

On the main screen, you can set a few basic options or switch to the advanced configuration editor. The options you can enable or disable on this screen are:

Always set the sender: This feature is disabled by default. If you enable this feature, it will change the header to always match the actual sender. Mail programs like Microsoft Outlook allow users to send mail on behalf of other users (for example, an assistant sending mail for the boss). If you enable this feature, users won't be able to do this, and the mail sent will actually reflect the real sender. This will make it easier for you to determine who sent mail if you are looking for a spammer.

Verify the existence of e-mail senders: This feature is enabled by default. If this feature is enabled, any time someone tries to send mail through your server via SMTP, Exim will check to make sure it is being sent from a domain actually on your server. If the sender does not exist on the server, Exim won't permit the e-mail to be sent. This feature helps to limit e-mail sender spoofing.

Use callouts: This feature is enabled by default. Exim will use callouts to make sure that a sender from a remote system actually exists before delivering mail to the recipient.

Discard e-mail for users over quota: This feature is disabled by default. Normally, Exim will store incoming mail in the mail queue for any user over his mail quota limit until the user clears some room in his mailbox or the message expires from the mail queue. With this feature enabled, any mail for a user who is over his mail quota will be immediately deleted rather than stored in the mail queue. This will help stop the mail queue getting overloaded, but users won't get any incoming mail while they are over quota.

The **System filter file** allows you to filter mail based on certain criteria you set up. By default, the filter file is set to a basic set of antivirus rules. This filter won't catch many viruses, but it won't hurt either.

The real power lies in the advanced Exim configuration editor. Here you can edit the configuration as you see fit. Every section of the Exim configuration file has an open text box where you can edit or add things. Exim can be very sensitive to incorrect edits; so make sure the changes you make are valid. The advantage of making edits to Exim's configuration in WHM rather than trying to edit the /etc/exim.conf file directly is that any changes you make will be preserved even if a new version of Exim is installed.

Chapter 8

To learn more about Exim and how to edit the Exim configuration file, visit http://exim.org/.

Don't try to make changes to your Exim configuration unless you know exactly what you are doing and why you need to do it! You might stop mail from being delivered to or sent from your server if you make a mistake.

The Mail Queue Manager

Mail that has not yet been processed, and mail that cannot be delivered yet, goes into the mail queue. The mail queue is a directory or directories on your server where mail files get stored while they are waiting for final processing. You can view the mail queue by clicking on the **Mail Queue Manager** feature in the **Email** section of WHM.

Exim Mail Queue				
Delete all messages in Queue | Attempt to Deliver all messages in Queue				
Loading.....				
There are currently 1 messages in the mail queue.				
1FI6NG-0007oc-D7	1.3K	8h	Delete	Deliver Now
mlambourne@gratte.com				

If you have more than one thousand messages in the mail queue when you access the **Mail Queue Manager**, then you will see a warning at the top asking you if you want to view all those messages. Click the button to view all messages. Note that this can take a while to display; so be patient. If you have less than one thousand messages, the messages will just be displayed on screen immediately.

You will be able to see the person the message is being sent to, the message ID number (which will allow you to find the message on your server if you want to do so), the size of the message how long the message has been in the mail queue, and you will have the option of attempting to deliver or delete individual messages or every message in the queue.

You can also click on the message ID number and see the content of the message (the raw mail file content). From the mail file view you can also attempt to deliver or delete the message.

If you attempt to deliver or delete mail from the queue, WHM will show you the progress including any error messages.

Mail Statistics

If you'd rather learn more about what your mail server has been doing this past 24 hours, then you will want to check out the **View Mail Statistics** feature in WHM.

```
                        Mail Delivery Stats
Generating Stats, please wait (this could take a minute)..... . . . . . . .


Exim statistics from 2006-05-28 04:04:53 to 2006-05-30 19:40:44

Grand total summary
~~~~~~~~~~~~~~~~~~~
                                   At least one address
    TOTAL          Volume   Messages    Hosts    Delayed       Failed
    Received        57MB      2628       1033    10  0.4%     2  0.1%
    Delivered       59MB      1440        51

Deliveries by transport
~~~~~~~~~~~~~~~~~~~~~~~~
                   Volume   Messages
    boxtrapper_autowhitelist   11MB       289
    mailman_virtual_transport  10KB         3
    remote_smtp        10MB      190
    virtual_address_pipe   14KB        6
    virtual_userdelivery  38MB       952

Messages received per hour (each dot is 3 messages)
~~~~~~~~~~~~~~~~~~~~~~~~~~~~~~~~~~~~~~~~~~~~~~~~~~~~~~~~~

00-01    53 ...............
01-02    85 ............................
```

Here you will see a variety of different statistics, including the volume of mail sent and received, the type of mail sent, how many messages were sent every hour, how long a mail took to process, which messages were relayed lately, top 50 senders and receivers by a variety of metrics, and the number and type of errors encountered by the mail server.

Mail Relayers

The MTA (in this case Exim) handles transferring mail to and from your server. Exim should only permit relaying (transferring of mail) to or from valid domains handled by your server. WHM automatically configures Exim to do just that, but using the **View Relayers** feature will allow you to check to see if someone is trying to bypass that protection (to send spam, for example).

If you want to see the mail that has been relayed on your server and who sent them, use the **View Relayers** feature.

		Top Email Relayers	
Below are list of users who have relayed mail. They are listed in the order by number of messages sent. You can click on the user/domain to view who they sent the messages to.			

User	Domain	Messages Sent	Total Bytes Sent
cpanel		72	6665239
nobody		24	115439
root		7	23051
ceriplex	ceriplex.com	1	3978

This will show you a table listing all of the relayers that have sent mail on your server lately. This will include the server itself (root, cPanel) and scripts (**nobody** if you don't have phpsuexec and suexec enabled, and **sending mail as nobody** disabled in **Tweak Settings**) as well as users from domains on your server.

If you click on the user or domain in the table, you will be taken to another table listing all of the messages that user or domain relayed. The information will include the time sent, message ID, sender, recipient, and the size of the message in bytes. This can help you track down a spammer if they are using your server to send mail.

Repairing Mail File Permissions

Mail is stored on the server in a file or series of files inside special directories. These files need to be set to certain owners and permissions. Sometimes, when mail is checked, the ownership or permissions of files get improperly changed. Most of the time this won't cause problems, but sometimes it can cause problems when delivering or trying to send mail.

If you are having problems, click on **Repair Mailbox Permissions** in WHM. This will check all mail files and make sure that they are set up properly. If there are problems, then the problems will be repaired by this feature if possible. Although you shouldn't have to use this very often, it is safe enough to use regularly should you need to do so.

Mail Tracing

If you want to see the path a message takes to be delivered to a remote e-mail account so that you can see if there are problems with your mail setup or perhaps with the remote account, use the **Mail Troubleshooter** feature.

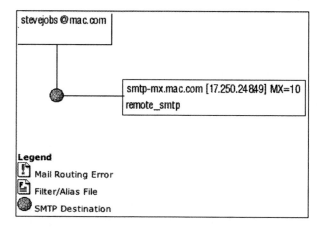

Type in an e-mail address, and a map will be displayed showing where the mail goes from your server. This can help you identify mail-configuration or mail-routing problems.

Managing Security

The data on your server is important to both you and your clients. You need to keep that data out of the hands of those people who desire to steal or destroy it. WHM does include a number of security-related features.

Although the security features in WHM are quite handy, true server security can only be achieved by careful server monitoring on your part as well as utilizing other tools as techniques to keep your server safe.

This book cannot go into depth on server security, so I recommend that you take time to learn more about server security. There have been hundreds of books written on the topic, and there are lots of websites that discuss security. See Appendix B (http://www.packtpub.com/web_host_manager/book) for links to popular security-related websites and tools.

Managing Wheel Group Users

Any user who is placed in the "wheel" group has the ability to attempt to log into the server as a superuser (root). Of course the user will still need SSH access and will need to know the root password, but it is still best to be careful which users you permit in the wheel group. To manage users in the wheel group from WHM, click on **Manage Wheel Group Users** in the **Security** section.

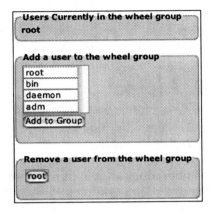

At the top is a list of all the users on the server. You can select any one and click **Add to Group,** and the user will be able to use the su command if he has shell access, and if he has the root password for the server.

In the last section, you will see a button with the username of every user currently in the wheel group (typically only root). If you click on a button, that user will be removed from the wheel group.

Shell Fork Bomb and Memory Overload Protection

In some cases, it may be possible for an unscrupulous user to overload your server if they have shell access. WHM can limit how much resources a shell session can use so that it is harder for a user to disable your server. To use this feature, click on **Shell Fork Bomb Protection** in the **Security** section of WHM.

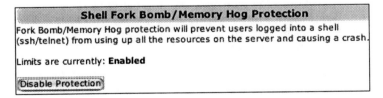

Click **Enable Protection** to enable the protection or click **Disable Protection** to disable the protection.

The Tweak Security Feature

WHM groups several security-related features into the **Tweak Security** feature in the **Security** section. Clicking on **Tweak Security** will allow you to manage the **open_basedir** and **mod_userdir** restrictions as well as restrict compiler access, disable the traceroute command, and restrict the processes that can send mail using SMTP.

PHP open_basedir Protection

Without **open_basedir** protection, PHP can access directories and files that are outside the account's home directory. This includes libraries or binaries stored centrally on your server (like NetPBM or ImageMagick). This can save users some disk space and hassle, since they will be able to use a single installation that you've installed on your server. However, this can also be a security risk, since PHP scripts may be able to access certain files or directories that they shouldn't. With **open_basedir** activated, PHP scripts will only be able to access files and directories in the home directory or web root of the account where the script is run from. **open_basedir** protection is turned off by default. To enable PHP's **open_basedir** protection, click on **Configure** under the **Php open_basedir Tweak** section.

---
php open_basedir Protection

Php's open_basedir protection prevents users from opening files outside of their home directory with php.
☐ Enable php open_basedir Protection.

Host   **Exclude Protection**

                                             ☐

You will see a list of all of the domains on your server. Check the first box at the top of the screen to enable PHP's **open_basedir** protection. You can exclude certain domains from this protection (trusted domains) by clicking on the checkbox in the **Exclude Protection** column next to that domain. When you have finished, click on **Save** at the bottom of the screen to apply your changes.

cPanel Inc.'s implementation of this feature has always been buggy, so you may have odd issues with scripts if you turn this feature on. Furthermore, there is no interface in WHM to control which directories are excluded from the open_basedir protection.

Mod_Userdir Protection

When you are adding new accounts on your server, you probably will want to leave **mod_userdir** protection off, since with it off users will be able to access their domains on the web before they propagate to your server, using the server's main

IP address or hostname followed by a tilde (~) and the user's cPanel username. For example, if you add the account domain2.com to your server with the cPanel username dom2, then the user will be able to access any files they place in their web root by visiting http://your.serverhostname.com/~dom2/file.html. This will allow them to view pages as they are getting their site set up before the domain itself starts reporting your server's nameservers.

However, there is a problem with this feature that fortunately not too many users know about, and it has to do with bandwidth. For example, let's pretend your server has two domains on it, domain1.com with the cPanel username dom1, and domain2.com with the username dom2. With mod_userdir protection off, both users can access their files with .../~dom#/file.html, but it is possible for domain1.com to steal bandwidth from domain2.com or vice versa if their domain currently resolves to your server. To steal domain2.com's bandwidth domain1.com only needs to use a URL like this: http://domain2.com/~dom1/dom1LargeFile.mov. Because domain2.com is used as the domain in the URL, but the file is coming from domain1.com's account (thanks to the ~dom1/ part of the URL), WHM will be tricked into thinking that this file (that is actually in domain1.com's account) is really in domain2.com's account, and the bandwidth for downloading that file will be counted against domain2.com instead of domain1.com as it should.

Finding someone who is stealing bandwidth in this way is easy once the domain logs have been processed, since the URL to the file will clearly show that it is coming from ~dom1/, and you can take action. However, you can't take away bandwidth usage from users on your domain once it is counted, all you can do is increase the total bandwidth limit for the customer by an appropriate amount to make up for the lost bandwidth (and suspended the offending account, of course). Still, this can cause problems if a user doesn't realize that the bandwidth stealing is happening and doesn't look at the web statistics for his domain.

For this reason, once you are finished adding new accounts to a server, you should enable **mod_userdir** protection to stop people from being able to steal bandwidth from other accounts.

Click on **Configure** in the **mod_userdir Protection** feature, and enable it by checking the first checkbox at the top of the screen; then you can enable or disable protection for individual accounts by clicking on the **Exclude Protection** checkbox next to each domain. Further, you can allow certain cPanel users to bypass the **mod_userdir** protection for certain domains by typing the cPanel username of the user in the text box next to the domain you wish to allow access to. Finally, click **Save** to save the changes you've made.

> If you offer shared SSL to users (so they can use a certificate you've purchased for your server itself to secure their own content), then you will want to make sure **DefaultHost** (nobody) is excluded, as well as the domain where the shared SSL certificate to be used is installed. Just remember that anyone using the shared SSL certificate will have that bandwidth charged to your shared SSL account, and not to themselves.

Restricting Access to the System Compilers

Even if you permit some of your users to access your server via SSH, you generally should not permit them to access the compilers (like GCC) on your server to compile binary programs, as this is a serious security risk.

> Generally speaking, no non-root user should have any need to compile binary files on your server. If necessary, you should offer to compile and install the file for them.

In order to restrict usage of the compilers on your server to certain accounts, click on the **Configure** link under the **Compilers Tweak** box.

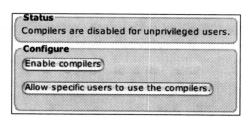

Click the **Disable Compilers** button to do just that. This will stop all users (except root) with shell access from using the compilers. If you choose to allow certain trusted users to access the compilers, click the **Allow specific users to use the compilers** button, and choose the cPanel users you want to grant access to. To disable the compiler restriction, click on the **Enable compilers** button.

Disabling or Enabling the traceroute Command

The `traceroute` command can be very useful in the root shell for diagnosing problems with connections between your server and other servers. However, it may be possible for a hacker to abuse the use of this command, so you can choose to disable the command completely. Click on **Configure** in the **Traceroute Tweak** box.

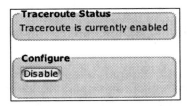

All you then have to do is click **Disable** to disable the user of the `traceroute` command, or click **Enable** to enable it.

SMTP Restriction

Many spammers will try to bypass your SMTP server to send mail (using a remote SMTP server to send mail from your server). Enabling the **SMTP Tweak** can help stop this from happening. Click on the **Configure** link in the **SMTP Tweak** box.

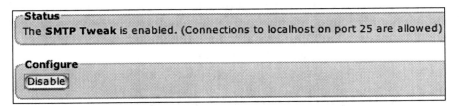

Then click the **Enable** button to stop any script or process from accessing remote SMTP servers except root, mailman, and Exim. If you want to allow connections to localhost (your own server) on port 25, then check the checkbox before clicking **Enable**. This will increase compatibility with some web scripts that attempt to send mail on your server by using a localhost (127.0.0.1) connection to port 25. Later, if you wish to disable this, just click on the **Disable** button.

Enabling or Disabling CGI SuEXEC

Normally, suEXEC is turned on for all CGI scripts. This means that Perl, Python, and other CGI scripts will run as the owner of the cPanel account. This makes tracking down problems much easier. Generally, you should leave suEXEC enabled. If it is causing problems, however, you can click on the **Enable/Disable SuExec** link in the **Service Configuration** section of WHM to change this setting.

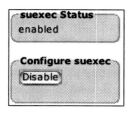

Click on **Disable** (or **Enable**), and the new setting will take effect immediately.

Remember, suEXEC (for CGI scripts) and phpsuEXEC (for PHP scripts) perform the same basic feature for CGI or PHP scripts; however, enabling or disabling one of these does not affect the other. SuEXEC is enabled by default, while phpsuEXEC is disabled by default.

Fixing Non-Secure CGI Script Permissions

WHM automatically scans your home directories looking for CGI files that have insecure permissions after every cPanel update check. However, you can run this check yourself at any time by clicking on the **Fix Insecure Permissions (Scripts)** item in the **Security** section of WHM. This will initiate the scan, and report any problems found. If some issue is found, the insecure settings will be changed to something more secure. You may want to run this feature more than once if it does find an insecure script to make sure that it has caught everything.

The Background Process Killer

WHM has the ability to search for common scripts that are often used but not permitted to be used by most hosts (like IRC-related scripts and compiled services or daemons). To enable this feature click on the **Background Process Killer** item in the **Server Health** section of WHM.

Background Process Killer

You can setup WHM to kill any of the following processes and send you an email when it find one of them. Some malicious users will choose to run an irc bouncer on their shell account even though this may be against your policy. Some of the really sneaky ones will rename their bouncer to something like 'pine' so the admin just believes that the user is just reading their mail. WHM can detect they are running an irc bouncer even if they rename it to something that looks non-malicous. Please check off any of the programs you do not want running on your server (we recommend that you check off all of the programs below as letting your users run irc bots and servers usually leads to denial of service attacks).

- ☑ BitchX
- ☑ bnc
- ☑ eggdrop
- ☑ generic-sniffers
- ☑ guardservices
- ☑ ircd
- ☑ psyBNC
- ☑ ptlink
- ☑ services

Trusted Users (optional, place a list of users that you want the process killer to ignore, one per line, in textbox below. root,mysql,named,cpanel and anyuser with a uid lower than 99 are already consider trusted and do not need to be added.):

Save

Here you can enable searches for commonly outlawed types of scripts or services by checking the box next to each listed item. If you want to permit certain trusted users to use these outlawed scripts or daemons, be sure to enter their cPanel username, one per line in the text box in the second section of this screen. Click **Save** to enable the changes you've made.

WHM will periodically scan for these scripts or processes, disable them if it finds them, and report the issue to you so you can take action.

This is a great idea, but unfortunately this feature doesn't work well. It often misses obvious processes or scripts that it should catch. However, when it does find something and reports it to you, it can be very helpful. Do not think that this will replace diligent monitoring done by you, though. Always check for violations regularly.

Scanning for Trojan Horses

Sadly, the **Scan for Trojan Horses** feature in the **Security** section of WHM is almost completely worthless unless you know exactly what you are looking for. Nominally, this feature offers to scan your server looking for potentially dangerous files that a hacker may have installed on your server. In practice, however, it reports so many false positives as to be completely useless. For example, on a clean, brand new cPanel server, this feature found over 350 different files that it thought might be a problem. (They were standard operating system files, not hacked at all.) This is one feature which is probably best to ignore.

Shutting Down Unneeded Services

Since the hardware you are using is designed for use as a web server, there are many services that are installed and active on normal desktop computers that may not be needed in a server environment like the **Common Unix Printing System (CUPS)**, which are printer drivers for Linux/Unix servers, (To find out more about CUPS, visit http://www.cups.org/.) To shut down any services that WHM feels are not needed, click on **Quick Security Scan** in the **Security** section of WHM. This will look for services that do not need to be enabled on a server and will try to shut them down. Any services it lists with a result of **[FAILED]** means that those services were not running (and so could not be shut down). If you see the word **done** next to a service, that one was running and WHM shut it down.

For security reasons, it is best to shut down any unneeded services, and remove unneeded software. After all, a hacker cannot exploit something that isn't available on your server.

Summary

In this chapter, you've discovered ways to keep an eye on what is happening on your server. This includes monitoring and restarting services, watching processes on your server to avoid abuse by users and other bottlenecks, monitoring mail, and improving security on your server.

In Chapter 9, we will look at some of the ways you can customize your server the features you offer your clients via the use of cPanel and WHM themes, and other third-party add-ons that work with WHM and cPanel. The chapter is worth reading, especially if you are interested in distinguishing your services from those of your competition.

9

Customizing your Server with Themes and Add-Ons

There is a lot of hosting competition out there, including many who use cPanel. You have to make your service stand out if you want to attract a lot of business. One way to do that is to customize the service you offer by using different cPanel and WHM themes, and adding new features to your hosting service through add-on modules and third-party products designed to work with cPanel servers. In this chapter, we're going to take a closer look at the features that WHM offers to make this customization possible, including:

- Adding, cloning, and deleting cPanel themes
- Working with different cPanel themes
- Adding, cloning, and deleting WHM themes
- Working with different WHM themes
- Adding, cloning, editing, and deleting cPanel language files
- Setting additional language configuration options
- Installing and managing add-on scripts
- Working with cPanel Inc.'s own add-on modules
- Looking at a selection of third-party add-ons

By the end of the chapter, you will be intimately familiar with all of the options you have to set your hosting business apart from others.

Working with cPanel Themes

It is possible to change the look of your client's cPanel accounts through the use of cPanel themes. cPanel comes with a few themes (which are just variations on a single theme), and you can install at least two more for free right from WHM. All the features that WHM offers for working with cPanel themes are in the **Themes** section of WHM.

Installing and Removing Other Free cPanel Themes from cPanel

To install the other free cPanel themes that cPanel Inc. maintains, click on **Addon cPanel Themes** in WHM. Currently, you have two choices.

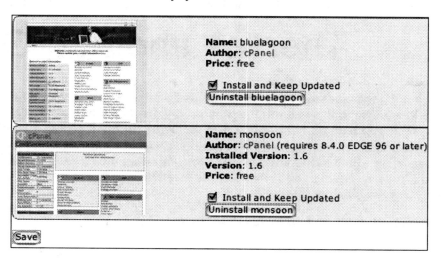

Check the box next to each one you want to install, and click the **Save** button. The themes you have chosen will be installed. If you later decide to uninstall these extra themes, click on the **Uninstall bluelagoon** or **Uninstall monsoon** button and the theme will be removed.

 Accounts assigned to themes that have been removed will revert to the standard "x" **XSkin** theme.

Installing a Third-Party cPanel Theme

To install a third-party theme, you should follow the directions that the theme developer provides, as many of them use shell commands rather than downloadable theme files to install their themes.

```
Cpanel theme tarballs should have a directory structure similar to the one shown below

  theme.cptheme
  |
  \----logout.html
  |
  \----index.html
  |
  \----images
  |   |
  |   \-----webmail.jpg
  |   |
  |   \-----passwd.jpg
  |   |
  |   \-----edit.jpg
  |   |
  |   \-----delete.jpg
  |
  \-----ETC

Theme Tar Ball: [              ]  ( Browse... ) (Upload)
```

However, if you have a cPanel theme file (which usually ends in .cptheme, or .tar. gz, or .tgz) and you want to use WHM to install the file, click on **Install a New cPanel Theme**. Click **Browse…** to find the file on your computer, and click **Upload** to upload it to your server. WHM will check to make sure it is a valid cPanel theme, and then proceed to install it.

Listing Currently Installed cPanel Themes

Clicking on **List Installed cPanel Themes** will list all installed cPanel themes (by their directory name as found in /usr/local/cpanel/base/frontend/), so you can print the list or copy it.

Cloning an Installed cPanel Theme

If you want to make a copy of a theme on your server so you can edit it without having to modify or remove the original, you will want to clone the cPanel theme. Click on **Clone a cPanel Theme**, and choose the theme to clone. The theme will be given a different name, and a copy will be made of it; then you can feel free to edit it or study it without affecting the original theme.

Downloading Installed cPanel Themes

To download a cPanel theme file from your server, click on **Download a cPanel Themeball** in WHM, and then click on the name of the theme you wish to download and the file download will begin. You can use this feature to back up your installed themes or move a theme from one server to another.

Removing cPanel Themes from Your Server

You can remove an installed theme by clicking on **Delete a cPanel Theme** in WHM. Then click the name of the theme you want to delete.

Remember, not all theme designers want you to install their themes using a theme file. Follow the proper directions from the theme designer for installing, backing up, and removing their theme. Some third-party themes require files in other locations, so using WHM may not properly install, copy, or remove that theme.

Do not delete the "x" XSkin theme, as cPanel requires this theme even if no accounts use it.

The XSkin Migration Tool

cPanel Inc. used to offer several other themes with older versions of cPanel. However, they were depreciated once the XSkin theme became the default. cPanel Inc. has provided a tool to automatically move accounts and packages from old style themes (like **default** and **Vertex**). Click on **x Skin Migration Wizard** to use it.

WHM will look for any accounts and packages that are currently set to use any depreciated theme and inform you which ones are currently using such themes. To switch users or packages to the default "x" XSkin or **Xmail** theme, click on the appropriate button and the changes will be made immediately.

This tool will only switch users to the default XSkin themes; you cannot use it to switch users to some other theme. All new cPanel servers do not come with these depreciated themes, and so it is likely that this feature will be of no use to you if you have a new server.

cPanel Themes Gallery

There are many available cPanel themes: some are free and others are available for a fee from third-party theme designers. To make you aware of what sort of themes are available and what their key differences are, we will examine most of the publicly available themes.

While I've tried to make sure this list is complete, there may be some new or obscure themes I may have missed. cPanel themes that do not have any support and do not work with modern versions of cPanel are not in this list.

cPanel's Other Themes

Although cPanel's default theme is "x", it isn't the only theme cPanel offers for free. These themes are not updated as often as "x", but allow hosts some different choices without forcing them to pay a third party.

Blue Lagoon

Blue Lagoon looks similar to the various XSkin themes except that it uses fewer graphics and so will load faster than XSkin. It supports cPanel Pro and many third-party add-ons.

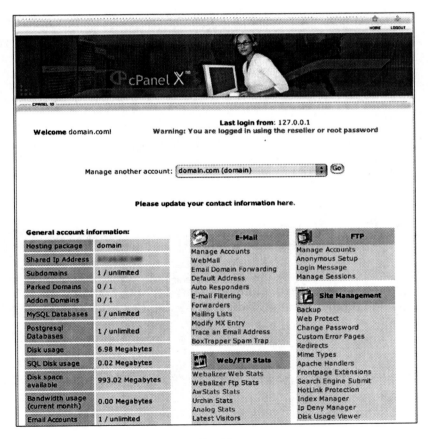

Each major section of features has a single graphic followed by a plain text link to each feature. The header of this theme was used by "x" for a while. Blue Lagoon has been around for many years, though it used to look much different. For a time, after Monsoon was created, cPanel Inc. considered discontinuing Blue Lagoon, but thanks in part to customer demand, decided retain it.

Monsoon

Monsoon is another theme that is light on graphics. It is a fairly new theme (only supporting cPanel 8.4.0E96 or later) and incorporates some of the look of the old-style Blue Lagoon theme along with modern cPanel features.

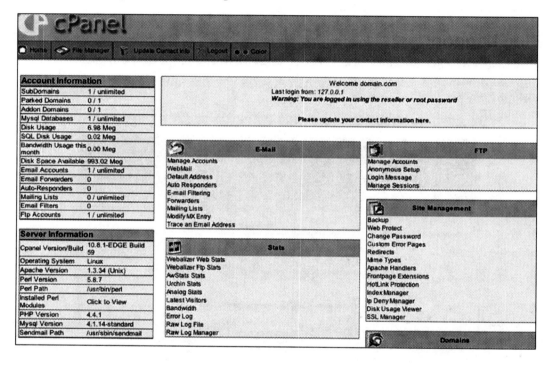

Monsoon supports cPanel Pro and many third-party add-ons. It also comes in two colors: blue (which is more gray than blue) and red (which is more pink than red). Clicking on one of the colors in the header allows the user to switch between them at will.

Xmail

Xmail is a theme based on "x" except that it only offers the user e-mail-related features.

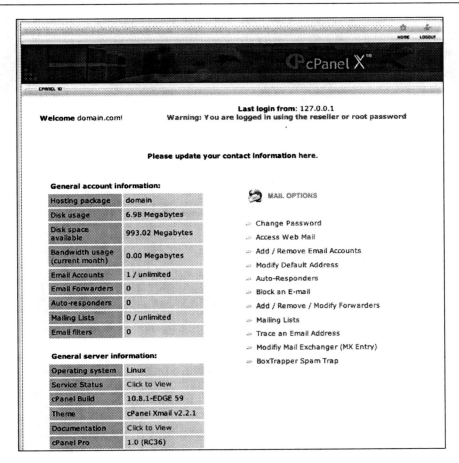

Xmail does not support cPanel Pro nor any third-party add-ons. You do have the ability to access all e-mail-related features, though, including forwarders, webmail, auto-responders, etc.

X2

X2 is an alternative form of cPanel's standard "x" XSkin theme. It looks almost exactly the same as "x."

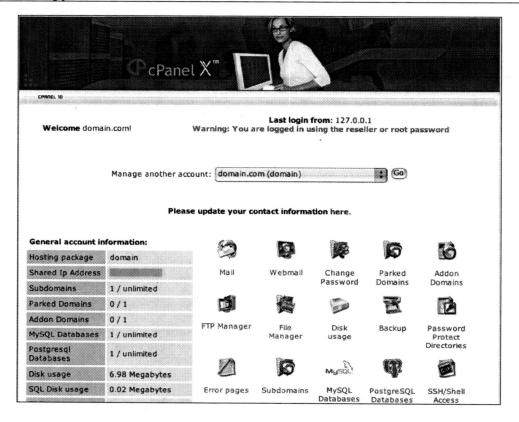

X2 does support cPanel Pro and many third-party add-ons. X2 removes some information from the standard "x" theme that some web hosts don't like to offer to clients.

Third-Party Themes

Since cPanel Inc. does not provide many themes with cPanel, and since themes are not easy for web hosts to create, many other companies have stepped in to provide themes that not only change the look of cPanel, but in some cases also add new features not available in cPanel's own themes. What follows is a discussion of all of the actively supported themes that I have been able to find, listed in alphabetical order. There may be others, and your web host may have created their own theme.

7Dana

Publisher: 7dana (http://www.7dana.com/)
Supports: cPanel Pro
Special Features: Sidebar with collapsible tree of links to cPanel features. .

7Dana is a free cPanel theme that was released on cPanel.net's support forum.

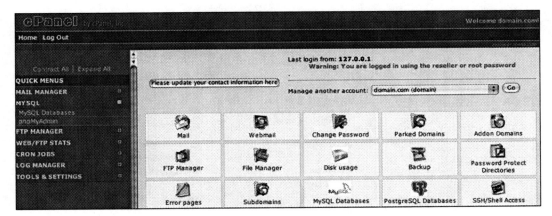

This theme has a center bank of icons like "x". Information about your account appears at the bottom of the screen.

Ace

Publisher: CPSkins (http://www.cpskins.com/)
Supports: cPanel Pro, some third-party add-ons
Special Features: Theme changer (CPSkins themes only), fast loading, multiple languages

Ace is a clean, primarily white theme with few graphics (except the header).

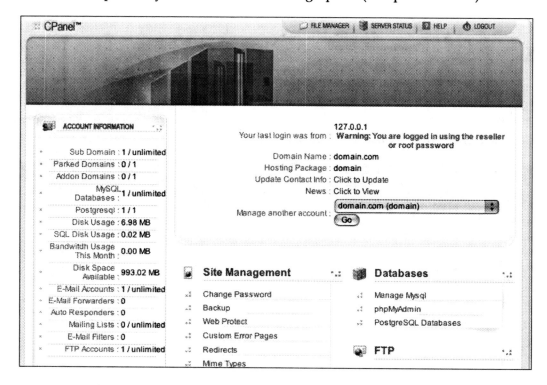

As with most CPSkins themes, your web host can enable a theme switcher that will allow you to choose another CPSkins theme.

BlueCrush

Publisher: CPSkins (http://www.cpskins.com/)

Supports: cPanel Pro, some third-party add-ons

Special Features: Theme changer (CPSkins themes only), fast loading, multiple languages

This is one of the few dark cPanel themes available.

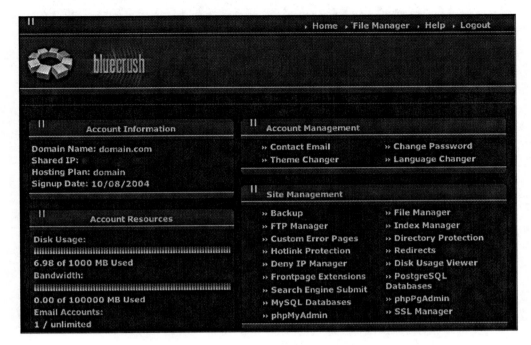

It doesn't have a lot of graphics, and supports the CPSkins theme changer.

CoolBreeze

Publisher: Netenberg (http://netenberg.com/)
Supports: cPanel Pro, Fantastico
Special Features: Fast loading, multiple languages

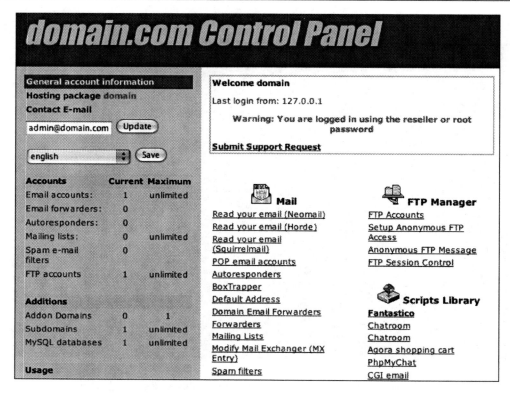

This is another theme that is designed to be quick loading and focused on providing every link and piece of information you need on one, easy-to-read screen. This theme has recently been discontinued in favor of the company's more flexible **Universina** theme (which includes the look of this theme as well as the rest of Netenberg's themes).

CPANELXP Evolution

 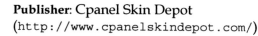

Publisher: Cpanel Skin Depot
(http://www.cpanelskindepot.com/)

Supports: cPanel Pro, some third-party add-ons

Special Features: Theme changer (CPANELXP Evolution, x, and x2 themes only), customizable by host and resellers, tool tips (optional), flash tutorial integration

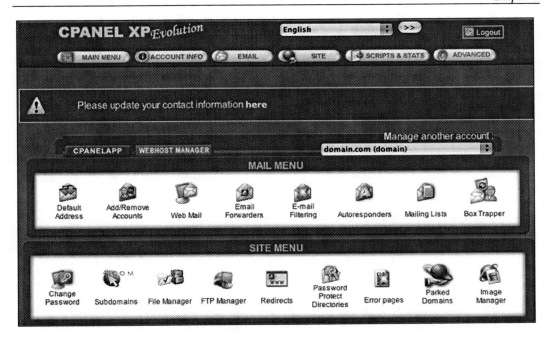

CPANELXP Evolution (Evo) is a theme that is reminiscent of the default blue theme for Microsoft Windows® XP. It also tries to extend cPanel in a number of ways. It supports a wide variety of languages, is completely customizable by web hosts and their resellers via a special web application called **CPAPP**, includes a basic help-desk feature, and integrates with a number of third-party products and scripts.

CPSkins

Publisher: CPSkins (http://www.cpskins.com/)

Supports: cPanel Pro, some third-party add-ons

Special Features: Theme changer (CPskins themes only), quick-loading, many theme colors, direct webmail login from the main screen, multiple languages

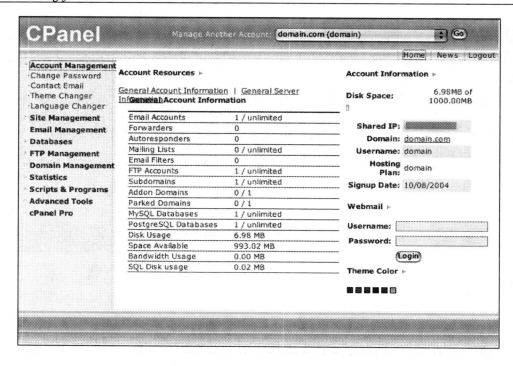

CPSkins is designed to be quick loading while allowing the user to choose from a number of different colors for the interface.

iCandy

Publisher: CPSkins (http://www.cpskins.com/)

Supports: cPanel Pro, some third-party add-ons

Special Features: Theme changer (CPSkins themes only), multiple languages

This theme is designed to look good, so it may take slightly longer to load. The icons are rather playful.

InteliSkin

Publisher: CPSkins (http://www.cpskins.com/)

Supports: cPanel Pro, some third-party add-ons

Special Features: Theme changer (CPSkins themes only), multiple languages, quick-loading

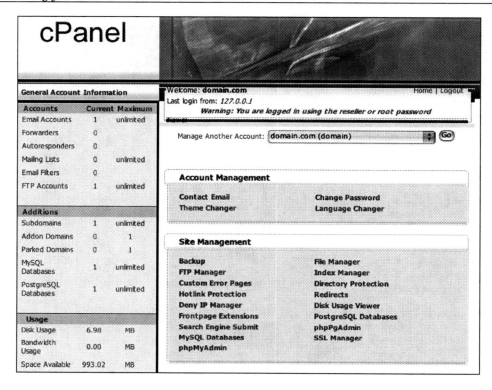

This theme is designed to be fairly quick loading and provide every link users need on a single screen.

Java

Publisher: PixelByPixel
(`http://www.pixelbypixel.com/`)
Supports: Fantastico
Special Features: Theme changer (PixelByPixel themes only)

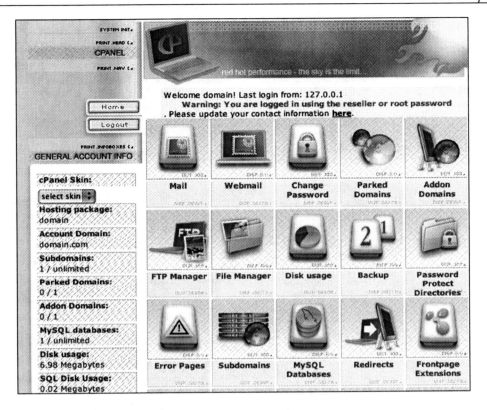

A theme designed to be very good looking. It includes a theme changer to switch between the two currently released PixelByPixel cPanel themes (**Java** and **Winterfall**).

Support may be a bit spotty for this theme. It does not support all of the modern features of cPanel at this time.

Radiance

Publisher: CPSkins (http://www.cpskins.com/)

Supports: cPanel Pro, some third-party add-ons

Special Features: Theme changer (CPSkins themes only), multiple languages, custom login screen

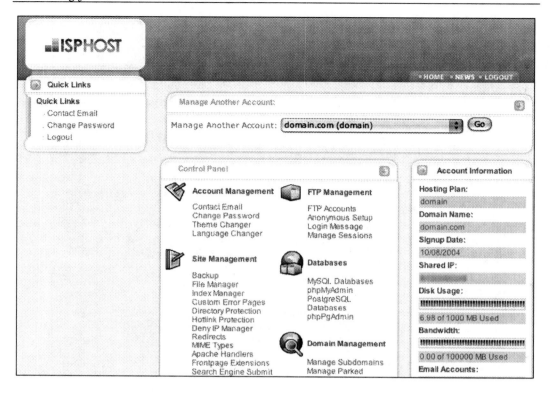

This theme is designed to make it easy to find and access all the features and information cPanel provides from a single screen. You can also install a special login screen so that cPanel's standard "please log in" screen looks like this theme.

RVSkin

Publisher: RVSkin (http://www.rvskin.com/)

Supports: cPanel Pro, all third-party add-ons that follow cPanel Pro guidelines

Special Features: Theme changer (RVSkin themes only), multiple languages, every item is customizable by both web hosts and resellers, sub-reseller feature, upsell feature, integration with nearly any item through custom pages and links, complete control over every offered feature by resellers, updated constantly to work with all recent versions of cPanel, custom themes

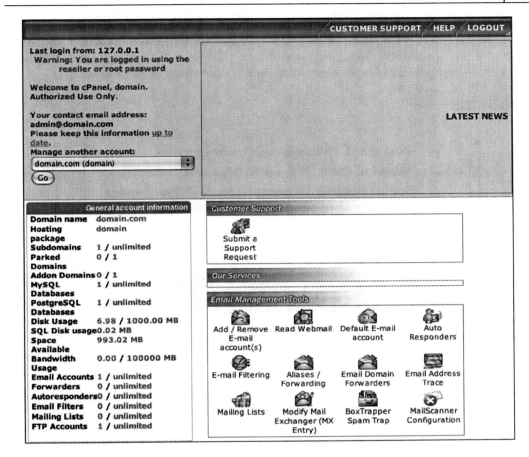

RVSkin was created to allow web hosts and resellers as much flexibility as possible, while still supporting every new feature cPanel adds via regular automated updates. RVSkin isn't just a set of themes, it is an entire cPanel management system. Resellers and server administrators love RVSkin because they can customize any feature or even add entirely new links or pages to cPanel.

RVSkin permits **upselling**. Upselling allows a web host or reseller to place links in cPanel to features that won't work until the user pays for them. RVSkin integrates with your billing software to allow a user to pay for additional features, space, bandwidth, etc., right from cPanel.

Sub-reselling allows resellers to offer basic reseller plans of their own using RVSkin. The features sub-resellers have are somewhat limited compared to the standard cPanel/WHM reseller interface, but it works as advertised.

Support for many languages is another strongpoint for RVSkin. It offers true multilingual support for almost every item in the cPanel interface. Resellers and web hosts can easily add their own languages if they wish and even post news in multiple languages (that gets displayed depending on the user's language preference).

SimSkins

Publisher: CPSkins (http://www.cpskins.com/)

Supports: cPanel Pro, some third-party add-ons

Special Features: Theme changer (CPSkins themes only), multiple languages, quick loading, many user-selectable colors

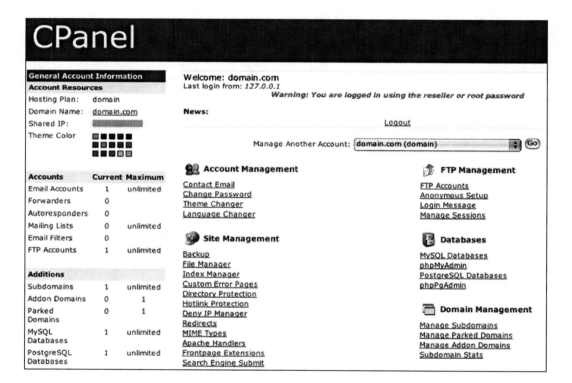

SimSkins is another largely text-only cPanel theme. It supports multiple languages, CPSkins theme changer, and even multiple theme colors.

Stainless Steel

Publisher: Netenberg (`http://netenberg.com/`)

Supports: cPanel Pro, Fantastico

Special Features: multiple languages, quick-loading

A dark-colored, quick-loading theme. This theme has recently been discontinued in favor of the company's more flexible Universina theme (which includes the look of this theme as well as the rest of Netenberg's themes).

Trix

Publisher: CPSkins (http://www.cpskins.com/)

Supports: cPanel Pro, some third-party add-ons

Special Features: Theme changer (CPSkins themes only), multiple languages, multiple colors, webmail login from main page

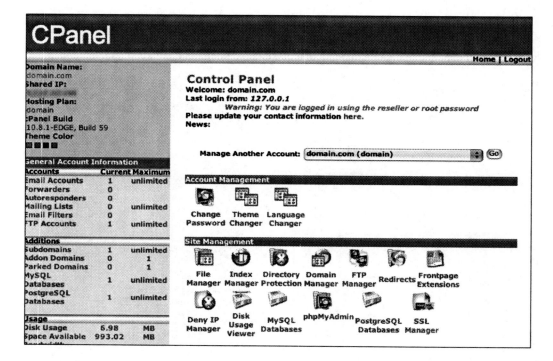

This theme is designed to be clean while still offering many graphic elements. The user can quickly switch between colors at will.

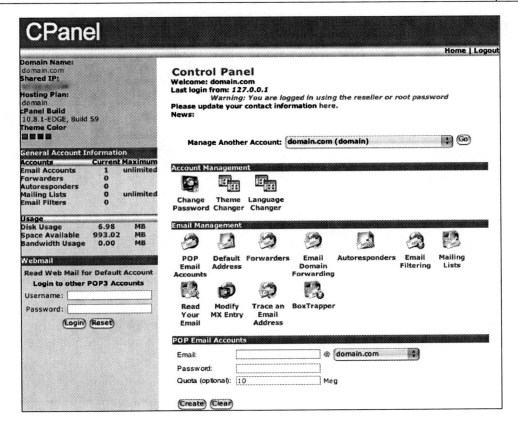

Trix also comes in an e-mail-only version for users who purchase e-mail-only plans.

Universina

Publisher: Netenberg (`http://netenberg.com/`)

Supports: Fantastico, cPanel Pro, and most third-party add-ons

Special Features: Theme changer (makes Universina look like a variety of different themes), multiple language support, create multiple accounts using a simple Comma Separated Values format (FTP, mail, databases, and more), highly customizable by both the server owner and reseller, more plain language descriptions of how features work, integrated FAQ, auto upgradeable, WHM add-on for management, favorite features function, improved feature control

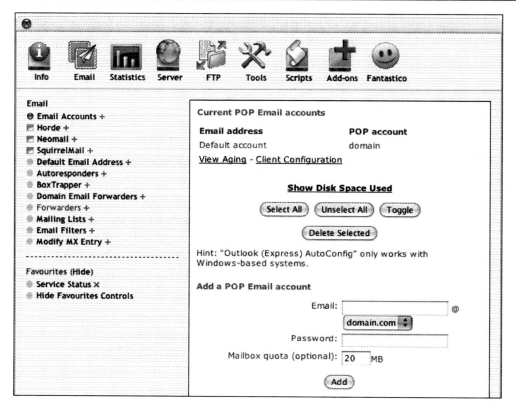

Universina is designed to be a more flexible cPanel theme than most others. It supports better language abstraction and more configuration options for users, resellers, and system administrators. By default Universina comes with themes that look like all of Netenberg's other themes (**XController**, **Coolbreeze**, and so on) as well as cPanel's own XSkin themes (several variations). However, creating new themes is designed to be fairly easy, and even resellers can customize themes and offer them to their clients.

Winterfall

Publisher: PixelByPixel
(http://www.pixelbypixel.com/)
Supports: Fantastico
Special Features: Theme changer (PixelByPixel themes only)

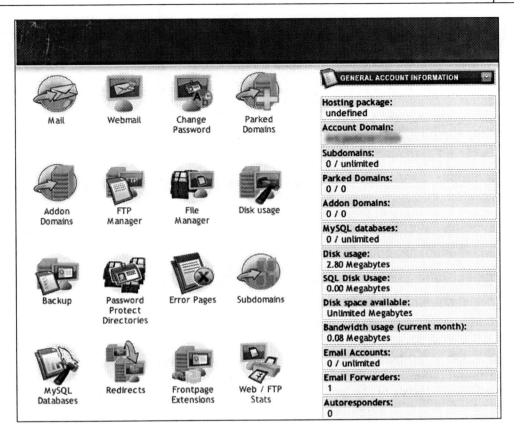

Winterfall is designed to be clean-looking but graphic-rich. Users can switch at will between the two currently released PixelByPixel cPanel themes (Java and Winterfall).

Support may be a bit spotty for this theme. It does not support all of the modern features of cPanel at this time.

XController

Publisher: Netenberg (`http://netenberg.com/`)
Supports: cPanel Pro, Fantastico
Special Features: Multiple languages

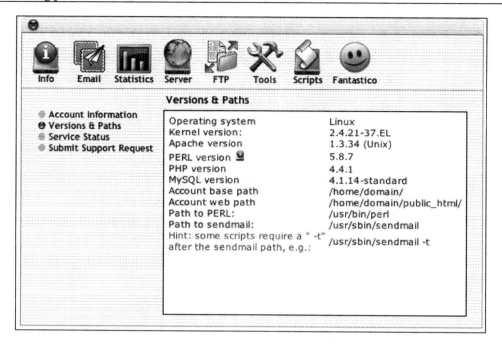

XController is designed to look similar to Mac OS X. It supports cPanel Pro features and Fantastico as well as several languages. This theme has recently been discontinued in favor of the company's more flexible Universina theme (which includes the look of this theme as well as the rest of Netenberg's themes).

ZabrinskiPoint

Publisher: Netenberg (http://netenberg.com/)
Supports: cPanel Pro, Fantastico
Special Features: Quick-loading

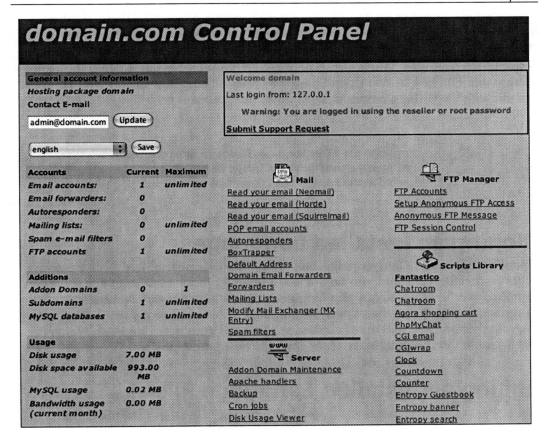

A bright, mostly text theme designed to be quick loading. It supports cPanel Pro features and Fantastico. This theme has recently been discontinued in favor of the company's more flexible Universina theme (which includes the look of this theme as well as the rest of Netenberg's themes).

Working with cPanel Theme Languages

Most modern cPanel themes (including cPanel's own XSkin theme) have support for multiple languages. However, since the only language that cPanel Inc. supports is (American) English, the XSkin themes do not come with any language files other than English.

If you want to make changes to the English language file that comes with cPanel, or if you want to create or edit some other language file to use with XSkin or one of cPanel's other free cPanel themes (Blue Lagoon or Monsoon), then WHM provides you with the features found in the **Languages** section.

Installing a New Language File

If you already have a language file completed (perhaps that you've created or obtained from another source), you can install it via WHM by clicking on the **Upload a Language File** link in WHM, and then selecting the language file on your computer and clicking the **Upload** button to send the file to your server.

 In order to use other language files with most themes, you need to make sure that the **Change Language** option is checked in the appropriate cPanel feature lists.

Cloning an Installed Language

Before trying to edit a language file, you should make a copy of it; this way it won't affect your customers, and you can switch them over to the new language file when you are done. To make a copy of a language file, click on **Clone/Create a New Language** in WHM and then select the language you want to copy or base your new language file on. You will then be asked what to call your new language. Name it, and click the **Do It** button to create or copy the new language file.

Editing an Installed Language File

If you want to make changes to an installed language file other than the default English file, click on **Edit a Language File** and select the file you want to edit. You will be presented with the entire content of the language file on screen with the default English text to serve as a guide.

Language Editor		
Main >> Languages >> Edit a Language File		
Variable	**English**	**spanish Translation**
ACAdmin	Admin User Name:	
ACAgora	Agora Shopping Cart	
ACHint	The Agora Cart is a free shopping cart program. Support can optionally be obtained through a mailing list setup specifically for Agora Users for a small fee of $25.00 per year. You can join the list by visiting: <a href="http://www.agoracgi.com/">http://www.agoracgi.com/</a>	

Place the translated text for each phrase in the text box to the right of the default English text. Continue this process until the entire file is translated. If you leave a translation blank, cPanel will use the default English text instead. Click **Save** to save the progress of your translation. (To make changes to the English language file, first clone it using the earlier directions.)

Downloading a Language File

If you prefer to work on a language file on your own computer rather than working in a web browser, you can download language files. The language files are actually plain text files you can edit with nearly any text editor.

Click **Download a Language File** in WHM, and click on the language to download. The file will be saved to your computer.

Remember, when you work with language files, do not change the name of the file, and always make sure that you are saving the text file with Linux/Unix line breaks and not with Windows or DOS line breaks, as this will render the file unusable.

Not all themes use the same format for language files. For example, if you have RVSkin installed, you won't be able to use the RVSkin language files with other cPanel themes as the format is slightly different.

Setting the Language for Web Statistics Programs

If you have more than one language file installed, you can tell the web statistics programs (AWSTATS, Analog, and Webalizer) to use their own special language files if the language has been changed in cPanel. To do this, click on **Advanced Language Configuration** in WHM.

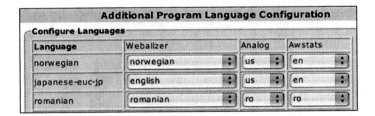

Language	Webalizer	Analog	Awstats
norwegian	norwegian	us	en
japanese-euc-jp	english	us	en
romanian	romanian	ro	ro

For each language you have installed, you will be able to pick a corresponding stats program language file from the drop-down list under the name of the stats program in question. Each stats program maintains its own, separate, language files; so there are no guarantees that the stats program has an appropriate language file. When you are done, click **Save** to apply the changes.

It may take 24–48 hours before the stats programs start using the new language in reports.

Deleting an Installed Language File

To remove an installed language file, click on **Delete a Language File** in WHM. Select the language you want to delete, and confirm your choice to have the language deleted from your server.

Working with WHM Themes

WHM also has the ability to use themes to change its look and layout. However, there are fewer WHM themes than there are cPanel themes. Further, only you and your resellers will see the themes; so it's not as big a concern for most people unless you really dislike the default "x" XSkin theme that WHM uses.

Installing and Removing Some Free WHM Themes

Although cPanel Inc. only provides a single WHM theme by default, they do make it easy to install two other WHM themes created by a third party and released for free. The two free themes also come in Spanish language versions.

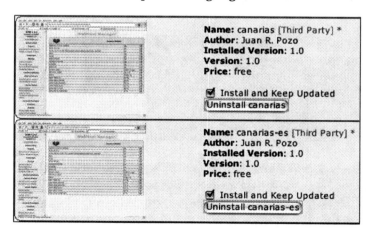

Click on **Addon WHM Themes** in the **Themes** section of WHM. Click on the checkbox next to each theme you want to install, and click on the **Save** button. WHM will then install your choices.

To remove any of these themes, click on the uninstall theme button under the description of the theme you wish to remove from your server. That theme will be removed immediately.

 These themes are maintained and supported by a third party, not cPanel Inc.

Installing Third-Party WHM Themes

You aren't limited to only those WHM themes you can get from cPanel Inc; there are some third-party providers of WHM themes as well. If you have a WHM theme file that you've created or that you've acquired from another location, you can use WHM to install the file by clicking on **Install a New WHM Theme**, locating the WHM theme file on your computer, and clicking on **Upload** to send the file to your server. WHM will verify that the file is a valid WHM theme and then install it for you.

Listing Installed WHM Themes

If you just want to see which WHM themes are available on your server, click on **List Installed WHM Themes** and you will see a plain text list of the names of all installed WHM themes.

Choosing the Default WHM Theme

By default, WHM uses the standard "x" XSkin theme (just as cPanel does). If you'd like to change the default WHM theme for yourself and for resellers who haven't explicitly chosen another theme, click on the **Set Default WHM Theme** link and then click on the name of the theme that you'd like to use as the default. Your change takes place immediately.

Changing the Current WHM Theme

If you don't want to use whatever WHM theme you've set as the default, you can choose another. This choice will affect anyone logged in as root. Resellers can choose their own theme separately. **Change WHM Theme** allows you to do just that. Click on the theme you want to use, and the change is applied immediately.

Downloading a WHM Theme

You can also download any installed WHM theme if you want to back it up or perhaps use it as the basis for a customized theme. Click on **Download a WHM Themeball** and select the theme to download. The resulting file is actually a tar.gz compressed file which you should be able to open using most popular file decompression utilities.

Removing Installed WHM Themes

The default "x" XSkin WHM theme does not offer a link to permit you to remove WHM themes; if you need to do so, you will have to it manually. Be careful not to remove a theme that a reseller (or yourself) is using or they may have problems accessing WHM.

To remove a WHM theme manually, log into your server via SSH as root and navigate to /usr/local/cpanel/whostmgr/docroot/themes/. There you can remove the directory named after the theme you wish to remove.

WHM Theme Gallery

Although there aren't many actively developed third-party WHM themes at the moment, here is a look at the ones I know to be available.

7Dana WHM

Author: 7dana

URL: http://7dana.com/ and http://forums.cpanel.net/showthread.php?t=40127

Special Features: Matches 7Dana cPanel theme, collapsible section headers in WHM

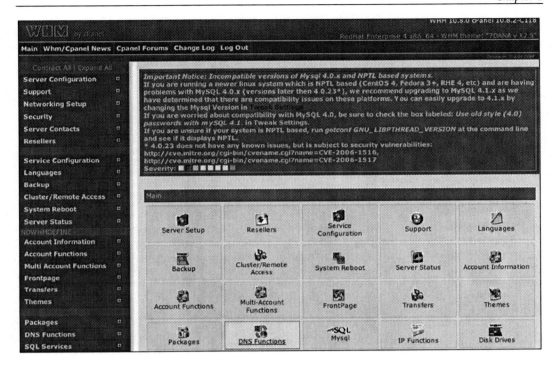

This theme matches the cPanel theme released for free by 7dana. This WHM theme is free as well. You'll find that the collapsible header sections are a very popular feature in WHM themes, including this one.

Canarias

Author: Juan R. Pozo

URL: n/a

Special Features: Collapsible section headers in WHM sidebar, English and Spanish versions

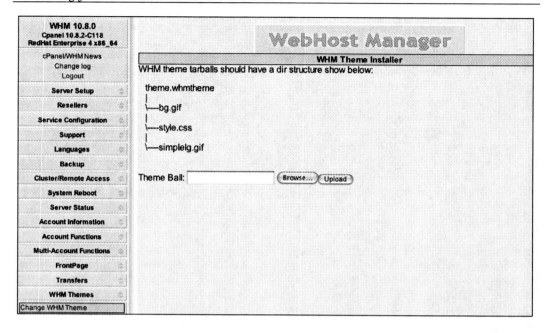

If you love orange, this is the theme for you! It offers collapsible headings in the WHM sidebar. This theme is starting to show its age and does not support all WHM features. However, it does come in a Spanish language version.

Radiance

Author: CPSkins.com

URL: `http:http://cpskins.com/`

Special Features: Matches Radiance cPanel theme by this company, collapsible section headers in WHM sidebar

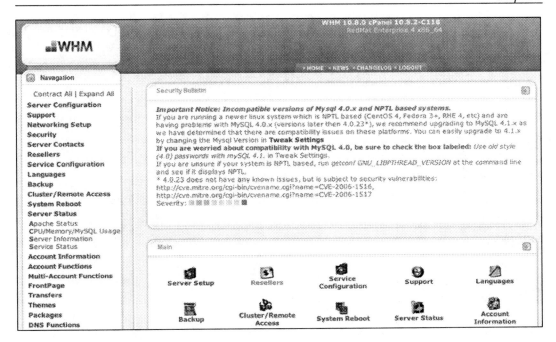

The only supported commercial WHM theme that I am currently aware of; it is designed to match the Radiance cPanel theme offered by this company. You get a clean layout with collapsible section headers in WHM.

TrueBlue

Author: Juan R. Pozo

URL: n/a

Special Features: Collapsible section headers in WHM, English and Spanish version also available

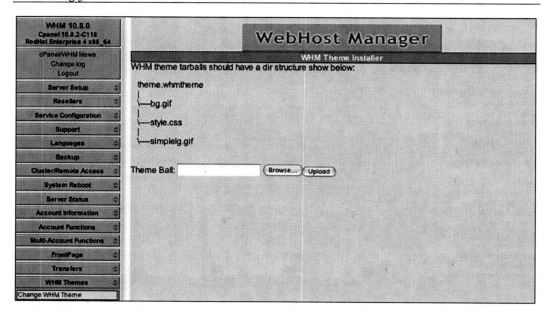

This theme is identical to Canarias except it's blue instead of orange. It has the same features and shortcoming.

Working with cPanel's Own Autoinstall Scripts Feature

The third-party add-on known as **Fantastico De Luxe** was the first product to add the ability to automate the installation process of popular web scripts into cPanel. This feature has proved wildly popular with users because it is not a simple process to install web scripts. This popularity has generated a number of competing solutions that do the same sort of thing.

cPanel Inc. added their own autoinstall scripts feature some time ago. Recently, they've updated this feature to make it easier for server administrators such as yourself to manage the scripts installed on your server.

Web scripts are very popular as they allow users to add features to their website without having to code the feature themselves. However, developers are human, and so security flaws are often found in these scripts. These security flaws can cause serious problems for the user who has the unpatched script installed and potentially cause problems for you as well, since hackers may use the flaw(s) to try to exploit your server or the user's account.

Choosing the Scripts to Offer

If you plan on allowing customers to autoinstall certain scripts, you first need to choose which scripts you plan on offering. To do this, click on **Install cPAddon Scripts** in the cPanel section of WHM.

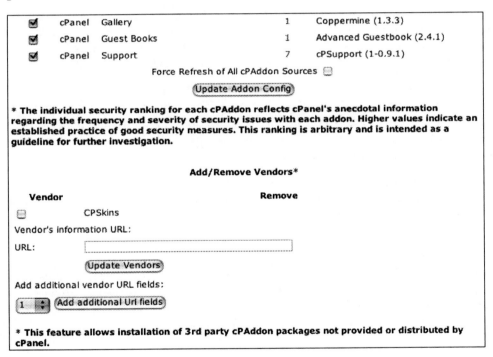

At the top of this screen, you can check the box next to each script that you'd like to offer in cPanel to your clients (assuming you've permitted them access to the **Scripts Library** feature). Then you can click the **Update Addon Config** button to have WHM fetch the latest available version of all of the scripts that you've selected from cPanel's own servers. If you check the box next to the **Force Refresh of All cPAddons**

Sources before clicking on the **Update Addon Config** button, it will force WHM to refetch all of the add-on scripts you've checked, even if the latest version is already available on your server.

All scripts that cPanel Inc. maintains for use with this feature are given a rating concerning how secure the script (on average) is likely to be. Higher numbers mean that the script has had relatively few security issues and that problems are dealt with quickly. Lower numbers mean that the script is less secure or still in testing.

Note that cPanel Inc. does not actually make most of the scripts they offer in this feature; they just package it so that it can be used by cPanel. When a script gets updated by the developers, it may be some time before the new version is added to cPanel.

At the bottom of this screen is the **Add/Remove Vendors** section. cPanel Inc. has designed this feature to allow third-party companies to add other scripts if they want to. At this time, I am only aware of one company that does so, CPSkins.com with its Auto-Installer v4 product, though others are certain to follow eventually.

To add a new vendor, just paste in the special URL that the company has provided to you under the **Vendor's Information URL** area. Then click **Update Vendors** to have WHM check for scripts that the company offers. Those scripts will appear in the list at the top of this screen. As with cPanel's own scripts, just check the boxes next to each script you want to offer to customers.

If a vendor offers more than one URL, you can add more URL input lines by selecting a number from the **Add additional vendor URL fields** drop-down box and then clicking the **Add Additional Url fields** button.

If you decide you no longer wish to offer scripts by a particular vendor, you can remove them by checking their name in the vendor list and clicking the **Update Vendors** button. This will remove all of that vendor's scripts. Users who have already used cPanel to install one of these removed scripts will still be able to use the script(s) they have installed; they just won't be able to add more, or remove, or upgrade the existing installation via the **Script Library** any more.

At this time, WHM still offers the old-style add-on script installation feature for legacy support, called **Addon Scripts (Deprecated)**, but you should avoid using this feature.

Moderating Script Installation

With the new cPanel script installation feature, you as the system administrator have the ability to force users to request permission to install a script that is available in the **Script Library**. If you want to restrict installation to only those you personally approve, use the **Manage cPAddon Scripts** feature in the cPanel section of WHM.

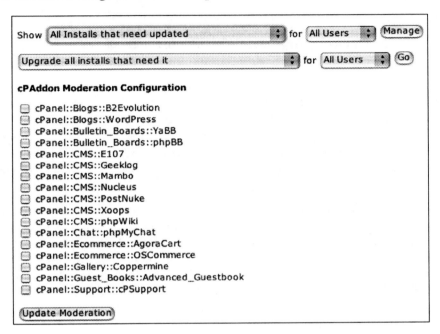

On this screen you will not only be able to moderate installation of scripts from the **Scripts Library**, but you can also monitor installations and even force an upgrade if a user hasn't upgraded their installed script to a more secure version yet.

To force users to request the ability to autoinstall a script, check the box next to the script you want to be able to moderate, and click the **Update Moderation** button. From then on, when users click on that script in the **Script Library**, they will be prompted to contact you to request installation permission.

You can control where you are contacted when a user requests installation permission as well as control how many times they can contact you and other moderation options using the features in **Tweak Settings** as discussed in Chapter 3.

Note that the script moderation feature will not stop users from manually installing scripts on their own or using a third-party script installation feature like Fantastico.

You can display (and then take action on) any installations that need to be updated, or only those installations that appear to have been manually removed by the user, or list all installations by choosing the appropriate item from the drop-down list at the top of the screen, picking either all users or a particular user from the drop-down list next to it and then clicking **Manage**. WHM will display all installs that meet your criteria. From here you can upgrade or remove individual scripts that users have installed.

If you prefer to force WHM to automatically upgrade all scripts that users have installed via the **Scripts Library** (if there is a new version available), or remove the script management information from cPanel for those scripts that are no longer installed where WHM expects them to be, just select the appropriate choice from the drop-down box on the second line of the screen and then choose all users or a particular cPanel user, and click on the **Go** button to force WHM to take that action.

If you force an upgrade to a script, the user who has that script installed may lose any special customization or added code and have the script set back to a stock version.

Working with cPanel and WHM Add-On Modules

Due to the popularity of cPanel, many products have been created that add new features to WHM or cPanel. cPanel Inc. has taken steps to make it easier for third parties to add features to WHM and cPanel in an organized way.

cPanel Inc. offers several of its own add-on features (typically to allow users to test new features before they are added to WHM or cPanel, or to allow access to certain optional features). However, many third parties can use the same mechanisms to add their own features to WHM and cPanel.

Managing cPanel's Own Add-On Modules

To install or remove one of cPanel's own add-on modules, click on **Addon Modules** in the cPanel section of WHM.

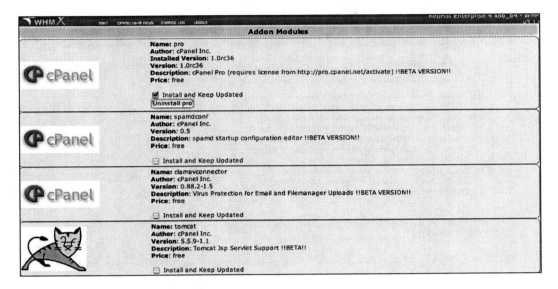

To install one or more of the listed modules (which are all free at the moment), select the **Install and keep updated** checkbox under the item description, and click **Save** to have WHM install the selected modules. Later, if you want to remove a module, click the uninstall module button under the module description, and that will immediately remove that module.

Module Gallery

Here are the modules that are currently available:

cPanel Pro: cPanel Pro isn't really a new version of cPanel as you might think. cPanel Pro is the name of the improved APIs that make it easier for third parties to add content to cPanel and WHM. It does include a few "example" modules that will probably become standard cPanel features at some point. **Boxtrapper** and **Statistics Software Configuration** are some examples of "Pro" modules that are now a standard part of cPanel. If you enable cPanel Pro, you currently get the **Leech Protection, Image Manager**, and **Submit a Support Request** modules in cPanel. You can disable these features using WHM's feature sets.

The only module from cPanel Pro that adds an item in WHM's **Addon** section is
Submit a Support Request. You and your resellers can both use this feature to set
up a quick link for requesting support, either via e-mail or by linking directly to your
help desk.

Support Request Configuration

This feature allows you to configure where support requests go when they are submitted through cPanel.

◉ Email support requests to [   ] or Pipe support requests to

[   ]

- ☑ Display the customer's browser in the body.
- ☐ Display the customer's browser in the subject.
- ☑ Display the customer's domain name in the body.
- ☑ Display the customer's domain name in the subject.
- ☑ Display the hostname of the server in the body.
- ☐ Display the hostname of the server in the subject.
- ☑ Display the customer's client ip in the body.
- ☐ Display the customer's client ip in the subject.
- ☑ Display the customer's username in the body.
- ☐ Display the customer's username in the subject.

○ Redirect the user to the following url: [   ]
○ Disable this feature.

(Save)

If you want the **Submit a Support Request** feature to allow your customers to
e-mail you, select the **Email support requests to** radio button, and type in an e-mail
address or the absolute path to a script that processes e-mail (for your help desk).
Underneath this section are a bunch of checkboxes for adding certain information
automatically to the subject or body of the e-mail message that is sent. Alternatively,
you can redirect users to a particular URL (of your helpdesk for example) by clicking
on the **Redirect the user to the following url** radio button.

The last radio button, **Disable this feature**, stops your customers from using this
feature (or you can disable it in the WHM feature lists). Remember, your resellers
will be able to use this feature to direct their customers to a different location.

Spamdconf: This feature allows you to better control cPanel's standard
SpamAssassin feature to help manage its load or feature set on your server.

Spamd Startup Configuration

Spamd Startup Options

The following options will be used upon execution of the spamd daemon.

PID File		Location of spamd pid file *(defaults to /var/run/spamd.pid when blank)*
Maximum Children		Number of spamd child processes spawned upon startup
Allowed IPs		Restrict connections to spamd to specific IP address *(i.e. 127.0.0.1)*
Maximum Connections Perl Child		Number of connections to spamd child before abandoning the process

Submit

You can change the location of the Process ID file that keeps track of what processes IDs the SpamAssassin daemon are running.

Maximum Children sets how many child processes the SpamAssassin daemon can run when started. More will allow SpamAssassin to process mail faster at the expense of server load and memory. Unless you are experiencing a problem, don't bother to change the default values.

Allowed IPs will let you specify only certain IP addresses that can access the SpamAssassin daemon.

Maximum Connections Perl Child controls how many connections can be made to each child of the SpamAssassin daemon before the process is abandoned.

Unless you know you're having problems, you shouldn't need to modify any of the features.

ClamAVConnector: This will install ClamAV on your server, which is a free and very well-maintained antivirus solution. When installed, users can use it to scan all of their mails, files on the server, and all files uploaded via the **File Manager** in cPanel. ClamAV also has the ability to find some phishing and scam e-mails, and block them.

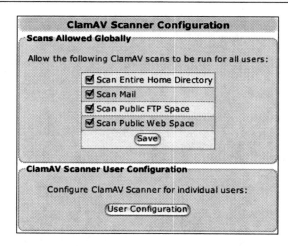

In the WHM add-on module for this feature, you can control what features users can access. The first section controls which features all cPanel users can access. The second section allows you to fine tune the feature set for individual users.

Tomcat: This is one of two different Java modules available; Resin is the other module. Never use both Tomcat and mod_resin as they do the same thing. Tomcat is probably the most well-known Java connector that allows Apache to serve server-side Java (.jsp) and Java applets. After installing this feature, you must use the **Install Serverlets** feature that you will find in the **Account Functions** section of WHM. This new feature will allow you to enable server-side Java support for individual accounts. Java can be very processor intensive, so don't enable this feature for many accounts, or you may overload your server.

Modresin: Resin is another Java connector that allows Apache to be able to serve Java. This module has a reputation for being less of a memory and CPU-load hog than Tomcat. Do not enable this if you already have Tomcat installed and vice versa.

Modmono: mod_mono is part of the Mono project (http://www.mono-project.com/) that aims to create a fully open-source alternative to allow servers to work with Active Server Pages (ASP) and .NET-enabled scripts. Note that the project is still in active development and may not support all of Microsoft's proprietary additions, but it enjoys wide compatibility. Once installed, you need to use /script/addasp to enable mod_mono use for particular accounts.

Modbandwidth: mod_bandwidth allows you to throttle web bandwidth usage of certain accounts to whatever level you set. There is no WHM module for this feature, either.

Modsecurity: mod_security is a content firewall for Apache (http://www.modsecurity.org/). It allows you to stop access to certain pages or features based on the content of the URL or post, or get payload from your web pages.

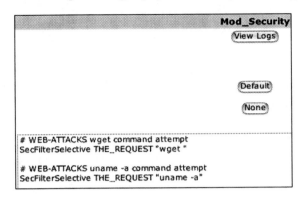

In the WHM add-on module, you can view the recent hits that mod_security stopped. The log shows which IP address attempted the illegal connection, what time it happened, and the URL or payload that caused the issue as well as what rule triggered the block and what domain it was attempting to access at the time.

In order for mod_security to be really effective, you need to add certain rules that mod_security will use to block access. Click **Edit Rules** to switch to the rules screen. On this screen you can add or edit rules (in the large text box), or install the default cPanel rule set that does a reasonable job of blocking dangerous connections without blocking valid connection attempts. Click **Default** to use the default rule set. They will be installed, and Apache restarted immediately. Or click **None** to disable all the custom rules and only provide basic mod_security protection. You can also switch back to the logs.

The trick with mod_security is finding good rules. Add too many and you can slow down your server. Add too few and malicious content might get through. If the rules are too broad, you might stop a lot of legitimate traffic (with a 403 or 406 error code). I recommend you use the default rule set until you find rules that work best for you.

Addonupdates: This module is for use with the old add-on scripts function in WHM, and it can check for updates for installed scripts. I don't recommend that you install this, since the new add-on scripts feature offers more flexibility.

Cronconfig: This module allows you to change when to run /scripts/upcp (cPanel's update feature) and /scripts/cpbackup (the WHM automatic account backup feature) each day.

Configure cPanel Cron

Main Menu

Command	Minute	Hour	Day	Month	Weekday	
upcp	6	4	*	*	*	Commit
cpbackup	0	1	*	*	*	Commit

The times are entered with the minute that it runs followed by the hour, the day, the month, and the weekday. Generally the default values (assigned by WHM) are going to work well. If you feel these two load-intensive scripts are running too soon or too late, you can modify the time they run so as to minimize their impact on your server.

Munin: Munin (http://munin.projects.linpro.no/) allows you to monitor servers to make sure they are up and running. The WHM add-on displays the Munin status page.

There is another add-on module, not in this section, that is created and supported by cPanel Inc.

GameServer Manager (currently in beta testing): The cPanel game server add-on (http://gs.cpanel.net/) aims to provide cPanel users and server administrators with an easy-to-use cPanel and WHM module to manage game servers for a number of popular online games like HalfLife 2, Call of Duty, and others.

This module isn't feature complete yet, but it has come a long way. It is capable of managing game servers running on the same server or on a remote server. You can find a lengthy thread on this module here: http://forums.cpanel.net/ showthread.php?t=30272.

Other Available WHM and cPanel Add-Ons

There are lots of other cPanel and WHM add-ons that do everything from auto-installing scripts (like Fantastico De Luxe and Auto-Installer v4) to allowing you to filter mail for spam and viruses (with MailScanner). There are so many that it is impossible to discuss them all here. Please look in Appendix B (http://www.packtpub.com/web_host_manager/book) for links to many popular add-ons and a description of what they do.

There is only one group of add-ons I will mention in-depth here, and that is add-ons that allow your users to auto-install even more web scripts.

Fantastico De Luxe

Fantastico De Luxe, http://netenberg.com/, is the most popular third-party add-on for cPanel servers. It was the first cPanel add-on product to ever allow end users to easily install popular web scripts, and it has grown over the years.

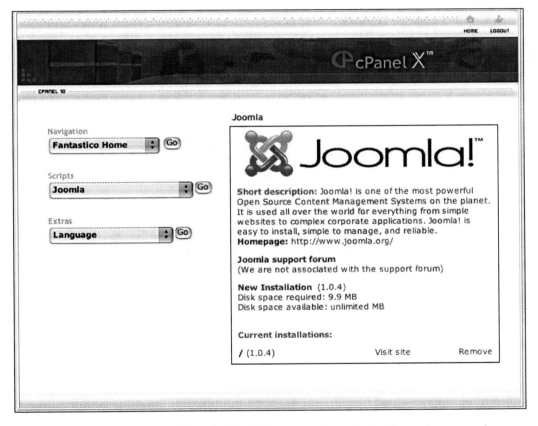

Fantastico De Luxe 2.x installs over 55 different scripts, including a few popular commercial scripts like SohoLaunch and PerlDesk. However, most of the scripts it offers to install are completely free. Users love it because it is more flexible than cPanel's own **Script Library** feature (added after Fantastico was already quite popular).

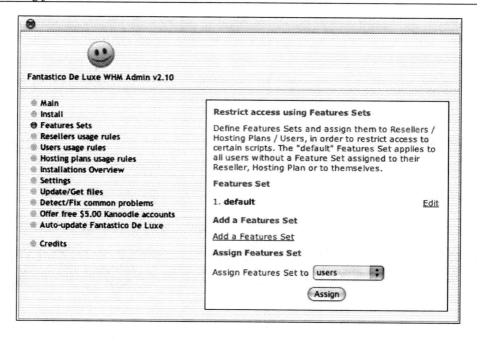

It allows you to monitor installations and even upgrade scripts for your clients. Fantastico always makes a full backup of any script that it upgrades, so if something goes wrong, the user can always fall back on the old version.

Fantastico De Luxe version 3 may be out by the time you read this (or will be released soon). Fantastico 3 will make it easy for script authors and hosts such as yourself to add custom scripts to Fantastico. You will also be able to charge for installation if you want to (with integration to some popular e-commerce solutions) and improve script monitoring and notification of new script versions.

Auto-Installer v4

Auto-Installer v4 (http://cpskins.com/) was recently released to work with the new cPanel add-on scripts functionality as well as add even more auto-installable scripts.

Blogs (10)	
B2Evolution (from CPSkins) *PHP/MySQL Blog System*	WordPress (from CPSkins) *PHP/MySQL Blog System*
LifeType *PHP/MySQL Blog System*	boastMachine *PHP/MySQL Blog System*
Nucleus *PHP/MySQL Blog System*	myBloggie *PHP/MySQL Blog System*
Serendipity *PHP/MySQL Blog System*	B2Evolution (from cPanel) *PHP/MySQL Blog System*
Textpattern *PHP/MySQL Blog System*	WordPress (from cPanel) *PHP/MySQL Blog System*

Bug Trackers (2)	
Mantis Bug Tracker *PHP/MySQL Bug Tracking System*	phpBugTracker *PHP/MySQL Bug Tracking System*

It adds more script options to cPanel's own **Script Library** feature. It offers even more scripts than Fantastico 2.x does. You can install and manage the additional scripts through the standard WHM add-on scripts management features discussed earlier. It relies on cPanel's own script installation features to handle installing, upgrading, and removing scripts.

Open Installer

There is one free project that aims to add more scripts to cPanel's **Script Library**, though it does not currently work with cPanel's new script installation features; I'm sure it will soon. This project is called, appropriately enough, Open Installer (http://www.openinstaller.com/), and they are in part supported by cPanel Inc.

To date, work on this project has been sporadic, and updates slow in coming. However, it's a project worth watching.

Installatron

Installatron is a multi-platform script auto-installer designed to work with numerous hosting control panels (including cPanel, Plesk, and DirectAdmin).

installatron

Installatron v3.3.6
[Administration] [Help]

Introduction
Installatron is an *auto-installer* that allows you to quickly install and manage free web scripts. Web scripts are programs/software that can enhance or add functionality to your website. Examples include guestbooks, forums, image galleries, and e-commerce systems.

Installing a Script
To install a script using Installatron:

1. Select a script from the list.
2. Allow the page to reload.
3. Click the `New Install <` button.

Blogs • CMSs • Portals	
b2evolution	*blog*
Pivot	*blog*
WordPress	*blog*
Feed On Feeds	*blog/rss*
Coranto	*cms*
Drupal	*cms*
Soholaunch	*cms*
TYPO3	*cms*
Joomla	*portal*
Mambo	*portal*
ocPortal	*portal*
PHP-Nuke	*portal*
PostNuke	*portal*
Xoops	*portal*

Installatron offers many of the same scripts as the other solutions, though there are a few different scripts offered. Installatron offers the ability to e-mail users when scripts they have installed are updated in Installatron. It also offers the (currently) unique ability to install scripts for users via the root shell. Its interface isn't as "cPanel-like" as the other solutions and may be somewhat more daunting to new users not already familiar with how auto-installation services work.

Summary

In this chapter, you've learned how to customize your server using cPanel and WHM themes, how to modify and add themes, and also how to work with add-on modules for WHM and cPanel.

In Chapter 10, we will look at the resources that WHM provides to give you help when you need it. Also, we'll discuss some other places you can turn to for help. Finally, we'll wrap everything up and crown you King or Queen of WHM!

10
Where to Go for Help with WHM

Let's face it; we've covered quite a lot in this book. Hopefully, now that you've nearly finished this book, you will feel more empowered and less intimidated than you did when you first started reading. No matter how many pages I write and you read, though, there are going to be issues that arise with your server that this book cannot cover. Sometimes, the unexpected happens, or you have a crisis that needs immediate attention. Where can you turn for help? That is the question this chapter will answer.

Help(ful) Resources in WHM

WHM has its own set of features that makes it easier for you to access a few of cPanel Inc.'s own support options as well as to find features in WHM.

The Interactive Knowledgebase

The idea behind the **Interactive Knowledgebase** feature in the **Support** section of WHM is a good one. If you want to know how to accomplish a task with WHM, or if you are having a problem, you type in a natural-language question, and WHM will look for features that can help you with your problem and display quick links to each one.

Sadly, the actual usefulness of this feature is rather limited. It can be nearly impossible to find something in the **Interactive Knowledgebase**. Even simple questions like "How do I restart Apache?" don't have answers in the knowledge base. Also, the natural language parser isn't the most intelligent. Any question with the word "quota" in it will return the two resolutions listed in the following picture, even if you are asking about how to set e-mail mailbox quotas.

Furthermore, even when there are answers, they just link directly to a potential fix. If you click on the fix, it will immediately take action in most cases. A better idea would be to provide a plain text answer on how to fix the problem in addition to a link to the potential fixes.

Despite these shortcomings, when the feature works, it can be rather handy; so it may be worth a try if you are having problems or need to know how to do things in WHM.

Links to cPanel Support

The **Support Center** feature in WHM provides handy links to all of the various online support features cPanel Inc. offers.

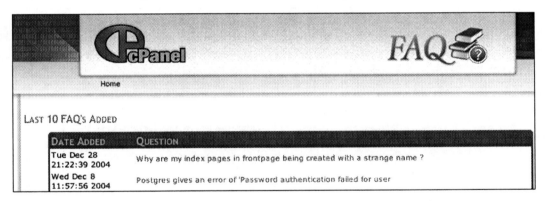

Support Center

- **cPanel/Web Host Manager FAQ**

    The cPanel/Web Host Manager FAQ provides easy access to frequently asked questions about cPanel and Web Host Manager.
- **Support Forums**

    The Support Forums provide a place to discuss current issues, third party addons, and other features.
- **Web Host Manager Documentation**
- **cPanel Documentation**
- **Contact cPanel.net**

    This form provides a way to contact the makers of cPanel and Web Host Manager. **You should contact your vendor for support before contacting cPanel.net**

    This servers' support access number is:
    You may need this to obtain support.

You will find five different links; two that are links to copies of resources on your own server, and three that are links to external resources from cPanel.net.

Just the FAQ

The **cPanel/WHM FAQ** is a link to `http://faq.cpanel.net/`. Here you can see answers to common questions, and fixes for common problems.

Even if you aren't having any problems, it is worth looking at the FAQ, as you will learn quite a bit about how cPanel and WHM work. However, it isn't regularly maintained, and so some of the entries are a bit out of date.

The Forum

The **Support Forums** link will take you to `http://forums.cpanel.net/`. We'll discuss the forums more later, but this is a very useful resource if you want to keep tabs on current issues and cPanel/WHM development.

Documentation

The **WHM** and **cPanel Documentation** links take you to copies of the WHM and cPanel documentation maintained by cPanel Inc. on your server. However, you can also access them online:

- cPanel Docs: `http://www.cpanel.net/docs/cpanel/`
- WHM Docs: `http://www.cpanel.net/docs/whm/`

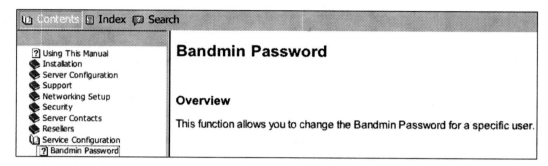

In the sidebar, you will find links to the various sections of the documentation. Clicking on a section causes the various topics covered in that section to appear. Click on the topic to see it.

 The documentation is good as a quick reference if you just want to know where and how to use a feature. Don't expect much elaboration, though. Also, the documentation may not immediately reflect all of the latest changes to cPanel and WHM.

Contacting cPanel

The **Contact cPanel** item is a quick link to the support request form available here: `https://tickets.cpanel.net/submit/index.cgi?support=1`

However, the link in your WHM automatically supplies cPanel Inc. with your server's unique support access number (which you will find listed in red near the **Contact cPanel** link in case you need to refer to it). This support access number is required to ask for assistance from cPanel.

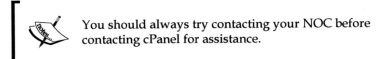 You should always try contacting your NOC before contacting cPanel for assistance.

Turning to your NOC for Assistance

If you can't find the answer on your own, you should turn to your NOC for assistance. Since they have physical access to your server, and have extensive experience with numerous operating systems and hosting control panels, they can be an invaluable source for quick, mission-critical assistance.

You should be aware of your NOC's support policies so that you can avoid surprises and unexpected expenses when you have a problem. Some provide free assistance via phone and e-mail for any problem or question you might have. Others may only provide you basic server reboot and hardware support. All NOCs should have some means of support available 24 hours a day, seven days a week, 365 days a year. Many will provide a certain level of assistance for free but may charge you if they need to log into your server to fix the problem.

Finding Help in the Forums

A good place for general assistance and to connect with other cPanel and WHM users is the cPanel.net forums: `http://forums.cpanel.net/`.

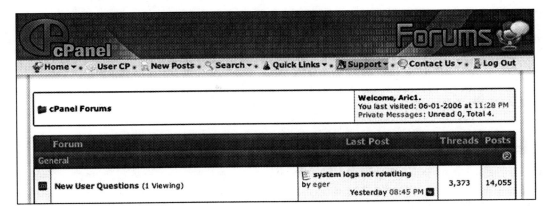

You will need a free account in order to use the forums, but once you have an account, you will be able to read and post freely, so long as you carefully observe the rules and post in the proper section.

You should use the **Search** feature (at the top of the forum screen) to see if anyone has posted a topic on an issue you are interested in before you post one yourself. The forums have been around for many years, and the most common problems have been discussed in depth at some point in the past.

The nice thing about the forums is that there is always someone willing to lend a hand to try to help you. cPanel Inc. staff also reads the forums and will sometimes chime in when appropriate.

The cPanel forums are not designed for users to post support requests for cPanel Inc. The staff do read the forums, but if you need direct assistance from them either file a support request or file a bug in Bugzilla as appropriate.

Assistance from cPanel Inc.

If you cannot get support from your NOC, or if you simply must have direct support, you can file a support request with cPanel Inc. The best place to do this is from the cPanel Support link in the Support Center in WHM on one of your servers (preferably the one with the problem you are reporting). However, you can file a support request on the Web here:

`https://tickets.cpanel.net/submit/index.cgi?support=1`

If you do not have your server's unique support access number (also viewable in the **Support Center** on your server), your request for assistance may be denied or given a lower priority.

If you submit a support request to cPanel Inc., make sure you're as clear and concise as possible. They will need to know exactly what sort of problem you are having and how to reproduce that problem. Don't ramble, though, get right to the point. cPanel Inc. sees a lot of support requests each day and, being concise will help them provide you with faster service.

cPanel Inc.'s Bugzilla Bug Tracking System

cPanel Inc. has a special web interface for users to report bugs in WHM and cPanel. If you think you've found a bug in cPanel or WHM and can reproduce it, or if you have a feature request for cPanel or WHM, you should file it in Bugzilla.

Bug List							Sat Jun 3 2006 03:06:07	
139 bugs found.								
ID	Sev	Pri	Plt	Assignee	Status	Resolution	Summary	
186	nor	P2	x86	confirmed@cpanel.net	NEW		[DEBIAN] Debian - easyapache Broken - Missing libz	
448	nor	P2	x86	confirmed@cpanel.net	NEW		[BUILDAPACHE] FD_SETSIZE not changed in FreeBSD 4.9	
592	enh	P2	All	enhancement@cpanel.net	NEW		WebDav support in EasyApache	
594	enh	P2	All	enhancement@cpanel.net	NEW		Combined format logging of SSL requests	

You can access the Bugzilla interface at `http://bugzilla.cpanel.net/`.

You can search and read most of the bug reports without a Bugzilla account, but if you want to post a bug or feature request, or vote for a bug (to let cPanel Inc. know that you consider this bug or feature request important), you will need to sign up for a free Bugzilla account first.

Before posting a feature request or bug, make sure that no one else has posted an entry about this already. Also, when you post the bug, try to be as specific as possible, and provide code examples or error messages if you can.

Remember not to post private information in Bugzilla, because all entries are public unless cPanel Inc. restricts access to the text of the entry.

Assistance from Other Sources

In addition to the other support methods mentioned, there are independent sources you can turn to for help.

Web Hosting Talk

Web Hosting Talk (WHT) is a forum dedicated to discussion of all aspects of the web hosting business. People looking for hosting as well as hosts all post here. The forums cover all aspects of web hosting, and support all hosting platforms and control panels, including cPanel. (Visit this forum at `http://webhostingtalk.com/`.)

The reason that this particular forum is worth a mention is because of the sheer number of people who visit it every day. This attracts a lot of businesses looking for customers also. If you need assistance, have a general question, or would like to promote your hosting service, this is a good place to come.

Be extremely careful to follow the rules for posting on WHT, because the forums are heavily moderated, and too many violations may get your account suspended.

Third-Party Assistance

There are a wide variety of companies and individuals who may be willing to provide you with ongoing assistance, and customer and server management for a fee. If your business outgrows your ability for you to handle it yourself, or if you need to provide assistance to customers while you sleep or are out of town, hiring a support company or systems administrator may be just what you need.

How do you find one that fits your budget while providing quality support to you and your customers? Typically, watch the various hosting forums, and ask other clients of the company or individual. If you see regular complaints about a service, then you might want to consider someone else.

However, remember that people are far more likely to complain about bad service than they are to take the time to praise good service, so a company may have a great track record and one or two ex-customers with an axe to grind, but this may not make them a bad company.

Search Engines to the Rescue!

If nothing else provides the answer you are looking for, don't forget to use your favorite Internet search engine. They often index web hosting forums and FAQ pages that may provide you with the answer you are looking for.

WHM: The Final Words

We've reached the conclusion of the main portion of this book. You're not completely done, however. There is some handy information to be found in the Appendices, including a discussion of handy scripts in the /scripts directory on your server (Appendix A), a list of links to handy resources (Appendix B), and even a glossary of important terms (Appendix C). You can download these Appendices from http://www.packtpub.com/web_host_manager/book.

I'd like to take this time to thank you for reading this book. I hope you've found this to be a useful resource and feel more comfortable with WHM now. Feel free to come back and revisit this text any time you need to.

Index

Thank you for buying
Web Host Manager

About Packt Publishing

Packt, pronounced 'packed', published its first book "*Mastering phpMyAdmin for Effective MySQL Management*" in April 2004 and subsequently continued to specialize in publishing highly focused books on specific technologies and solutions.

Our books and publications share the experiences of your fellow IT professionals in adapting and customizing today's systems, applications, and frameworks. Our solution based books give you the knowledge and power to customize the software and technologies you're using to get the job done. Packt books are more specific and less general than the IT books you have seen in the past. Our unique business model allows us to bring you more focused information, giving you more of what you need to know, and less of what you don't.

Packt is a modern, yet unique publishing company, which focuses on producing quality, cutting-edge books for communities of developers, administrators, and newbies alike. For more information, please visit our website: www.packtpub.com.

Writing for Packt

We welcome all inquiries from people who are interested in authoring. Book proposals should be sent to authors@packtpub.com. If your book idea is still at an early stage and you would like to discuss it first before writing a formal book proposal, contact us; one of our commissioning editors will get in touch with you.

We're not just looking for published authors; if you have strong technical skills but no writing experience, our experienced editors can help you develop a writing career, or simply get some additional reward for your expertise.

Printed in the United Kingdom
by Lightning Source UK Ltd.
125204UK00001B/157-166/A